Praise for *Synergy and Sparks*

"*Synergy and Sparks* is a smart, timely guide for leaders who want to connect, inspire, and lead with purpose. This book is a must-read for anyone serious about leading with impact in today's workplace."

—Tramel Dodd
Chief of Staff, People and Culture, Reddit

"*Synergy and Sparks* is a practical and actionable must-read for leaders in today's complex and rapidly changing world. Mills describes the key components of effective leadership and makes them come to life with inspiring stories of both success and failure that create a 'how-to' guide with both personal and professional applicability."

—Mario Rizzo
President, Property-Liability, The Allstate Corporation

"Mills's unique perspective—blending performance techniques with leadership strategies—is both enlightening and practical. With a wealth of practical examples, this guide empowers leaders to inspire and drive meaningful change."

—Sarah Wang
Deputy General Counsel & HRVP, AstraZeneca

"Mills has devoted his life to human communication, of the most productive and generous kind. This book is that life's wisdom in one digestible serving. Swallow these lessons whole. Use them for good."

—David Murray
Executive Director, Professional Speechwriters
Association and author of *An Effort to Understand*

"*Synergy and Sparks* held up a mirror to my own leadership wins and flops and somehow did it without judging me. If you've ever wondered how to lead with confidence, communicate with purpose, or survive a team meeting without screaming into a 'Live, Laugh, Love' throw pillow, this is the book for you."

—Mark Salisbury
Peabody and Emmy Award–winning director and animator

"*Synergy and Sparks* reshaped the way I understand influence, leadership, and human connection. Whether you're leading a team, building a movement, or sharing a message with the world, *Synergy and Sparks* will ignite your thinking and elevate your impact."

—Rohullah Hassani
Founder and CEO, United Leaders Global

"Collaborative communication is at the heart of every high-performing team and thriving learning culture. This book brilliantly captures the power of dialogue, active listening, and shared understanding in building environments where ideas flow freely and innovation thrives."

—Mahipal Goud
Vice President, Learning & Development, Capgemini

"Mills brings tremendous clarity and insight to a core element of leadership: communication. Over the years we have benefited greatly from his expertise."

—Githesh Ramamurthy
Chairman/CEO, CCC Intelligent Solutions

"*Synergy and Sparks* artfully explores how inclusive dialogue, mutual respect, and shared purpose ignite both innovation and connection. This book is a must-read for leaders and learners committed to building cultures where every voice matters and every conversation sparks progress."

—Arti Gusain
Associate Vice President, Infosys Leadership Institute

"Thank you, G. Riley Mills, for the validation and reminder that authenticity can often be a leadership superpower. I am a former actor now leading a team of learning professionals in the corporate world. I strive daily for a genuine approach in my daily interactions that mimics the honesty that an actor requires for true success."

—Andrea Gillman
Manager, Learning & Development, S&C Electric Company

"This powerful and timely publication offers us both a personal narrative and a professional blueprint for how organizations can adapt to crisis, evolve leadership practices, and reimagine communication in a rapidly changing world. A must-read for leaders seeking to future-proof their teams and foster resilience in uncertain times."

—Alistair Cumming
Head of Talent Development, Lidl

"*Synergy and Sparks* is a must-read for any leader wanting to hone their skills and capability in this fast-moving world. This is a great read, as expected, from the cofounder of Pinnacle Performance. The concepts shared in this book certainly elicited synergy and sparks from me!"

—Therese M. Dickerson
Senior Vice President, Director of Learning Development,
Bank of Hawaii

"*Synergy and Sparks* offers new and developing leaders practical tips to proactively empower their teams. Read this book and your team will quickly notice the positive, lasting impact you have as a leader."

—Krysta Van Ranst
Founder and Learning Business Partner, Building PPL

"*Synergy and Sparks* highlights the importance of gratitude and real connections in leadership. With relatable stories and straightforward advice, it shows how kindness can uplift your team and create a positive workplace. Whether you're new to leadership or looking to improve, this book offers valuable insights that everyone can benefit from."

—Melanie Waters
Global Learning Strategist

SYNERGY AND SPARKS

SYNERGY AND SPARKS

UNLOCK **EXCELLENCE** THROUGH COMMUNICATION, COLLABORATION, AND INFLUENCE

G. RILEY MILLS

WILEY

Copyright © 2025 by G. Riley Mills. All rights reserved.

Published by John Wiley & Sons, Inc., Hoboken, New Jersey.
Published simultaneously in Canada.

No part of this publication may be reproduced, stored in a retrieval system, or transmitted in any form or by any means, electronic, mechanical, photocopying, recording, scanning, or otherwise, except as permitted under Section 107 or 108 of the 1976 United States Copyright Act, without either the prior written permission of the Publisher, or authorization through payment of the appropriate per-copy fee to the Copyright Clearance Center, Inc., 222 Rosewood Drive, Danvers, MA 01923, (978) 750-8400, fax (978) 750-4470, or on the web at www.copyright.com. Requests to the Publisher for permission should be addressed to the Permissions Department, John Wiley & Sons, Inc., 111 River Street, Hoboken, NJ 07030, (201) 748-6011, fax (201) 748-6008, or online at http://www.wiley.com/go/permission.

The manufacturer's authorized representative according to the EU General Product Safety Regulation is Wiley-VCH GmbH, Boschstr. 12, 69469 Weinheim, Germany, e-mail: Product_Safety@wiley.com.

Trademarks: Wiley and the Wiley logo are trademarks or registered trademarks of John Wiley & Sons, Inc. and/or its affiliates in the United States and other countries and may not be used without written permission. All other trademarks are the property of their respective owners. John Wiley & Sons, Inc. is not associated with any product or vendor mentioned in this book.

Limit of Liability/Disclaimer of Warranty: While the publisher and author have used their best efforts in preparing this book, they make no representations or warranties with respect to the accuracy or completeness of the contents of this book and specifically disclaim any implied warranties of merchantability or fitness for a particular purpose. No warranty may be created or extended by sales representatives or written sales materials. The advice and strategies contained herein may not be suitable for your situation. You should consult with a professional where appropriate. Further, readers should be aware that websites listed in this work may have changed or disappeared between when this work was written and when it is read. Neither the publisher nor authors shall be liable for any loss of profit or any other commercial damages, including but not limited to special, incidental, consequential, or other damages.

For general information on our other products and services or for technical support, please contact our Customer Care Department within the United States at (800) 762-2974, outside the United States at (317) 572-3993 or fax (317) 572-4002.

Wiley also publishes its books in a variety of electronic formats. Some content that appears in print may not be available in electronic formats. For more information about Wiley products, visit our web site at www.wiley.com.

Library of Congress Cataloging-in-Publication Data is Available:

ISBN 9781394338122 (Cloth)
ISBN 9781394338139 (ePub)
ISBN 9781394338146 (ePDF)

Cover Design: Wiley
Cover Image: © Jose A. Bernat Bacete/Getty Images
Author Photo: © Tocky Bonner
SKY10122439_072125

syn·er·gy

/ˈsinərjē/

noun

The interaction or cooperation of two or more organizations or agents to produce a combined effect greater than the sum of their separate effects.

spark

/spärk/

noun

A trace of a specified quality or intense feeling.

For Jo

Contents

Introduction	*xv*
PART I COMMUNICATION	**1**
1 The Stagecraft of Leadership	**3**
2 Solving the Attention Dilemma	**19**
3 Thriving During Uncertainty	**33**
PART II PRESENCE	**49**
4 Boosting Confidence and Maintaining Credibility	**51**
5 Elevating Your Leadership Impact	**67**
6 Why Authenticity Matters	**81**
PART III INFLUENCE	**95**
7 Unlocking the Science of Engagement	**97**
8 Creating Outcomes by Design	**111**
9 How Leaders Drive Passion and Purpose	**125**

PART IV STORYTELLING 141

10 The Undeniable Power of Narrative 143

11 Managing Change Through Storytelling 157

12 Choosing a Business Story to Tell 171

PART V COLLABORATION 185

13 Establishing Trust and Mutual Respect 187

14 Enhancing Performance Through Feedback 201

15 Mastering Challenging Conversations 215

PART VI CONNECTION 229

16 The Case for Empathy in Leadership 231

17 Cultivating Authentic Dialogue 245

18 Building Unbreakable Teams 259

Afterword 273
Notes 277
Acknowledgments 309
About The Author 313
Index 315

Introduction

From a little spark may burst a flame.

—Dante Alighieri

We all remember where we were when we first heard the news. And most of us recall the flood of emotions we felt: fear, confusion, anxiety. Suddenly, we all stopped what we were doing and asked the same collective question: *what in the world is happening right now?*

For me, the first sign that something was amiss came in January 2020 as I packed a bag for our annual company retreat. Once a year, the global communication skills training firm I cofounded, Pinnacle Performance Company, selects a location to bring together every member of our team for an event we call Summit. This gathering is an opportunity to connect, sharpen our skills, and explore new ways to enhance our products and offerings. It's a time for fun, team bonding, and personal development. That year, we chose Sedona, Arizona, as our destination, and those of us based at the Chicago headquarters couldn't wait to escape the cold and snow for some sand and sunshine.

As I packed my swimsuit and imagined lounging poolside with a piña colada, I received a call from a team member, one of our instructors based in China. He was having trouble leaving Shanghai due to what he described as a "flu" going around and a low-level advisory to "mask up" while traveling. No big deal, he said. After some delays, he eventually made it to Sedona, and we enjoyed a productive retreat.

A week later, back in Chicago and still energized from Summit, I received another call—this time from one of our London-based instructors. He shared news of a virus outbreak in Asia that was beginning to cause concern in the United Kingdom. He suggested we monitor the situation and, given Pinnacle's global footprint, prepare a contingency plan in case the virus spread. I presented this to Pinnacle's leadership team, most of whom were unaware of the virus, and we agreed to keep an eye on any developments.

As we now know, developments proceeded quickly.

On January 31, after the death toll had reached 200, the World Health Organization (WHO) declared a global health emergency. Three days later, the United States followed suit, and a little over a month after that, the WHO declared COVID-19 a pandemic. Global lockdowns and quarantines—the first in living memory for many— soon followed. For a company like Pinnacle, whose business model relied on international travel and in-person coaching and training, we suddenly found ourselves in a precarious situation. Our previously packed calendar of workshops and coaching sessions vanished overnight.

Amid the pandemic-induced chaos, we gathered the Pinnacle team (virtually, of course) to assess the situation and devise a plan. Our first priority was to check in with our clients. We asked them how they were coping, what their current needs were, which priorities required immediate attention, and how we could support them during this uncertain time. We then set to work—reimagining and redesigning our offerings to suit the needs of the current moment. We adopted new technologies, produced videos that could quickly reach remote teams, and piloted new products. Our team worked tirelessly—sometimes around the clock—to create a suite of more robust, flexible, and refined products than we had ever offered.

As the pandemic raged, business leaders around the world, many now managing fully remote teams, suddenly had to address technology gaps, adaptation fatigue, stress, and burnout, as employees were often asked to do more with less. Resource allocation and cash flow were severely affected in many organizations, compounded by the struggles of leaders learning to build trust and maintain productivity in a remote environment.

Many companies struggled to adapt during the pandemic, resisting change or failing to evolve in ways that met their customers' needs, which ultimately led to their closure. By contrast, those that emerged successfully from the pandemic did so largely because their leaders were agile, leaning into transparency and curiosity, and adapting quickly to address urgent client needs. Flexibility, collaborative skills, and open communication shifted almost overnight from desirable traits to essential qualities for leaders striving to retain talent and remain profitable.

Think about how different your work is today compared to before the pandemic. Before COVID, very few people worked remotely on a regular basis, and those who did often did so for personal or medical reasons. Prior to COVID, Zoom had about 10 million daily participants. By April 2020, as remote work surged, that number skyrocketed to 300 million.[1]

Today, in this post-COVID landscape, leaders face complex challenges in team collaboration and communication. New research from Gallup found that engagement levels for managers fell from 30 percent in 2023 to 27 percent in 2024.[2] Hybrid work, widely adopted during the pandemic, created new obstacles, as virtual environments often left employees feeling disconnected. Only 34 percent of employees today feel effectively connected to their colleagues.[3] One study found that 52 percent of employees reported feeling burned out in the past year, and 37 percent felt so overwhelmed it negatively affected their job performance.[4] Leaders faced the challenge of balancing accessibility and intentionality to prevent burnout, all while adapting to rapidly evolving customer expectations. Additionally, maintaining a strong corporate culture remotely has continued to be a concern, with 80 percent of workers believing they will have some degree of remote work flexibility moving forward.[5]

As COVID slowly receded from the headlines and my international work resumed, I saw firsthand the numerous challenges organizations faced. Through these partnerships, I encountered some glaring shortcomings and concerns that were strikingly consistent across industries and sectors. Nearly every leader I spoke with shared a similar story: with the sweeping changes since the pandemic, coupled with new challenges in managing their teams, bosses and managers were feeling overwhelmed. The processes and strategies that had served them well in the past no longer seemed effective in a post-COVID world, making a new approach to leadership essential.

Many managers found themselves struggling due to gaps in essential leadership and management skills. Budget cuts and resource constraints during the pandemic often led to promotions without adequate training, leaving new leaders feeling overwhelmed and unprepared. These leadership deficiencies created significant challenges for their team members, who frequently felt frustrated and unsupported, as though they were being set up to fail. In fact, 63 percent of people considered quitting their present job solely because of poor workplace communication.[6]

Today, less than half of the world's managers (44 percent) receive any form of management training.[7] Promoting employees to leadership roles without providing them with the necessary skills often leads to failure—failure to communicate a clear vision, drive profitability, and retain top talent. The consequences of this lack of training are significant: global employee engagement levels reached an 11-year low, fueling the "Great Resignation" of 2021, when employees left their jobs in record numbers.[8] According to Gallup, 79 percent of employees worldwide are currently disengaged with their work, a 2 percentage point increase from the previous year. Gallup estimates that if the world's workplace was fully engaged, \$9.6 trillion in productivity could be added to the global economy, the equivalent of 9 percent in global GDP.[9]

Additionally, as younger workers begin to enter the workforce, a generational clash is emerging, driven by distinct differences in how older and younger employees communicate and collaborate. A recent survey by General Assembly found that over 25 percent of executives hesitate to hire recent college graduates because of concerns over their limited interpersonal skills, including communication, adaptability, and collaboration. This lack of "soft" skills is also affecting managers, many of whom are already stretched thin following a wave of mid-level management layoffs.[10] New research from Intelligent.com revealed that one in five managers have considered quitting due to the stress of overseeing Gen Z employees. The study also found that 75 percent of managers believe these younger workers require more time and resources than employees from other generations.[11]

While businesses can't afford to dismiss Gen Z graduates solely for lacking critical interpersonal skills—especially as many haven't yet had the chance to develop them—it's clear that leaders in this new era of work will have their hands full. Bridging this generational gap will require a concerted effort to support and nurture the development of these essential skills. And leaders, take note: 71 percent of younger workers will leave a job within two to three years if they feel their skills aren't being developed.[12]

These challenges inspired me to write *Synergy and Sparks* to share the tools and lessons I've developed over 20 years of helping leaders achieve exceptional results. A foundational precept of my previous books, and the work we do at Pinnacle, is this: the burden of engagement always lies with the speaker. This idea is even more important today than it was when we started this work over 20 years ago.

xix

Introduction

The world is moving faster, technology is creating more distractions, and people's attention spans are shrinking.

When you deliver a presentation or call your team to a meeting, you are asking them to part with their most valuable asset: their time. Your audience doesn't owe you their attention or engagement; you have to earn it and keep it for as long as you can. And as any experienced leader knows, every second you keep them engaged is a privilege; every moment of their attention, a gift. Engagement should never be taken for granted, despite one's rank or role. It must be hard-fought and won, a result of thorough preparation and effective delivery. As a leader, everything you achieve comes from your behaviors and your actions. And like a character in a film or play, your decisions will dictate how others perceive you and whether you will move closer to achieving your given objective.

Synergy and Sparks approaches communication and collaboration from a unique perspective, drawing on performance techniques and psychological approaches used by professional actors to engage and inspire others. As director/author Declan Donnellan reminds us, "We live by acting roles, be it father, mother, teacher or friend. Acting is a reflex, a mechanism for development and survival."[13]

To be clear, this book is not about acting—and you won't become a great actor by reading it. Instead, it explores how techniques drawn from the world of acting—such as body language, adaptability, vocal dynamics, intentionality, and active listening—can enhance your effectiveness as a leader. Since ancient Greece, influential leaders have either worked with acting coaches or borrowed from performance techniques to better engage and influence others. In this book, I'll show you how to apply those same methods to elevate your leadership presence. We'll also explore the neuroscience behind the idea that we are all "performers" in our daily lives, and how every meeting, presentation, or team interaction is an opportunity to take the stage, command attention, and inspire action. Together, we'll delve into both the art and science of powerful communication.

Erving Goffman, a prominent 20th-century sociologist, likened everyday interactions—both personal and professional—to theatrical performances. In his 1956 book, *The Presentation of Self in Everyday Life*, he introduced the idea that, as humans, we navigate "front" and "back" stages, casting ourselves as protagonists in each setting. Goffman argued that in our interactions, we aim to control the impressions we make on others, much like actors performing on a stage.

This idea of "life as theater" is linked to the Latin word *persona*, meaning "a mask worn by actors."[14] Just as actors adapt their performances to their audience, people adjust their behavior based on whom they're interacting with. Goffman used the term *performance* to refer to any activity someone does in front of observers. Our "self" shifts with each "stage" we enter—be it at school, work, or social gathering. Each setting has its own rules, values, and expectations. Within every stage, there are also front and back regions, like in a theater, where we manage different aspects of our public and private selves. We speak differently to our children or parents than we do to our boss or clients.[15] According to Goffman, we are all "social actors," and "the part one individual plays is tailored to the parts played by others present."[16]

General George S. Patton, a key figure in the defeat of Nazi Germany during World War II, is often quoted as saying, 'Half of leadership is theater.' He understood that a leader's presence and presentation play a crucial role in shaping morale, perception, and effectiveness within a team or organization.[17] The connection between a successful leader and a professional actor is a compelling one: both recognize that communication isn't a static thing—it's a dynamic event; an exchange of facts, ideas, and emotions; the outcome of intentional actions. In fact, a Carnegie Institute of Technology study found that 85 percent of a person's financial success comes from their "human engineering"—meaning their ability to effectively communicate and collaborate.[18] In today's corporate landscape, effective communication is a vital component of impactful leadership. As Warren Buffett famously said, "If you can't communicate, it's like winking at a girl in the dark—nothing happens."[19]

The concepts of synergy and sparks stem from my experience working professionally in television, film, and theater, as well as my work coaching CEOs and executives across the globe. Together with my cofounder, David Lewis, I've spent more than two decades developing and refining the Pinnacle Method—a system that has empowered thousands of executives worldwide. It is the dynamic synergy between connection and motivation—the synergy that ignites sparks—that drives impactful outcomes and fosters lasting change.

Synergy and Sparks is organized into six parts, each focusing on what I believe are the essential pillars of modern leadership: *communication, presence, influence, storytelling, collaboration,* and *connection.* Each part provides valuable insights, practical examples, data, and tools that leaders can use to boost their effectiveness and create meaningful impact.

In Part I, "Communication," we'll delve into valuable lessons that business leaders can learn from professional actors: how to prepare effectively, craft compelling content, and deliver messages that resonate with an audience's wants and needs. We'll also explore engagement strategies, examining how leaders can capture and sustain attention in a world full of distractions and change.

In Part II, "Presence," we'll focus on the power of body language and vocal dynamics in enhancing your influence. We'll explore how a confident yet authentic delivery style can quickly establish credibility, build trust, and create meaningful connections with an audience.

In Part III, "Influence," we'll explore the science of engagement and the pivotal role influence plays in effective leadership. You'll learn how to ask strategic questions that drive you closer to your goals, answer questions effectively in the moment, and discover why inspiring purpose and passion within your teams is a proven formula for success.

In Part IV, "Storytelling," we'll explore why humans are inherently wired for stories and examine the power of narrative to engage and influence. We'll cover the five essential business stories every leader should master and I'll provide simple frameworks for crafting impactful stories and anecdotes.

In Part V, "Collaboration," we'll discuss how to build stronger teams, break down silos, and foster effective working relationships by encouraging team members to take risks and innovate. We'll also explore effective strategies for providing constructive feedback and handling challenging conversations—essential skills for successfully managing high-stakes situations.

In the final section, Part VI, "Connection," we'll examine the importance of building relationships and connecting with your network of contacts and team members. We'll discuss strategies for creating trust and fostering a work environment where individuals feel valued and motivated. We'll also detail how leaders can influence the mood of a team or meeting to cultivate optimism, trust, and productivity.

As you explore *Synergy and Sparks* and apply these ideas and insights to your life and work, focus on progress, not perfection. Acknowledge your strengths as a leader while identifying opportunities for growth. Stay open to new ideas and approaches—experiment with the concepts presented, adapt what resonates for you, and make them your own. Becoming a better leader is a journey, not a destination. Embracing change is key to growth and evolution.

I hope this book offers valuable insights to help you build the influence needed to inspire your teams, enhance productivity, and achieve lasting success.

Welcome to *Synergy and Sparks*.

Part I

Communication

Chapter 1

The Stagecraft of Leadership

Your voice is your currency. Spend it like you're a billionaire.
—Kevin Smith

Buckingham Palace and the Queen's Christmas Address

In 2018, I was offered an extraordinary opportunity—one I never could have imagined when I cofounded Pinnacle back in 2005. I was invited to London, on behalf of the Queen of England, to address the Royal Household at Buckingham Palace. Like most people, I had never been inside the 775-room palace, so, of course, I was thrilled to receive the invitation. I eagerly spent the next few weeks designing a custom program, tailoring content that I hoped would resonate with this unique audience, and preparing to deliver a memorable session.

Just days before my departure, I was at my daughter's high school soccer game when I ran into my friend David Murray, executive director of the Professional Speechwriters Association. When I told David about my upcoming engagement with the Queen's team, he was excited for me but posed a question that struck me with an unexpected wave of uncertainty: "How do you think they're going to feel about an American coming to teach them about communication?" Until that moment, I hadn't considered the potential challenge of connecting with a British royal team. Despite my experience—having written two books on communication and working with executives worldwide for more than 15 years—I suddenly felt a surge of self-doubt. What if they didn't respond to me? What if I couldn't bridge the gap?

As the game ended and we parted ways, David wished me well and mentioned something interesting: the Queen's 1957 Christmas address to the nation, her first televised speech. I'd never seen it, but David said it was a powerful example of the Queen's poise and grace, particularly a very human moment at the end of the broadcast when her face lights up with pride after delivering her message so flawlessly. He promised to send it to me, and I left the conversation slightly reassured, knowing I had that video in my back pocket if I needed it.

On arriving in London and passing through Buckingham Palace's multiple security layers, I was escorted into the most beautiful training room I'd ever seen. Ornate ceilings, dramatic doors, and priceless artwork filled the space, and I couldn't help but pause, taking in the grandeur—especially considering I grew up in a small farm town in Minnesota. But as the Royal Household team began to assemble, the old doubts crept back in. What if they didn't respond to my content? What if I couldn't make a meaningful connection?

Then, something unexpected happened. After introducing myself and setting the agenda, I decided on a whim to reference the Queen's 1957 Christmas address. I asked the group if they had ever seen it. Surprisingly, none of them had, and a few had never even heard of it. I could see their curiosity piqued, so I asked if they'd like to watch it. They enthusiastically agreed, and we all watched the Queen's first televised Christmas message as a group.

That spontaneous choice turned out to be a brilliant icebreaker. Not only did it instantly build a bond between me and the Queen's staff, but it also gave them a rare glimpse of their boss in a completely different light. By sharing something they hadn't seen before, I established

4

Synergy and Sparks

credibility and earned their trust. The session, which had started with my own nerves, quickly turned into an engaging and meaningful experience, setting the tone for a day of connection and collaboration with the Royal Household.

How Leaders Connect with Their Audiences: Objective and Intention

Constantin Stanislavski, the founder of the Moscow Art Theatre and the father of modern acting, always believed that the best communication occurs when there's a moment of understanding between two human beings—whether that happens onstage or off. Stanislavski focused extensively on authenticity and true emotional connections between actors to create compelling performances, and many of his concepts and methods can be used by nonactors to improve leadership communication and influence.

Effective leaders, much like skilled actors, begin by identifying a clear *objective*—a specific goal or outcome they intend to achieve with their audience. As Stanislavski explained, "Life, people, circumstances . . . constantly put up barriers . . . . Each of these barriers presents us with the objective of getting through it . . . . Every one of the objectives you have chosen . . . calls for some degree of action."[1]

Whether you are a salesperson motivating a client to buy, a human resources manager implementing a new process, or a clownfish named Nemo trying to get back to your family, you are pursuing something—a goal or result—that is important to you. Both actors and leaders pursue specific objectives at every moment, and the success of their message depends on their ability to influence emotions. Ken Howard, an Emmy and Tony Award–winning actor and Harvard professor, explains it this way: "Just like an actor, an effective communicator must have a clear objective and then take deliberate actions to fulfill it . . . capturing attention, leaving an impression, and

5

The Stagecraft of Leadership

persuading others to act—whether that means buying a product, choosing you over competitors, or making a critical decision."[2]

Throughout history, leaders have honed their communication skills by drawing on the techniques of professional actors, dating as far back as 360 BCE, when the actor Satyrus transformed the Athenian statesman Demosthenes into one of the most dynamic orators of all time. Demosthenes had struggled to capture the attention of his audiences, feeling frustrated that his speeches, despite his intense effort, were often ignored. Satyrus noticed that Demosthenes's delivery lacked the expressive qualities needed to truly engage an audience. To demonstrate the power of delivery, Satyrus taught Demosthenes how physical presence and vocal modulation could dramatically enhance the impact of a speech. Satyrus's guidance was instrumental in helping Demosthenes shift from focusing solely on content to honing his delivery, significantly improving his impact as a speaker.[3]

In the Academy Award–winning film *The King's Speech*, Great Britain's King George VI, struggling with a debilitating stammer, reluctantly seeks help from an unorthodox speech therapist, an Australian actor named Lionel Logue. Through unconventional techniques, which combined vocal exercises with breath work, Logue helped King George find his voice and the confidence needed to deliver a crucial wartime radio speech meant to inspire and unite the British people on the brink of World War II.

In 1960, ahead of the first televised US presidential debate in history, John F. Kennedy enlisted Hollywood director Arthur Penn to help him refine his on-camera presence. Penn advised Kennedy to look directly into the camera lens during the debate and keep his responses concise. Those tips, along with Kennedy's calm, confident demeanor, helped him appear more polished and credible than his opponent, Richard Nixon. This debate is often credited with giving Kennedy an edge with voters, showcasing the power of presence.[4]

Margaret Thatcher, Britain's first female prime minister, also sought acting guidance to strengthen her public image. Initially perceived as dowdy, with a shrill voice, Thatcher's advisor, television producer Gordon Reece (with an assist from actor Lawrence Olivier), arranged for her to study with a coach from the Royal National Theatre. This training helped Thatcher lower her vocal pitch, develop a more commanding tone, and refine her physical appearance, contributing to her authoritative persona.[5]

Before becoming president of the United States, Ronald Reagan enjoyed a successful career as a well-known movie star. Having spent years in Hollywood, Reagan developed a confident on-camera presence, an ability to project warmth and charisma, and a knack for storytelling—skills that proved essential in politics. Other notable leaders have also worked with acting coaches, including Barack and Michelle Obama, Bill and Hillary Clinton, Arnold Schwarzenegger, Oprah Winfrey, Justin Trudeau, and Robert F. Kennedy. All have employed acting techniques to refine their speaking skills. Boxer Mike Tyson performed in a one-man show on Broadway directed by Spike Lee, and Supreme Court Justice Ketanji Brown Jackson, a longtime theater lover, recently made her Broadway debut acting in *& Juliet*. Even Dale Carnegie, the legendary author of *How to Win Friends and Influence People*, began his journey as an actor. His experience on stage helped shape his understanding of effective communication, which later became central to his teachings.

Before becoming the president of Ukraine, Volodymyr Zelenskyy launched his career as a comedian and actor, most famously portraying the president of Ukraine in the sitcom *Servant of the People*—a role he would later step into in real life. His acting background enhanced his ability to deliver impactful speeches and connect with audiences, shaping public opinion both domestically and internationally, especially during Ukraine's protracted conflict with Russia.

7

The Stagecraft of Leadership

In the 2024 presidential election in the United States, candidates Donald Trump and Kamala Harris both tapped into actor-based techniques to motivate and inspire the electorate. Trump's extensive television appearances over the years, from *Saturday Night Live* to *WrestleMania*, sharpened his skill in commanding public attention. Harris, in turn, worked with an acting coach to prepare for debates and interviews. By borrowing from the actor's toolkit, leaders like Trump and Harris enhance their ability to connect, communicate, and inspire—an invaluable advantage in the political arena.

Influencing an audience involves aligning your intention with your delivery. This can be achieved by activating specific "intention cues"—something we'll explore in Chapter 5. By consciously managing elements such as vocal dynamics, body language, and facial expressions, a speaker can shape how their audience perceives them, ultimately influencing emotions and motivating action. The Pinnacle Method, a three-step process for impactful communication, is based on this principle. It provides a clear framework to guide you through these steps:

Step 1: Analyze your audience.

Step 2: Identify a desired outcome.

Step 3: Modify your delivery accordingly.

This methodology combines a strategic psychological approach rooted in neuroscience with the actor's mindset of objective and intention to drive meaningful behavior change. I'll break down the three-step process in more detail shortly, but first, let's define two key concepts: objective and intention.

Objective

An *objective* for a speaker or actor represents something they want or need from their audience; it is the goal being pursued that drives their communication and actions. For example, the objective for an actor playing detective Hercule Poirot might be to identify the killer before they strike again, while the objective for Dorothy in *The Wizard of Oz* is to return home to Kansas to reunite with her family. Every action Poirot and Dorothy take, and every interaction in which they engage, should be in service to that purpose.

Similarly, a leader in a corporate setting must approach their objectives with the same clarity and focus. Whether you're a sales manager motivating your team to hit a target, a real estate agent persuading your buyer to make an offer, or a teacher making US history come alive for your students, success depends on pursuing a clear objective. Entering a meeting or presentation without a well-defined goal is like running a race without knowing where the finish line is: it undermines purpose and makes success difficult to achieve.

Having a specific objective also helps leaders demonstrate passion and purpose, focusing their message and enhancing their delivery, just as it does for professional actors. As Stanislavski observed, "When an actor is completely absorbed by some profoundly moving objective . . . he throws his whole being passionately into its execution."[6] One key difference between actors and leaders lies in their relationship to objectives. In a scene, actors are often driven by conflicting goals, which is what generates the tension and drama. By contrast, a leader's role is to *align* the objectives of their team members, minimizing conflict and fostering collaboration in the pursuit of a common purpose.

Intention

The second part of the equation is intention. In our 2012 book *The Pin Drop Principle*, we described intention as the "rocket fuel" behind your words. In our book *The Bullseye Principle*, we explored how intention helps speakers connect with their audience and hit the bullseye with their message. Put simply: intention determines

9

The Stagecraft of Leadership

outcome, creating an emotional resonance that propels you toward your objective. Steven Bartlett, the popular British entrepreneur and podcaster, puts it this way: "Intention is nothing without action, but action is nothing without intention. Progress happens when your intentions and actions become the same thing."[7] Setting a strong intention and expressing it clearly through your words and delivery will help create a compelling message.

Intentional communication can "make sparks fly"—not just in fiery debates, but in dynamic, engaging conversations that energize and influence. When we speak with purpose, we spark energy, creativity, and connection, turning ordinary interactions into moments of growth and insight. Communicating with intention is about cultivating meaningful exchanges that achieve results and inspire action. As the late scholar and business thinker Sumantra Ghoshal aptly said, leadership is about "making happen what otherwise would not."[8]

In a corporate setting, information presented should always be intentional—illuminating a specific point of view. Intentions help your audience understand how you want them to feel about the information you're providing. When setting an intention, use active verbs with strong emotional impact, such as *excite, motivate, reassure, persuade,* and *challenge*—each of which has the power to engage emotions effectively.

Powerful verbs play a vital role in how people process and remember messages. Leaders who aim to inspire or motivate others often tap into feelings that make their message memorable, fostering a sense of shared purpose. As the French writer and aviator Antoine de Saint-Exupéry beautifully put it, "If you want to build a ship, don't drum up men to gather wood, give orders, and divide the work. Rather, teach them to yearn for the far and endless sea."[9] Studies, including Gallup research, show a strong correlation between passionate, engaged leaders and higher team motivation and productivity.[10]

10

Synergy and Sparks

People naturally gravitate toward leaders who energize and empower them, seeing them as guides rather than mere informers. Conversely, when leaders choose weak intentions for their message, such as *inform*, *update*, or *review*—or fail to choose an intention at all—they risk reducing their communication to passive awareness. Strong intentions, by contrast, energize your delivery, drive behavior, and enhance congruency between your verbal and nonverbal cues. Actors learn early in their training the importance of intention, knowing that it dictates the power of their performance. As Robin Roberts from *Good Morning America* aptly puts it, "Once you know your intentions, once you know that, the rest will fall into place."[11]

The Pinnacle Method

As mentioned previously, the Pinnacle Method is a three-step approach designed to help communicators align their messages in ways that influence emotion and motivate action.

Step 1: Analyze your audience. Effective communication begins with understanding who you are addressing. One common mistake leaders make is thinking about their content before they think about their audience. Entering a presentation or client meeting without a clear understanding of the audience can lead to disconnection or confusion. Just as a tailor wouldn't make a suit for a customer without first taking measurements, the same concept applies to a leader delivering a speech or presentation. Here, too, tailoring your message to your audience's specific characteristics becomes essential for a successful outcome. Key factors to consider include demographics (age, education, occupation, and cultural background), psychographics (attitudes, beliefs, knowledge, and potential reactions), and situational elements (setting, audience size, time of day, seating arrangement, and event structure).

Step 2: Identify a desired outcome. Regardless of the nature of your message—whether good, bad, simple, or complex—it's important to define how you want your audience to feel and what action you want them to take. By aligning your objective with an active intention, such as inspiring, challenging, or motivating your audience, you ensure that your message resonates and influences an audience's attitude, knowledge, or behavior.

Step 3: Modify your delivery accordingly. Often overlooked, this step involves adapting your vocal and visual cues to align with your message, remembering that every aspect of your communication, including tone, expression, and gestures, contributes to the impression you create. Synchronizing these elements with your intention ensures clarity and congruency. For example, smiling when delivering good news, accelerating your speaking pace to convey excitement, or maintaining appropriate eye contact while providing feedback can all significantly enhance the impact of your message.

Self-Awareness: The Key to Authenticity and Growth

Self-awareness is the ability to understand one's own thoughts, emotions, and behaviors, along with the impact they have on others. For a professional actor, self-awareness is essential, as it enables performers to be fully present and aware of how their choices—voice, body language, and movement—affect both their scene partners and the audience. By connecting deeply with their characters and understanding their own emotional responses, actors can convey emotions truthfully and realistically, enriching their performances.

In the business world, self-awareness is equally crucial for leaders, enabling them to recognize their strengths and weaknesses, manage stress, and avoid reactive decision-making. While studies show that 95 percent of people think they are self-aware, only 10–15 percent actually are.[12] In his book *Your Brain at Work*, David Rock says, "Without this ability to stand outside your experience, without self-awareness, you would have little ability to moderate and direct your behavior moment to moment."[13]

Many leaders struggle with self-awareness, often due to the Dunning-Kruger effect—a cognitive bias where individuals with limited skills or knowledge overestimate their competence.[14] In simple terms, those who are mediocre at something often believe they're better than they actually are. This inflated self-perception, driven by overconfidence, can blind them to areas where they need to grow and improve. After all, confidence without competence is just bluster. As the saying goes, "Confidence is quiet; insecurity is loud."

Working with someone who lacks self-awareness can be difficult, often leading to resistance to feedback, heightened conflict, and struggles with empathy. These challenges can create frustration and stress for those around them, making collaboration more tense and less productive.

On the flip side, when leaders have strong self-awareness, their teams enjoy a wide range of benefits. Self-aware leaders are more attuned to their strengths, weaknesses, and biases, which enables them to make more informed, balanced decisions. They also have a clearer understanding of their impact on others, which helps them create a more collaborative, supportive team environment. By addressing issues early, offering effective support, and boosting morale, these leaders increase productivity and engagement—ultimately helping to retain top talent and reduce turnover. Moreover, self-aware leaders are open to feedback and committed to ongoing personal and professional growth.

13

The Stagecraft of Leadership

Self-awareness is a key component of emotional intelligence. Self-aware leaders also recognize their personal triggers—what upsets them or gets under their skin—and can manage their emotions and reactions as a result. They understand the impact of their words and actions on their teams, adjusting them as needed to build trust and respect.

A Case Study in Self-Awareness: Ben Francis

Ben Francis, founder of Gymshark, the British fitness apparel brand, embodies self-aware leadership. Starting as a Pizza Hut delivery driver in Birmingham, England, he founded Gymshark at 19 from his parent's garage. Frustrated by the lack of stylish, affordable gym wear, he and his friend Lewis Morgan created their first products by hand. Using social media and influencer partnerships, Francis quickly grew Gymshark, making it the United Kingdom's fastest-growing company by 2016.[15]

As the company expanded, Francis recognized gaps in his leadership skills, particularly in the areas of communication and people management. After receiving candid feedback describing him as "erratic" and "hot-headed," Francis initially dismissed it, but a conversation with his partner Robin helped him see the truth.[16]

Realizing Gymshark needed a more experienced leader to meet the needs of the moment, Francis made the "heartbreaking" decision to step down as CEO in 2017, appointing Steve Hewitt to focus on operational growth while he worked on his leadership skills. "I'm proud of my decision," said Francis, years later, "I would recommend it to anyone else in the position I was in . . . . Remove your ego and build the team in a way that's truly best for your business."[17] By 2021, Francis resumed the CEO role, and Gymshark is now a billion-dollar brand.

Francis's journey demonstrates how self-awareness drives leadership growth. By embracing feedback and focusing on self-improvement, he became the CEO Gymshark needed, showing that self-awareness is key to both personal and organizational success.

Read the Room: Mastering Social Awareness

Social awareness is the ability to observe and empathize with others, including those from diverse backgrounds and cultures. It directly influences one's ability to understand the unique social and ethical norms that guide behavior within a group or organization. When a person is able to develop social awareness, they can accurately interpret and respond to the behaviors of those around them, fostering stronger relationships and deeper understanding.

For professional actors, social awareness is key to creating authentic relationships with their fellow actors in a scene. Being fully present and attuned to the wide range of physical and vocal cues being communicated from the other performers in a scene is essential to being able to respond or react in a genuine, truthful way. By truly observing and understanding people—their motivations, priorities, and nuances—we ultimately foster empathy. And empathy, as we will explore throughout this book, is foundational to building trust and strong connections, whether onstage or in a boardroom.

Social awareness is crucial in business to navigate the complexities of interpersonal and group dynamics. In a rapidly evolving world—shaped by technology, globalization, and the shift to remote work—leaders increasingly need this skill to manage teams dispersed across different time zones and continents.

Additionally, as younger generations enter the workforce, they bring new priorities and expectations that can differ significantly from those of older team members who are approaching retirement. Cultural differences must also be taken into account, too, as team members in India, for example, may have different working styles compared to their colleagues based at a company's headquarters in

Silicon Valley. Social awareness enables leaders to minimize misunderstandings and foster stronger, globally connected relationships. By recognizing how cultural and generational nuances affect collaboration and communication, leaders can better align, motivate, and sustain productivity within diverse teams.

A Case Study in Social Awareness: The Starbucks Incident

A notable example of an organization demonstrating social awareness during a crisis occurred in 2018 when an incident at a Philadelphia Starbucks led to the wrongful arrest of two Black men.[18] The incident highlighted concerns about racial bias and triggered a nationwide debate. It also stood in stark contrast to the chain's brand, as Starbucks has long positioned itself as a "third place"—a welcoming, inclusive environment between home and work, where anyone can feel comfortable. The brand's image was built on a concept of warmth, community, and a commitment to diversity and inclusivity. The incident, however, painted a starkly different picture: two Black men, simply waiting for a friend, were racially profiled and subsequently arrested after a store manager called the police. This directly clashed with Starbucks' values and corporate messaging.

The public outcry suggested that Starbucks had failed to fully train its employees to handle incidents requiring social awareness and bias sensitivity, exposing a gap in execution that seemed contrary to the brand's commitment to inclusivity. In response, Starbucks CEO Kevin Johnson quickly issued an apology, vowing that Starbucks would do "whatever we can to make things right . . . and make any necessary changes [to] prevent such an occurrence from ever happening again."[19] Johnson subsequently met with the two men involved and then took additional action by closing more than 8,000 Starbucks stores so employees could get antibias training. The move showed social awareness by acknowledging an underlying issue and actively addressing it in a public way. Starbucks has since integrated ongoing training in and dialogue for inclusivity, demonstrating a longer-term commitment to socially aware practices.

Social awareness is essential for today's leaders, as it enhances emotional intelligence and helps them understand and address the diverse emotions, motivations, and needs of their teams. However, building social awareness is a gradual process—one that evolves through continuous personal and professional interactions. As leaders continue to hone these skills, they'll need to navigate new challenges—such as distractions created by technology and the shrinking attention spans of their teams.

In Chapter 2, we'll explore how to effectively manage these distractions and keep their teams focused in an increasingly digital world.

Chapter 2

Solving the Attention Dilemma

Every word has consequences. Every silence too.
—Jean-Paul Sartre

Are We Killing Communication?

Years ago, my teenage daughter and I were cleaning out a closet in her bedroom when we stumbled on my old pager, a relic of early 1990s communication technology. She had no clue what it did, so I explained its function. Her response was priceless: "So let me get this straight," she said, "What this device did was it told you someone wanted to reach you, but it didn't tell you who they were or what they wanted. And if you wanted to call them back, you couldn't use the device to do that?" I nodded, and she replied, "That sounds like the dumbest technology ever. Why would anyone want that?"

This interaction underscores the dramatic shifts in communication and technology over the years, altering how we connect with one another and how we send and receive messages. In a TEDx Talk I delivered in Shanghai, I explored this very evolution, highlighting two fundamental desires in communication: the desire to understand and to be understood. While technology continues to advance, fulfilling these desires has become more challenging—even though the technology itself has made certain tasks easier.

The ways in which we get information, and the speed and frequency at which we receive it, is much different now than it was in 1990.

Today, we have more information available to us at the touch of a button than at any other time in history. As AI evolves, it will continue to transform the way we work and live—streamlining tasks, enabling smarter decisions, and reshaping industries through automation and intelligent systems. And while many of the advances in technology have made our lives easier, there is also a downside to this avalanche of information, mainly increases in noise, distraction, and misinformation.

If you pause to consider the positive impact of the internet on modern work life, it's easy to identify examples where it has made things better. For example, the internet has erased geographical boundaries, creating the opportunity for instant communication between people around the world. It enables meaningful relationships, easier collaboration, and the exchange of ideas across different cultures and time zones. The internet provides access to vast amounts of information and knowledge, democratizing education and enabling people to stay informed. The internet has also increased speed and efficiency, making it possible to collaborate in real time without delays, enabling remote work, international partnerships, and flexible schedules.

Yet, these benefits often come at a cost. While online communication offers convenience, it can reduce face-to-face interactions—vital for developing empathy, interpreting nonverbal cues, and building genuine relationships. Human beings, especially children, are wired for connection, often instinctively mirroring each other's movements and emotions. An overreliance on digital interactions, however, can lead to social isolation, especially among workers from younger generations who've never known life without the internet. A recent study revealed that adults spend an average of 6 hours and 40 minutes per day in front of screens.[1] As psychologist Herbert A. Simon presciently warned us back in 1971, "The wealth of information means a dearth of something else . . . a poverty of attention."[2]

The addictive design of many online platforms further exacerbates communication challenges, leading psychologists to label them "experience blockers."[3] Nearly all of our digital lives today are now dominated by commercial spaces that are focused on buying and selling our attention. These platforms are designed to keep us hooked, often at the expense of genuine connections and real-world interactions. In a 2017 interview, Sean Parker, the first president of Facebook, openly acknowledged the platform's core goal: "How do we consume as much of your time and conscious attention as possible?"[4] The hours spent on social media or online gaming can also increase anxiety and can cut into time that could otherwise be invested in more meaningful, fulfilling activities. Over the past century, as machines have competed more for our attention, the amount of time people spend listening to each other during their waking hours has nearly halved, dropping from 42 percent to 24 percent.[5]

A 2015 Pew Research report found that 25 percent of teens were online "almost constantly." By 2022, this figure had nearly doubled to 46 percent.[6] Such high levels of online engagement mean that even when Gen Z team members are in real-world activities—attending meetings, sharing meals, or conversing—they are often mentally immersed in the digital world. This can affect their connections with family, friends, and colleagues, often leading to strained relationships.

Another major shift in technology's influence occurred in 2007, when Steve Jobs introduced the iPhone at the Macworld conference in San Francisco.[7] This device was revolutionary for consumers, combining a music player, camera, web-browsing capabilities, and a touchscreen mobile phone, all in one compact form. The next version of the iPhone went even further—enabling users to download apps, transforming the smartphone into a tool for watching live events, accessing information instantly, and staying connected from almost anywhere.

Again, consider the pager, that antiquated communication device I mentioned previously. In the early 1990s, the pager was considered cutting-edge. By contrast, today there are more than eight billion

21

Solving the Attention Dilemma

mobile phone subscriptions in the world—more phone subscriptions than there are people—and these devices have claimed a near-constant presence in our lives.[8] In the executive coaching work I do around the world, it's not uncommon to see participants carrying two or three phones with them. For today's leaders, the smartphone has become as ubiquitous as a wristwatch for past generations, but it also creates one of the primary barriers to genuine communication and collaboration.

Massachusetts Institute of Technology professor Sherry Turkle captured this paradox, observing that, because of smartphones, "We are forever elsewhere."[9] And research backs this up, finding that people's minds wander about 47 percent of the time.[10] Turkle's insight reminds us that, even in the presence of others, our attention is often divided, diminishing our ability to be fully engaged and present. Professor Earl Miller, also of MIT, concurs, stating, "Your brain can only produce one or two thoughts in your conscious mind at once." He added, "We're very, very single-minded."[11]

In fact, research from the University of Texas at Austin found that simply having a phone within reach—even if it's off—reduces one's focus and cognitive capacity. "It's not that participants were distracted by notifications," the researchers said, "The mere *presence* of their smartphone reduced cognitive capacity."[12] David Greenfield, founder of the Center for Internet and Technology Addiction, explains why. "Your cortisol levels are elevated when your phone is in sight or nearby, or when you hear it or even *think* you hear it," said Greenfield. "It's a stress response, and it feels unpleasant, and the body's natural response is to want to check the phone to make the stress go away."[13]

One effective way to combat technology distractions, such as cell phone addiction, and maintain focus is by creatively incorporating technology into teamwork and collaborative learning. By turning technology from a potential distraction into a valuable tool, we can enhance engagement and productivity. Dr. Paul Pavlou, dean of the Miami Herbert Business School at the University of Miami, highlighted this approach in his 2021 research. He found that students who had unlimited access to smartphones in the classroom performed worse than those whose phones were banned. However, when students were instructed to use their phones as learning tools in a structured, collaborative context, their performance significantly improved. This research underscores the idea that when technology is purposefully integrated into team-based learning, it can actually boost focus and learning outcomes.[14]

Active listening, as we'll explore in Chapter 17, is crucial for building rapport and strengthening relationships. However, in today's world, smartphones often serve as a significant distraction. In fact, 69 percent of parents admit to being distracted by their phones, highlighting just how pervasive this issue has become.[15] And, sadly, our children notice. A survey of children ages 6 to 12 conducted by *Highlights* magazine found that 62 percent reported their parents were "often distracted" when the child tried to communicate with them. And when they were asked the reasons why their parents were distracted, cell phones topped the list.[16] It's not surprising that Stanford psychiatry professor Anna Lembke describes the smartphone as a "modern day hypodermic needle, delivering digital dopamine 24/7 for a wired generation."[17]

For leaders, overcoming digital distractions is key to fostering meaningful connections and facilitating effective teamwork. Managing one's relationship with technology involves something that I highlighted in Chapter 1: intention. While the internet and our smartphones have undeniably made life easier, it's important we control them rather than the other way around. This means using social media and screen time intentionally. If you find yourself reaching for your phone, ask why—and make sure you have a clear reason beyond boredom or habit.

Being intentional with regard to one's smartphone use is not as difficult as it seems. Many devices have built-in features that limit app

23

Solving the Attention Dilemma

use or set screen time goals. Decide in advance how many hours you're comfortable spending on social media, games, or other "high-use" apps and stick to it. Turn off nonessential notifications to avoid constant distractions and set "Do Not Disturb" periods for focused activities. Monitoring screen use can reveal which apps dominate your time and attention and can assist you in making better decisions. Balancing smartphone use requires mindful choices and gradual adjustments to reshape habits. Finding a strategy that fits your lifestyle will not only allow you the opportunity to manage your workday better but it can also free up time to connect meaningfully with the important people in your life.

Capturing and Commanding Attention

In 1890, the influential US psychologist William James offered profound insights into the nature of attention, defining it from a psychological perspective. For him, attention wasn't just a passive state but a deliberate act of focusing. This meant it also involved an intentional withdrawal from some aspects of our environment to engage more deeply with others.

Attention is actually composed of multiple networks spread across various regions of the brain, working together to form the *attentional system*.[18] James famously likened attention to a "spotlight"—a metaphor that highlights how our minds illuminate certain details while leaving others in the shadows.[19] This ability to focus selectively helps us navigate complexity, make decisions, and act with clarity and purpose. In today's world, filled with constant stimuli, James's insights on attention are more relevant than ever, highlighting the power and necessity of focus.

Gloria Mark is a professor of informatics at the University of California, Irvine, and one of the foremost experts on human focus. "My research over nearly two decades shows that our attention spans are declining, averaging just 47 seconds on any screen," says Mark, "We are experiencing a fundamental shift in how we think, how we work, how we focus, and how we achieve fulfillment. We can all feel it—in our burnout, Zoom fatigue, endless notifications, and our inability to maintain our attention. Technology has been designed with the intent to augment our capabilities and help us produce more, but we are also distracted and exhausted in our everyday use with it."[20] When we think about attention, it's useful to remember that it's not a continuous flow. Instead, attention fluctuates moment by moment across three types: sustained, transient, and kinetic.

- *Sustained attention* is the capacity to concentrate on a task or activity for an extended period, particularly when that task is repetitive or monotonous. Examples include attending a work meeting, listening to someone share a story, or reading a lengthy report. A key characteristic of sustained attention is that its effectiveness tends to diminish over time. To effectively deliver information in a meeting or presentation, it's essential to engage your audience by carefully considering both your delivery and the structure and organization of your material. This is because our ability to maintain attention is shaped by a complex interaction of cognitive, motivational, and emotional factors.[21]

- *Transient attention* refers to brief, involuntary shifts in focus caused by external stimuli, such as a sudden noise or a quick interruption. Unlike sustained attention, which involves conscious focus over longer periods, transient attention is fleeting and often distracts us. Examples include a colleague popping in with a question or a meeting notification pinging on your phone. To manage transient attention effectively, create a distraction-free workspace, schedule time for deep work, and communicate your need for uninterrupted focus to others.

- *Kinetic attention* is a fluid state of attention characterized by rapid shifts, such as transitioning between applications, social media platforms, and websites, or alternating between a computer and a smartphone.[22] If you've ever observed a teenager doing homework on their computer while simultaneously watching television and occasionally checking messages on their smartphone, you've witnessed kinetic attention in action. Mark's research indicates that we often struggle to use kinetic attention effectively, and our attempts can lead to stress, fatigue, or burnout, as the rapid shifts in focus drain our cognitive resources.

To understand our attachment to smartphones and social media—and the negative impact they can have on our attention—it's helpful to examine their effects on our brains, which often occur without our conscious awareness. Much like slot machines, smartphones, and apps are designed to stimulate dopamine releases, fostering habitual use. We experience a momentary pleasurable sensation when someone "likes" our Facebook post or comments on our Instagram photo. A text or WhatsApp notification, for example, offers an instant dopamine rush, sparking curiosity about who sent it and what the message contains. While dopamine release feels pleasurable in the moment, it doesn't lead to lasting satisfaction. Instead, it simply drives a desire for more—more messages, more notifications, more engagement. This cycle of constant stimulation can quickly become addictive, and, as you might expect, it carries notable downsides.

In research conducted by Carnegie Mellon University's Human-Computer Interaction Lab, 136 students were asked to take a test. Some were required to turn off their phones, while others kept their phones on and received random text messages. The students who were interrupted by messages performed, on average, 20 percent worse on the test. Other studies involving similar scenarios have found even greater declines in performance, with some showing a 30 percent drop.[23]

A report by Google found that social media, email, and news apps create a "constant sense of obligation," leading to unintended stress.[24] A study published in the *Journal of Experimental Psychology* found that receiving a notification but not responding is as distracting as answering it.[25] And while many people feel they are good at multitasking, studies show that only 2 percent of the population actually do it well, and these "supertaskers are true outliers."[26] Years of laboratory research have shown us that the only way two tasks can be performed simultaneously, without a drop in performance, is if at least one of them requires minimal effort,[27] for example, listening to music while typing an email. Otherwise, rapid shifts in focus or activities can cause anxiety or stress. And the reason for this is simple: when a task is interrupted or left incomplete, it creates a lingering tension from the unmet urge to finish it, constantly reminding us—again and again—to go back and complete it.[28]

Smartphones can also influence the behavior of those around us. For example, when one person takes out a smartphone—whether at a dinner table, in a meeting, or even in a casual social setting—it frequently triggers others to do the same. In this example, people often feel a subtle pressure to mirror the actions they observe, even if they weren't planning to check their own devices. This effect can quickly shift the dynamic of any gathering, moving attention away from real-time connections and potentially reducing the quality of face-to-face interactions.

Numerous Broadway actors have stopped live performances to confront audience members who were using their phones in the theater. Patti LuPone, the Tony-winning stage legend, actually went a step further. In 2015, during a performance of the play *Shows for Days*, she noticed an audience member texting and, without hesitation, simply walked down into the audience and snatched the audience member's phone, before exiting the scene and proceeding offstage. In that same performance, there were four separate instances of cellphones ringing, which led LuPone to call it "the worst day of my career onstage, all because of the inconsideration—not of the entire audience, but just a few people . . . they ruin it for everyone."[29] Think about the meetings at your organization. Does your company foster a culture of respect and courtesy with regard to phone or computer use during meetings or presentations? If not, it might be time to start implementing some simple ground rules.

Technology, and the distractions that accompany it, can have a negative effect on productivity for leaders and their teams. The average CEO of a Fortune 500 company gets just 28 uninterrupted minutes a day.[30] Research conducted by the University of California, Irvine found that the average worker is interrupted or switches tasks every three minutes and five seconds.[31] These interruptions have a *switch cost effect*, causing the worker to take an average of 25 minutes to get back to their original task.[32] Distractions and interruptions also affect the *quality* of work that takes place. Researchers at Michigan State found that interruptions of less than three seconds doubled the rate of errors on a task.[33] However, intentional interruptions—like taking a walk or practicing breathing exercises—can be highly beneficial, offering mental breaks that help replenish cognitive energy.[34]

In a world where our attention is constantly under siege, reclaiming focus becomes an act of intention and defiance. Our attention, though limited, is one of the most powerful assets we have. By choosing to direct it with purpose—and helping others do the same—we elevate our experiences, deepen our relationships, and strengthen our capacity to lead and connect.

The Power of Surprise

Bill Gates, the philanthropist and cofounder of Microsoft, has dedicated much of his wealth and influence to global health issues, especially malaria. As chair of the Gates Foundation, he has invested heavily in research to combat the deadly disease that is spread by mosquitoes.

In a memorable 2009 TED Talk, Gates delivered a presentation on malaria with a twist that stunned the audience. Rather than relying on a standard PowerPoint filled with statistics, Gates chose an unconventional and provocative approach that left a lasting impression. He placed a container of live mosquitoes on stage and then released them into the audience, saying, "There's no reason only poor people should have this experience." The room, charged with a blend of laughter and tension, quickly grasped his powerful message: empathy and urgency are crucial in tackling the malaria crisis. The crowd erupted into applause, appreciating how Gates masterfully blended a striking visual, dark humor, and a provocative moment to drive home his point. Only then did Gates relieve the audience's anxiety, assuring them the mosquitoes he'd unleashed were not infected with malaria.[35]

The ability to persuade and influence others with your communication—whether in a meeting, presentation or during a one-to-one interaction—is an essential component of effective leadership. And as I have mentioned previously, the burden of engagement always lies with the speaker to keep an audience's attention and ensure that their message is received in the manner it was intended. This task can be challenging, as people's lives are frequently filled with distractions and heavy workloads. Like Bill Gates and his mosquitoes, it is up to you to overcome such obstacles by influencing the emotions of your audience and motivating action. One easy way to do this is by understanding the value of surprise and how to employ it strategically to keep your audience engaged and interested.

Hooks, Humor, and the Pattern Interrupt

The start of a meeting or presentation is crucial—not only for establishing your credibility and hinting at the value of your information but also for setting a strong hook. A *hook* is a powerful, attention-grabbing device designed to make the audience sit up, lean in, and feel compelled to hear more. Thoughtfully selected and relevant to your content, a hook should resonate with listeners and set the tone for the message you're about to deliver.

Effective hooks could include a surprising visual aid (such as the one Bill Gates used), a thought-provoking question or statement ("How many of you would like to work fewer hours and earn more money?"), a compelling story or anecdote that draws listeners in emotionally, or a current event that relates directly to your topic. You can also grab your audience's attention with a surprising fact, a compelling demonstration, or a thought-provoking statistic. When done effectively, a hook piques curiosity, engages your listeners, and sets the tone for a memorable presentation. Research has even shown that curiosity makes people more energetic.[36]

Many studies have explored how long people can stay focused during a speech or presentation before losing interest or becoming distracted. One study found that receptivity is greatest in the first 5 minutes of a lecture, and then begins to decline after 10 minutes.[37] Another study from Finland found that remote viewers began feeling drowsy after just 10 minutes.[38] And both of these studies align with an annual experiment by biology professor John Medina at the University of Washington, which consistently shows a similar outcome. According to Medina, "After 9 minutes and 59 seconds, the audience's attention is getting ready to plummet to near zero."[39]

Humor, when appropriate, is another excellent tool to use for engagement. Surprise is crucial to humor because it disrupts expectations, creating an unexpected twist that triggers laughter. If your audience is laughing, they're listening. When a punchline or humorous element catches the audience off guard, it activates a cognitive shift, releasing tension and sparking amusement. A self-deprecating joke or a funny story, strategically placed in a speech or presentation, can offer a jolt of energy to a room and help a leader stay connected to their audience. Humor can lighten the mood, build connection, and make complex or heavy topics feel more approachable, helping the audience stay attentive and receptive. Ultimately, humor not only entertains but also enhances retention, leaving a memorable impact on the audience.[40]

One of the most effective ways to use surprise strategically in a meeting or presentation is through the use of a *pattern interrupt* (or *changeup*)—a deliberate shift that breaks the usual flow and reengages your audience. Pattern interrupts disrupt the predictable listening patterns that can lead to disengagement. They are employed in much the same way screenwriters use plot twists or new characters to give fresh momentum to a story. As Stanislavski often preached, "A constant supply of spontaneity is the only way to keep a role fresh, on the move. The unexpected is often the most effective lever."[41] Introducing a pattern interrupt at key moments during a meeting or presentation snaps your audience out of routine and renews their focus on your message.

Pattern interrupts can take many forms, such as changing speakers, posing a direct or rhetorical question, introducing a striking visual, soliciting feedback, sharing a relevant story, switching topics, incorporating a brief physical activity, or even taking a quick break. These techniques reset your audience's attentional clock, keeping your presentation or meeting compelling and memorable. Additionally, whenever possible, strive to make your meetings and presentations a dialogue versus a monologue. By doing so, you increase engagement and maximize your influence, making it easier to accomplish your desired outcomes.

As it turns out, we are all hardwired to enjoy new experiences. According to research, the most effective way to capture someone's attention and make an impact may be the element of surprise. Jeffrey Loewenstein, an expert on leadership and creativity, examined the

31

Solving the Attention Dilemma

potential that surprise can have on changing opinions, influencing people, and creating a long-lasting and wide-reaching impact. "Surprise not only generates this emotional reaction," said Loewenstein, "it also is a push to learn, and an experience that people get excited to share with others. Put those things together and surprise becomes a powerful tool for social influence."[42]

Other research backs up this idea as well, finding that surprise makes people more aware of their environment and actually assists with concentration and engagement levels.[43] This can play a key role in someone's ability to engage with and retain the information you're presenting. As experts have discovered, surprise "builds new neural pathways in our brains, leading us to think more flexibly and creatively."[44]

Capturing and maintaining an audience's attention is crucial for leaders, as it ensures their message is not only heard but also understood and retained. Much like magicians, who captivate through surprise and anticipation, leaders can draw people in by creating an atmosphere of intrigue and possibility. As my friend, the acclaimed magician David Goldrake—whose 2023 Las Vegas show was named "Best Magic Show" by the *Las Vegas Review-Journal*—wisely puts it, "We have an inherent need for mystery. A sense of wonder keeps us feeling childlike."[45] In times of change and uncertainty, curiosity and a sense of wonder become even more powerful.

In Chapter 3, we'll delve deeper into the challenges of thriving during such times, and explore how leaders can inspire resilience and adaptability while navigating the unpredictable.

Chapter 3

Thriving During Uncertainty

In the middle of difficulty lies opportunity.

—Albert Einstein

A Focus on Futuring

Several years ago, I had the opportunity to deliver a presentation at Utrecht University of Applied Sciences in the Netherlands, outside Amsterdam. After my talk, a gentleman named Frank Evers introduced himself. Frank was an education designer at the university and the cofounder of a company called PerfectStorm. He explained that his work focused on "futuring"—a process he described as developing tools to envision and articulate both distant and immediate futures. In essence, Frank's role involved studying trends in education and learning to anticipate the skills and strategies that would need to be developed and employed for future success. His mission was to help organizations prepare for the evolving landscape of work by creating actionable plans and implementing tools to stay competitive in a rapidly changing world.

At that time, my eldest daughter was about to begin the daunting and often stressful college application process, exploring various majors. Curious about Frank's perspective as an education futurist, I asked him which field of study he thought would best prepare her for professional success in the future. His response was surprising. Evers explained that, for this younger generation, choosing a specific major was far less important than cultivating the agility needed to thrive in an ever-evolving work environment.

Even back then, Evers had foreseen many of the shifts we're witnessing today, especially in the post-COVID era. He predicted that a new approach to education would be necessary—one that would go beyond specialization to cultivate what he called a "professional, adaptive, value-driven change leader."[1] For my daughter's generation, he suggested, professional success would hinge on the ability to learn new skills quickly, to carry these skills fluidly across roles, and to transition smoothly between organizations and careers. Collaborative abilities, along with the confidence to communicate and work across generational lines, would also be essential. "Many of the jobs our children will hold haven't even been invented yet," said Evers, "Virtually every study on the future of work highlights a job market in flux." He added, "My work is to create an educational system where students learn to be the designers of their own future."[2] In essence, what Evers was emphasizing here was the vital importance of *adaptability*.

The Adaptability Advantage

Adaptability is the ability to remain flexible and responsive in the face of changing conditions, challenges, or environments. It involves adjusting one's mindset, behavior, and skills to meet evolving demands, enabling individuals to succeed even in uncertain or transitional situations. An adaptable person is open to learning and growth, readily embracing new approaches and solutions. Research from Harvard University, the Carnegie Foundation, and the Stanford Research Center all agree that 85 percent of job success is driven by strong interpersonal skills, while only 15 percent is attributable to technical expertise and knowledge.[3]

For professional actors, adaptability is a crucial skill. In a field filled with unpredictability, actors constantly face new challenges and must quickly adapt to different roles, directors, and cast members. When hired for a production, they often have limited time to rehearse or get to know their team, yet actors are expected to perform intense emotional or physical scenes with people they may have just met. This requires them to be open, flexible, and ready to build trust swiftly.

Actors also need to adapt emotionally and physically to embody diverse characters, which sharpens their ability to view situations from multiple perspectives. They may play a benevolent British priest in a film one week and a brutal murderer onstage the next. Their adaptability extends beyond just the performance—it also influences how they build relationships with cast and crew, to create a safe space for collaboration, and maintain flexibility in their approach, even when things go differently than planned on set.

In the corporate world, teams are faced with many of the same challenges. People leave, new people are hired, mergers or acquisitions take place, and downsizing happens, requiring everyone to do more with less, just a few of the situations requiring flexibility and nimbleness. According to Hannah Rosen, author of *The End of Men*, "What the economy requires now is a whole different set of skills: You need intelligence, you need an ability to sit still and focus, to communicate openly, to be able to listen to people, and to operate in a workplace that is much more fluid than it used to be."[4]

Since the mid-2010s, we have witnessed unprecedented shifts that have reshaped how we communicate and collaborate in the workplace. As hybrid work models and fractional leadership become more common, organizations are facing new challenges in fostering engagement and connectivity among dispersed teams. While remote work offers employees flexibility and autonomy, it also makes it harder to maintain a sense of belonging and team cohesion. And while these changes have unlocked remarkable opportunities for connection and innovation for many, they have also introduced challenges, disruptions, and uncertainty for others.

For leaders working in today's interconnected and rapidly evolving world, understanding global sentiments is more essential than ever for fostering collaboration, driving progress, and enhancing overall well-being. As change accelerates and brings significant shifts to our work processes and environments, it doesn't just alter what we do; it reshapes how we relate to each other. And these transformations often trigger emotional responses, affecting how we connect, communicate, and work together. The ability to navigate these emotional shifts and adapt to new ways of working has become an essential skill for leaders, with 65 percent of managers believing that frequent communication is the most important element when leading a team through transition.[5]

The Gallup Global Engagement Study measures employee engagement levels worldwide. This study delves deeply into various aspects of human well-being, covering emotional, social, and economic dimensions. Gallup's latest findings provide a compelling snapshot of how ongoing changes in the business landscape are affecting global workforce engagement and detachment. They also highlight significant challenges for leaders tasked with managing teams across diverse regions.

Gallup's research uncovered two key factors driving worker disengagement: weak leadership and a toxic work culture. Ineffective leadership—marked by a lack of clear guidance, feedback, and recognition—was a major contributor, alongside overwhelming workloads and environments tainted by micromanagement, unhealthy competition, and a disconnect from the company's core mission and values.[6] These findings underscore the urgent need for leaders to implement strategies that reignite employee enthusiasm, cultivate a sense of purpose, and rebuild a culture of engagement within their organizations.

By recognizing and responding to shifts in workers' priorities and expectations post-COVID, leaders can provide a clear, compelling vision to guide their teams through periods of uncertainty. As my late friend and collaborator, Michael Clayton McCarthy—whose notable career included writing for *Saturday Night Live* and *Sesame Street*—often reminded me, the essence of effective communication is to transform "fear into calm, attitude into gratitude, and chaos into clear, purposeful direction."[7] Take a moment to reflect on your team or organization. How engaged do you feel they are right now? What's one change you could make today to improve employee satisfaction? If you're uncertain, the best approach is simple: ask your employees directly.

Engaged employees—those who feel emotionally invested and committed to their work—consistently drive higher productivity, foster innovation, and enhance customer satisfaction. Now is the time to create a workplace that inspires and empowers employees to excel. By prioritizing creative collaboration during times of uncertainty, leaders can unlock their teams' full potential, building a resilient and high-performing workforce. In upcoming chapters, I'll delve into key areas for leaders to focus on to cultivate these outcomes.

Adaptable leaders are open to diverse perspectives, adjust their methods when needed, and embrace leadership styles outside their comfort zones. By fostering adaptability, they boost productivity, engagement, and resilience. Adaptable teams are better equipped to navigate challenges, adopt new technologies, and respond to shifting priorities, improving performance. Leaders can cultivate adaptability by offering learning opportunities, encouraging risk-taking in a safe environment, and providing constructive feedback to support growth. These actions help teams thrive in an ever-changing work landscape.

Research from Constellation Research reveals a striking statistic: 52 percent of Fortune 500 companies from 2000 have either gone bankrupt, been acquired, or ceased to exist.[8] Iconic brands like Radio Shack, Circuit City, and MySpace stand as cautionary tales of businesses that struggled to adapt to evolving technologies and changing market trends. Meanwhile, new companies—many offering products and services that seemed unimaginable just two decades ago—have emerged as integral parts of our daily lives. This rapid shift highlights the dynamic nature of today's corporate landscape, emphasizing the need for young professionals to stay agile, embrace innovation, and continually adapt to remain relevant in a fast-paced world.

Let's take a moment to look at a company that once enjoyed massive popularity and profits, but failed to innovate, leading to significant challenges for its growth and survival.

The Rise and Fall of BlackBerry

In the early 2000s, if you were a business professional, you likely owned a BlackBerry—the smartphone that defined that era. At its peak in September 2011, BlackBerry had a staggering 85 million subscribers worldwide and was widely credited with pioneering the modern smartphone.[9] Owning a BlackBerry during this time was more than just practical; it was a status symbol. The device became the go-to choice for world leaders, corporate executives, and celebrities alike. Former president Barack Obama, for instance, was so attached to his that he famously fought to keep his beloved "CrackBerry" when he took office.[10] BlackBerry's reputation for secure, real-time email and its iconic physical keyboard made it an indispensable tool for professionals at the time. In 2009, BlackBerry held about 20 percent of the global smartphone market, particularly thriving in enterprise environments where its security features were highly valued.[11]

BlackBerry's challenges began in 2007 with the launch of the iPhone, marking a major shift toward touchscreen technology and app-centric ecosystems. BlackBerry's co-CEOs, Mike Lazaridis and Jim Balsillie, underestimated the significance of this change. Internally, BlackBerry executives reportedly dismissed the iPhone as a niche device, seeing it as overly focused on multimedia rather than productivity. This mindset led to a delayed response, as leadership downplayed the iPhone's threat to BlackBerry's core business, failing to recognize the industry's changing direction and the growing consumer demand for devices that seamlessly combined business functionality with entertainment.

The repercussions were dramatic: BlackBerry's once-dominant market share collapsed. The brand went from being a top-selling smartphone in 2009 to holding less than 1 percent of the market by 2016, the same year it ceased its smartphone production entirely.[12] As one BlackBerry insider eventually admitted, "The problem wasn't that we stopped listening to customers. We believed we knew better what customers needed . . . than they did."[13]

The demise of BlackBerry serves as a powerful reminder that change initiatives often fail due to a combination of human, organizational, and strategic factors. Other key issues are a lack of transparency and insufficient involvement from people across all levels of the organization. Without clear communication and engagement, employees often feel disconnected and uninvested in the change process. Additionally, a lack of imagination or forward-thinking can prevent organizations from adapting to shifts in technology or market trends, leading to missed opportunities.

Moreover, when leadership fails to provide a clear, compelling vision, confusion, resistance, and apprehension can take root among employees. A vague or uninspiring direction makes it harder for teams to understand the purpose of the change and how they fit into the larger picture. Furthermore, even the best-laid plans can falter if leadership doesn't equip the organization with the necessary systems, frameworks, and training to successfully implement change. Without the right resources and support, employees are left ill-prepared, and the initiative is likely to stall. Ultimately, for change to succeed, it requires not only a strong vision but also a comprehensive strategy that involves clear communication, adequate support, and a focus on innovation.

39

Thriving During Uncertainty

People are at the heart of any change initiative and a leader must carefully consider this fact. Does the change feel empowering or does it feel imposed on them? Ignoring the emotional and psychological aspects—such as natural feelings of fear and anxiety—can lead to disengagement and even resentment. People often view change as either positive or negative, an opportunity or a threat, largely depending on how they expect it to affect their time, credibility, or personal reputation. However, the emotional impact of change is often overlooked. Dirk Hoke, the CEO of Volocopter, the German aircraft manufacturer, reminds us, "When we fail [at managing change], it's often because we haven't considered the emotional part."[14]

By thoughtfully framing the rollout of your change initiative and positioning it as a positive opportunity, you can help your team see it as a chance for growth rather than a source of anxiety. When people view change in a positive light, they experience what psychologists call *eustress*—a form of beneficial stress that energizes and motivates. Eustress can lead to greater engagement, inspire goal setting, and drive individuals to reach new heights. For example, the excitement of taking on a challenging new project or stepping into a leadership role can spark a sense of purpose and ambition, pushing people to develop new skills and embrace growth.

By contrast, the opposite of eustress is *distress*, a type of stress that arises from feelings of threat, uncertainty, or danger. Distress occurs when change is perceived as overwhelming, unpredictable, or beyond one's control. For instance, a sudden restructuring without clear communication or support can cause employees to feel anxious or fearful, leading to resistance, burnout, or disengagement. Distress not only harms morale but can also hinder performance, creating a cycle of anxiety that prevents people from adapting successfully.

Ultimately, the key is to manage how change is framed and communicated. By providing clarity, support, and a sense of purpose, you can help your team experience the motivating effects of eustress rather than the paralyzing effects of distress.

The Emotional Journey of Change: Surfing the Curve

According to *Forbes*, 31 percent of CEOs are fired as a result of their inability to manage change.[15] As a leader responsible for overseeing change, it's essential to recognize that change is inherently emotional, and team members will react in different ways. Understanding these varied responses and managing them effectively is key to successful transformation.

In 1969, Elisabeth Kübler-Ross, working with terminally ill patients, introduced the Kübler-Ross model, commonly known as the five stages of grief. Though originally developed to explain the grieving process, it has since been widely adapted and expanded to provide insights into how individuals experience and manage organizational change.

The Kübler-Ross Change Curve outlines seven key stages, each representing a distinct emotional response to change: *shock, denial, frustration, depression, experimentation, decision*, and *integration*.[16] Consider any recent change initiative at your organization—whether it was a merger, workforce reduction, or a complete restructuring—and recall the emotional journey it triggered among team members. For a manager or boss, recognizing and responding to the unique needs of individuals at each stage is crucial for maintaining employee morale and productivity (see Figure 3.1).

In the initial *shock* stage of the Change Curve, the person is surprised or in disbelief about what they are experiencing. *What is going on right now?* Here, it is important to acknowledge people's concerns or fears and respond with empathy and understanding.

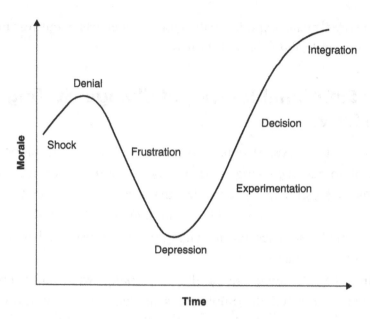

Figure 3.1 The Kübler-Ross Change Curve

Next, they hit the *denial* stage and their mood and morale often drop as they find themselves questioning their circumstances. *This can't be happening!* In this stage it is a leader's job to explain what is happening—and reiterate why—to keep them aligned and focused.

The third stage is *frustration* where team members might start to feel anger or resentment at the workload or what is being asked of them. *I hate all of this!* During this period, it is important to maximize communication and be there to address concerns.

Next, we arrive at the *depression* stage. This is generally the lowest point of the change journey, where morale sinks and energy dips. *I can't do this anymore!* Here, workers might feel burned out or hopeless, so it is important for a boss to spark motivation and keep them going.

Finally rising from the lowest point of the journey, people now see light at the end of the tunnel as they arrive at the *experimentation* stage.

This isn't so bad, I guess. Here, it's important to help team members develop capabilities to succeed, such as training them on new platforms or providing guidance on new processes.

The sixth stage is *decision*, as now your team members can finally see the finish line and start to feel more positive. *Hallelujah!* Their efforts and hard work have paid off, so offer them encouragement as they near the end of the initiative.

The final stage of the journey is crucial: *integration*. The change has been successfully implemented and embraced throughout the organization. *Congratulations, we did it!* As the initiative concludes, thank your team members for their dedication and hard work. It can also be helpful here to gather feedback on how they felt the initiative was managed to understand their experience and identify areas for future improvement.

Understanding the Change Curve can enhance leadership by providing insight into the emotional journey people often undergo during change. With this knowledge, leaders can anticipate different stages, communicate more effectively, offer tailored support, and create a safe environment that fosters resilience.

Harnessing Team Creativity

In today's corporate world, building a team that embraces creativity and innovation brings a wealth of advantages. Creative teams tackle challenges with improved problem-solving frameworks and enhanced adaptability, enabling them to respond quickly to shifting customer needs and unforeseen disruptions. Creating a safe and empowering work environment further elevates employee morale and productivity, as individuals are inspired to work for an organization that values dynamism and forward-thinking.[17] High morale boosts engagement, making it easier to retain top talent and attract new team members. Additionally, creativity fuels passion for the company's mission and helps alleviate workplace stress and anxiety, fostering a positive and resilient culture.[18]

Leaders in today's modern work environment are increasingly seeking creative talent. According to the 2020 World Economic Forum's "Future of Jobs Report," "creativity" was ranked among the top skills employers seek.[19] And this focus is well-founded: organizations today need individuals who can brainstorm, generate innovative ideas, and then integrate those ideas and concepts with emerging technologies to develop new products and services. Albert Einstein famously declared, "Imagination is more important than knowledge."[20] When Einstein made this statement, he wasn't suggesting that creativity inherently outweighs expertise; he was emphasizing that a playful and imaginative approach to problem-solving is often crucial for discovering innovative solutions. In other words, while knowledge is essential, it's the ability to think creatively that often leads to breakthrough insights.

The Art of Agreement: How "Yes, And" Drives Collaboration

Actors and writers in film, television, and theater spend their days collaborating creatively to bring productions to life, telling stories that capture the human experience. Often beginning with nothing more than a blank page and an initial idea, they develop concepts through intense collaboration, transforming them into art. Actors and writers draw from personal experiences and their collective imagination in every aspect of their work. They also learn to set their egos aside, finding ways to compromise and collaborate with others during the creative process.

In improvisational theater, the concept of "Yes, And" empowers actors to build scenes together in a spontaneous, collaborative, and constructive manner. This technique, popularized by theater innovators like Viola Spolin and her son Paul Sills, as well as the renowned improv theater, The Second City, in Chicago, encourages actors to accept and expand on each other's ideas. The principle was further developed by Del Close, the legendary actor and improv teacher, with whom I had the privilege of acting alongside early in my career.[21]

The "Yes, And" technique has two key rules. First, "Yes" means accepting the reality established by another actor. For example, if one actor says, "We're underwater," the other accepts it rather than contradicting it. Second, "And" means adding new information to build on that reality, like saying, "Look over there—a shark!" Together, "Yes" and "And" foster a supportive environment, encouraging active listening and collaboration, which keeps scenes dynamic and unpredictable.

Leaders can use "Yes, And" to foster collaboration, trust, and momentum within their teams. Instead of dismissing ideas, they should encourage team members to build on each other's contributions. This approach makes individuals feel heard and valued, motivating them to engage more deeply and contribute their best. For example, instead of rejecting an idea, a leader might say, "Yes, and what if we also try . . . ?" This response affirms the idea and sparks further innovation.

By modeling "Yes, And," leaders create a culture where team members feel confident sharing ideas without fear of rejection. This fuels collaboration and problem-solving. Research shows that when people believe their work contributes to a larger purpose, they are more likely to exceed expectations.[22] In short, "Yes, And" helps leaders create an environment where ideas flow freely, momentum builds, and teams feel connected to the bigger picture, driving both engagement and success—especially when change abounds.

US essayist George Scialabba once declared, "Creativity is intelligence having fun."[23] For anyone who faced the unprecedented

45

Thriving During Uncertainty

challenges of the COVID pandemic, it's clear that agility and creative thinking during times of change can mean the difference between success and failure, survival and extinction. Creativity enables us to engage our intellect in playful and innovative ways, finding joy in exploration and discovery. It reminds us that intelligence goes beyond solving problems; it's also about imagining possibilities and bringing new ideas to life.

Steve Jobs blended creativity with technology to shape Apple's iconic products, like the iPhone. Drawing inspiration from his passion for art, he believed in the fusion of technology, design, and simplicity. His interest in typography and calligraphy, particularly during college, influenced Apple's distinctive aesthetic. Jobs's design philosophy and attention to detail showed how creative leadership can drive revolutionary innovation.[24]

Google stands as one of today's most influential and innovative technology companies, and a key factor in its success is their "20 Percent Time" initiative, a work arrangement first detailed in 2004, that allows employees to dedicate 20 percent of their work time on projects of their choice.[25] "We encourage our employees, in addition to their regular projects, to spend 20 percent of their time working on what they think will most benefit Google," stated founders Sergey Brin and Larry Page in their initial IPO letter. "This empowers them to be more creative and innovative."[26] The creative freedom fostered at Google has led to remarkable innovations, with the 20 Percent Time initiative sparking breakthroughs such as Gmail and Google News. These developments have not only enriched Google's product portfolio but also significantly boosted employee motivation.[27]

Best Buy, the multinational electronics retailer, encourages creativity and innovation through its "Pitch Fest" program, which invites employees at all levels and roles to submit ideas and suggestions. Inspired by the popular show *Shark Tank*, this initiative allows leadership to tap into the diverse insights of its workforce. According to

Jennie Weber, Best Buy's chief marketing officer, the event "is a really great way to get both big and small ideas from the teams that are directly interfacing with consumers every single day."[28]

Today's leaders can learn from Google and Best Buy's approaches to creativity and collaboration, which serve as powerful models of innovation. Every breakthrough starts with a simple idea, nurtured through vision, persistence, and experimentation. Over time, these ideas evolve to reshape industries and the world. At the heart of every great innovation is creativity—the spark that drives progress. As Constantin Stanislavski said, "You can kill the king without a sword, and you can light the fire without a match. What needs to burn is your imagination."[29]

In Chapter 4, we'll delve into the importance of presence for a leader—how being fully engaged, authentic, and grounded can significantly shape their ability to inspire others and lead with credibility and confidence.

Part II

Presence

Chapter 4

Boosting Confidence and Maintaining Credibility

It is not the mountain that we conquer, but ourselves.
—Sir Edmund Hillary

The Cybertruck Debacle: Lessons in Preparation

Elon Musk, the unconventional entrepreneur behind groundbreaking companies like SpaceX, Tesla, and the media platform X, currently holds the title of the world's richest person. Known for his unorthodox approach to leadership and management, Musk has become one of the most recognizable figures of our time. In 2019, after years of intensive research and development, Musk and Tesla unveiled the highly anticipated Cybertruck—an all-electric pickup with a striking, angular design that immediately turned heads and sparked conversations worldwide. Marketed with "shatterproof" windows, Musk boldly claimed the Cybertruck was "literally bulletproof to a 9 mm handgun."[1]

At a highly publicized presentation in Los Angeles, Musk took the stage to enthusiastic applause. Dressed in all black, he introduced the Cybertruck, which rolled into view amid smoke, flashing lights, and pounding music. To demonstrate the strength of the truck's "Armor Glass" windows, Musk invited Tesla's chief designer, Franz von Holzhausen, to join him on stage and instructed him to throw a steel ball at the truck's window to showcase its resilience. "Are you sure?" von Holzhausen asked, to which Musk responded confidently, "Yeah." But when von Holzhausen hurled the steel ball, the unthinkable happened: the window shattered on impact. A moment of stunned silence followed as the audience processed the unexpected outcome.[2]

Undeterred, Musk and von Holzhausen decided to try again, this time aiming for a different window. Yet again, the glass failed, shattering under the force of the steel ball and leaving Musk visibly embarrassed before the audience.

Footage of the mishap, accompanied by a surge of internet memes, went viral, reaching millions worldwide. The failed demonstration had swift repercussions, causing Tesla's stock to plummet by more than 6 percent and erasing an estimated $768 million from Elon Musk's personal net worth.[3] It's safe to say that this outcome was far from what Tesla's leadership had envisioned for the rollout. Reflecting on the incident a year later in a conversation with podcaster Joe Rogan, Musk admitted that inadequate preparation was at fault, stating, "At Tesla, we don't do tons of practice for our demos . . . we don't have time for that."[4]

This example underscores the critical role of preparation when delivering a high-stakes message. Psychologists have long observed a direct correlation between preparation and confidence levels: the more familiar you are with your content, the more secure you feel when delivering it. Competence and confidence go hand in hand.[5] Preparation helps reveal potential risks and ensures you are positioning yourself for success. Interestingly, four years after the infamous Cybertruck launch, Musk and von Holzhausen returned to present a new, redesigned model. This time, von Holzhausen threw a baseball—rather than a steel ball—at the Cybertruck's upgraded windows. To Musk's relief, the windows held firm, allowing Tesla (and Musk) a moment of redemption in the public eye.

Synergy and Sparks

Laying the Groundwork for Success

As mentioned in Chapter 1, the first step in the Pinnacle Method is to thoroughly analyze your audience before delivering any important message. By understanding your audience and what matters to them, a leader can craft and deliver a message that truly resonates. Each person interprets your message through their own distinct lens, shaped by their personal experiences and core values.

During any communication—whether in a meeting, a presentation, or a performance review—a message rarely travels directly from speaker to audience; it's always filtered through the audience's unique attitudes, experiences, biases, and assumptions—a concept we call the *prism of priority*. Author Virginia Woolf reminds us that "words are full of echoes, of memories, of associations. They have been out and about, on people's lips, in their houses, in the streets, in the fields, for so many centuries."[6] Every word you speak carries layers of meaning shaped by its past uses and the listener's perspective.

We all possess biases rooted in our unconscious tendency to categorize, as well as the challenge of fully understanding experiences beyond our own. Effective leaders need to actively recognize and confront these biases to ensure their communication is fair, inclusive, and impactful. Assumptions based on factors such as age, gender identity, ethnicity, socioeconomic status, religion, political beliefs, or sexual orientation hinder understanding and weaken our shared humanity.[7] By reflecting on one's own assumptions and remaining open to diverse perspectives, leaders can craft messages that truly resonate with all audiences.

When preparing for a meeting or presentation, consider how your audience might feel about the information you're presenting and how they might perceive you as the messenger. What emotions do you hope to evoke? What benefit or value can you provide them? What questions might arise as they process what you're saying?

To connect with your audience on a deeper level, start by asking yourself, what matters to them? What matters to them at this moment? Why should they care? By exploring these questions, you can begin to craft a message that resonates beyond the surface.

To reinforce customer-centric decision-making, Jeff Bezos famously introduced the concept of the "empty chair" in Amazon meetings: during discussions or decision-making sessions, Bezos would place an empty chair at the table to symbolize the voice of the customer. This served as a constant reminder that, even though the customer wasn't physically present, their needs and perspective should always be at the forefront of every decision. This was meant to reinforce the principle that all decisions, whether related to product development, business strategy, or customer service, should prioritize the customer experience. Think about the meetings at your organization. How effectively do you keep the wants and needs of your customers at the forefront of what you do?[8]

Applying Stanislavski's Seven Questions to Leadership Communication

Constantin Stanislavski, the renowned Russian acting master, developed several key questions to help actors deeply understand their characters and deliver truly authentic performances.[9] These questions were later distilled and formalized by acting teachers and practitioners who studied and adapted Stanislavski's methods, eventually becoming known as "Stanislavski's Seven Questions." Originally designed for the stage, these questions can be adapted to offer valuable insights that can be applied beyond acting. For leaders in the corporate world, they provide a powerful framework for enhancing communication, fostering empathy, and connecting more effectively with teams and stakeholders.

Question 1: Who Am I?

Stanislavski emphasized the importance of actors understanding their character's identity, motivations, and how they're perceived. Similarly, as mentioned previously, leaders can benefit from self-awareness—understanding how they're viewed by their audience. Acknowledging your influence, authority, and credibility not only boosts confidence but also enhances the impact of your communication.

Question 2: Where Am I?

Actors must connect with the spaces their characters inhabit for believable performances. Leaders, too, should consider the physical and emotional environment in which they present or communicate. Whether it's a formal boardroom, a casual team meeting, or a virtual setting, understanding the audience's perception of the space and the emotional tone of the environment can help you tailor your approach.

Question 3: When Am I?

In theater, time frames a character's actions. For leaders, timing is equally critical. In leadership, this means recognizing the right moment to take action, make decisions, or influence others. Such awareness helps ensure that actions are timely and aligned with the broader context. A leader must consider when to intervene or step back, determining whether a situation requires immediate action or a more measured approach.

Question 4: What Do I Want?

Actors define a character's objectives to drive their actions. Similarly, leaders should identify a clear goal for their communication. Whether it's gaining approval, securing funding, or advocating for change, a well-defined objective gives focus and purpose to the message and provides a benchmark for evaluating success.

Question 5: Why Do I Want It?

Every objective is driven by purpose. Leaders who have a deep understanding of the why behind their messages are able to communicate with both clarity and impact. Intention also plays a crucial role, as it shapes not only your delivery but also the emotional resonance with the audience. When your purpose aligns with your audience's needs, it inspires action.

Question 6: How Will I Get What I Want?

Actors use vocal techniques, body language, and gestures to influence their scene partners. Similarly, leaders can leverage all of the those, plus deliberate word choices and strategic questioning to strengthen their message. Vocally adjusting one's tone, pace, and emphasis can evoke a desired emotional response and guide the audience toward a goal.

Question 7: What Must I Overcome to Get What I Want?

In both acting and leadership, obstacles are inevitable. For leaders, recognizing and addressing potential barriers—be they logistical, cultural, or interpersonal—is key to achieving success. Anticipating challenges enables creating proactive strategies, such as preparing counterarguments or crafting creative solutions.

Using Stanislavski's seven questions during the preparation process not only strengthens a leader's ability to navigate obstacles but also fosters a deeper understanding of the audience's needs and perspectives. This approach embodies the same commitment to readiness that Stanislavski encouraged in his actors, ensuring a more impactful and successful delivery.

Overcoming Speech Anxiety and Self-Doubt

An actor performing on a stage and a business professional delivering a presentation share a common goal: to engage their audience while effectively conveying a message. Both must strike a balance between preparation and spontaneity, ensuring their delivery feels authentic and compelling. They also face similar challenges, such as nervousness or speech anxiety, driven by the pressure to perform well under scrutiny.

Not surprisingly, people prefer to receive information or advice from a confident source.[10] Ultimately, both actors and presenters must harness their fears as fuel to connect with their audience, turning vulnerability into presence and pressure into power. As I learned from the years I spent performing with a Chicago-based circus, a person's full potential lies just on the other side of fear.

Studies reveal that 77 percent of people experience anxiety speaking in front of others.[11] This common fear, known as *glossophobia*, stems from psychological, physiological, and situational factors. At its heart is a fear of negative evaluation—worrying about judgment, mistakes, or unmet audience expectations. This fear activates the body's fight-or-flight response, flooding the system with adrenaline and triggering physical symptoms like a pounding heart, shortness of breath, or trembling hands, which often heighten nervousness. Past experiences, perfectionism, and self-doubt can further intensify this anxiety. For a corporate leader, the high stakes of presenting in a meeting or presentation—where their ideas, credibility, and reputation may feel vulnerable—can amplify anxiety. Additionally, when a leader is deeply invested in the topic and holds themselves to high standards, the pressure intensifies, further elevating feelings of stress and uncertainty.

Experts suggest that the speech anxiety many people experience isn't entirely negative; in fact, it has deep evolutionary roots tied to survival. Our ancestors depended on social belonging to ensure their safety and access to resources, so the fear of rejection became an adaptive response to protect their place in a group. "Feeling nervous about rejection, as well as experiencing anxiety or fear in general, are completely normal human emotions," explains Dr. Taylor Wilmer, a licensed clinical psychologist. "In small, manageable doses, these emotions serve an important purpose by helping to keep us safe."[12] These feelings of nervousness can heighten awareness, improve focus, and prepare the body for challenges, making them a natural response to situations where success feels critical.

Wendy Suzuki, a professor of neural science and psychology and dean of the College of Arts and Science at New York University, highlights the purpose of anxiety and argues that anxiety can guide us in the right direction. "Most people just want to get rid of all their anxiety," says Suzuki. "They don't want to think about it; they want to kick it out the door." However, Suzuki contends that paying close attention to our anxiety can help us focus on what truly matters in any given moment. "You worry about your work, your finances, your relationships. These are things that matter to you. And so what your anxiety is doing is really showing you what matters most."[13]

The Sweet Spot: Balancing Stress and Performance

The relationship between anxiety and performance has been studied extensively. In 1908, psychologists Robert Yerkes and John Dillingham Dodson introduced the Yerkes-Dodson law, which illustrates how stress affects the execution of a task, offering insights into finding the optimal balance between pressure and peak performance (Figure 4.1).

Yerkes-Dodson suggests that experiencing *moderate* levels of stress can significantly enhance performance by providing the motivation and focus necessary to tackle challenges effectively. However, when stress exceeds this optimal level, it can overwhelm individuals, leading to diminished performance due to heightened anxiety, distractions, or even burnout. On the other side of the curve, insufficient stress can result in underperformance or boredom, as a lack of stimulation fails to engage energy or motivation. Professional actors and athletes welcome a little adrenaline pumping before a show or sporting event, and use it to energize or supercharge their performance; leaders should do the same. The Yerkes-Dodson model emphasizes the importance of finding that right balance, where moderate stress creates a sense of challenge without becoming overwhelming. Within this optimal range of arousal—much like an athlete or actor—individuals are at their best, performing tasks with greater efficiency and success.[14]

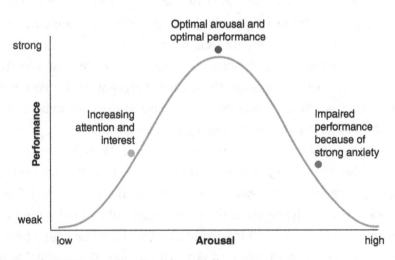

Figure 4.1 Yerkes-Dodson law bell curve

Navigating Imposter Syndrome

One of the leading causes of speech anxiety is *imposter syndrome*, a psychological pattern in which individuals doubt their own skills, talents, or accomplishments and experience a persistent fear of being exposed as a fraud. Despite clear evidence of their competence, people with imposter syndrome often falsely attribute their success to luck, timing, or external factors, rather than recognizing their own abilities or efforts.[15] While environmental stressors such as racism and discrimination can significantly contribute to imposter feelings among marginalized individuals, imposter syndrome is a challenge that affects a broad spectrum of workers, not just those from underrepresented groups. Research indicates that as many as 82 percent of people experience imposter syndrome at some point in their lives.[16]

The concept of *imposter syndrome* (or *imposter phenomenon*) was first introduced in 1978 by clinical psychologists Pauline Clance and Suzanne Imes, focusing initially on high-achieving women. Over time, the term *imposter syndrome* has expanded to describe the feelings experienced by individuals from all backgrounds, including men. Notable figures like David Bowie, Maya Angelou, and Sheryl Sandberg have publicly shared their struggles with imposter syndrome. Even Tom Hanks, the legendary actor and two-time Oscar winner, is not immune. Reflecting on his experiences, he admitted, "No matter what we've done, there comes a point where you think, 'How did I get here? When are they going to discover that I am, in fact, a fraud and take everything away from me?'"[17]

Interestingly, a study conducted by Stanford Medicine researchers reveals that physicians were at a 30 percent increased risk of reporting impostor syndrome symptoms versus workers in other US professions. This study, believed to be the largest of its kind, found that one in four physicians feel inadequate or fraudulent despite a proven track record of competence and years of training. This highlights not only the widespread nature of the phenomenon but also its unique prevalence within the medical field, where the pressure to be perfect and constantly perform at a high level is particularly intense.[18] One eye-opening study from the *Harvard Gazette* found that stress and burnout for doctors costs the health care system $4.6 billion a year.[19]

For leaders, overcoming imposter syndrome begins with redirecting focus toward their talents and accomplishments. Additionally, it's important to remember that most audiences are rooting for you—they want you to succeed and are eager to learn from the insights you're sharing. Cultivating an inner voice that is supportive and empowering—rather than negative or overly critical—is essential. As author Brené Brown wisely put it, "Don't walk through the world looking for evidence that you don't belong, because you will always find it. Don't walk through the world looking for evidence that you're not enough, because you will always find it. Our worth and our belonging are not negotiated with other people. We carry those inside."[20] It's also helpful to remember that our inner voice is shaped not just by those around us but also by the media we consume. What does your inner voice say to you? Is it kind or cruel? How does it shape your view of yourself and others—do you see the best or the worst?

The Perfection Paradox

Visualizing success can be a powerful tool for anyone preparing to deliver a speech or presentation. However, for leaders, the relentless pursuit of perfection can become a hidden trap—one that stifles authenticity, increases anxiety, and ultimately hinders performance. One of the first things I do when coaching an executive is help them shift away from the idea of "perfection"—a goal that is both unhelpful and unattainable—and instead guide them toward the pursuit of excellence. The great acting coach Lee Strasberg once noted in an interview, "Whatever step anybody has achieved is always only the prelude to something more. It's an unending series of steps. There's no point at which you get to the top floor. Nobody knows where the top floor is."[21] An excessive focus on perfection not only leads to inevitable disappointment but often signals that a leader is allowing their ego to take control. As Julia Cameron, author of *The Artist's Way: A Spiritual Path to Higher Creativity*, explains, "The perfectionist is never satisfied. The perfectionist never says, 'This is pretty good. I think I'll just keep going.' To the perfectionist, there is always room for improvement. The perfectionist calls this humility. In reality, it is egotism," says Cameron. She added, "Perfectionism is not a quest for the best. It is a pursuit of the worst in ourselves, the part that tells us that nothing we do will ever be good enough."[22]

Overcoming imposter syndrome and speech anxiety starts with recognizing and acknowledging the feeling; awareness is the first step toward addressing it. Sharing your experiences with trusted colleagues, mentors, or a therapist can help normalize these emotions and reduce their power. Grounding yourself in facts—such as maintaining a record of your achievements and the positive feedback you've received from bosses, clients, or peers—can counteract negative self-perceptions.

Reframing mistakes as opportunities for growth rather than evidence of professional inadequacy can also shift your perspective, encouraging a focus on improvement instead of unrealistic or unattainable standards. Finally, embracing imperfection and internalizing the idea that the goal is progress, not perfection, helps prioritize continuous improvement over chasing impossible ideals.

Showtime: Meeting the Moment

The opening night of a play shares many parallels with delivering an important presentation or leading a critical meeting. In both scenarios—whether you are an actor stepping onto the stage or a leader addressing your C-suite—clear objectives have been defined and a purposeful intention has been set. The stakes are high, with expectations soaring as the audience eagerly anticipates the information you are about to share. Success in either context depends not only on preparation but also on the ability to engage, connect, and adapt to the needs of your audience. Both require a strong sense of presence, confidence, and the skill to communicate in a way that inspires trust and leaves a lasting impression. Just as an actor relies on rehearsal and craft, a leader must prepare their message with clarity and purpose, recognizing that their audience's experience hinges on the effectiveness of their delivery.

The more prepared someone is before delivering a presentation, the more relaxed, confident, and composed they will appear on the day. Just as an actor must thoroughly know their lines and embody a specific, believable character, a leader must project confidence, clarity, and credibility while fully understanding the material they are presenting. Achieving this level of preparation requires both time and effort.

One key step during the preparation process is rehearsing out loud, ideally in front of a practice audience that can provide constructive feedback. Great presenters never step onto the stage without first doing a dress rehearsal, much like an actor preparing for opening night. Steve Jobs was renowned for his meticulous preparation for Apple product launches, often rehearsing his presentations in the campus auditorium for his team up to a month in advance.[23] Additionally, it is also helpful to record your practice sessions and review them afterward to make necessary adjustments and improvements.

An often overlooked yet essential element of effective presentations is the mastering of transitions during the preparation process. Smoothly moving from one topic to the next creates a natural flow, making the presentation easier for the audience to follow and keeping their attention engaged. Clear transitions act as signposts, guiding your audience through the narrative of your message with clarity and precision. Whether it's a pitch, a team meeting, or a high-stakes presentation, the time invested in rehearsing your transitions ensures your delivery is seamless, impactful, and memorable.

On the day of a high-stakes meeting or important presentation, it is not uncommon for nerves to start creeping in as the big moment approaches. Warming up the body physically—through stretches or light movement—can help release tension and reduce nervousness, allowing a leader to feel more grounded and confident as they step into the spotlight. A leader, much like an actor, must stay calm and focused in order to deliver a compelling and impactful message. One effective way to achieve this is by centering attention on one's breath, which helps to calm the mind and sharpen focus.

Breathwork: Inhale Confidence, Exhale Stress

Breathing is essential for a speaker because it significantly influences both physical and mental performance. Controlled, intentional breathing helps to calm nerves, regulate energy, and reduce anxiety, enabling a leader to appear composed and confident. Proper breathing also powers the voice, adding strength, resonance, and clarity to the message. By contrast, shallow breathing can make the voice sound weak or strained, diminishing a leader's authority and impact.

Breathwork also helps a leader center their thoughts, enhancing focus and minimizing distractions. Mindfulness fosters a sense of control, enabling the leader to stay fully present and engaged with both their message and audience. Moreover, effective breath control reinforces physical poise, instilling self-assurance for a leader as they step into the spotlight. According to Dr. Aditi Nerurkar, a physician at Harvard Medical School, breathing fully, feeling the air expand in your belly, stimulates the vagus nerve, which sends a message to your brain that says, "We can calm down."[24]

If you feel speech anxiety starting to hijack your confidence before a meeting or presentation, you can quickly calm yourself and regain focus using a technique called *box breathing*. This form of controlled breathwork, with ancient roots in Indian practices, has been widely adopted by Navy SEALs and other special operations units to manage high-stress situations. Many actors also rely on box breathing during their warm-ups to reduce nerves and prepare both mentally and physically for their performances.

Box breathing gets its name from its structured, four-step process, which forms a box with equal phases of breathing (see Figure 4.2). By intentionally slowing your breath, you can relax your mind and body, increase oxygen intake, and release built-up tension.

To practice box breathing, start by inhaling deeply through your nose for a count of four. Once you've fully inhaled, hold your breath for another count of four. Next, exhale slowly through your mouth for a count of four, then hold your breath again for a count of four before beginning the cycle once more. Continue repeating this

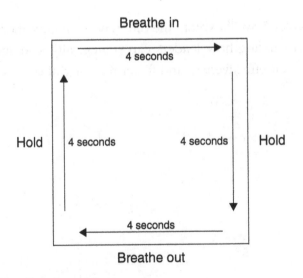

Figure 4.2 Box breathing

process several times, allowing yourself to feel progressively calmer and more centered with each cycle.

In moments of more intense anxiety, employing a *physiological sigh*—a calming pattern pioneered by Dr. Andrew Huberman at Stanford University—can offer a quick and effective way to restore focus and calm.[25] This simple technique involves taking two quick inhales through the nose, followed by a long, slow exhale through the mouth. The first inhale fills the lungs, while the second fully expands the air sacs, functioning as a reset button for both the respiratory and nervous systems. Repeating this cycle a few times can rapidly reduce stress, making it an invaluable tool for an actor or leader preparing to deliver a high-stakes message.

Preparation and focus are the cornerstones of a leader's ability to present themselves as both confident and credible. By investing time in rehearsal, refining key messages, and understanding the needs of their audience, leaders can ensure they communicate with clarity and authority. The more prepared they are, the more naturally they can inspire trust and influence others, reinforcing their leadership presence.

In Chapter 5, we'll explore the different communication channels in detail, discussing how leaders can strategically leverage them to maximize their effectiveness and foster meaningful connections.

Chapter 5

Elevating Your Leadership Impact

My presence speaks volumes before I say a word.

—Mos Def

First Impressions Last: A Meltdown in Las Vegas

Michael Bay is an acclaimed US filmmaker celebrated for his visually spectacular action films, including *Bad Boys*, *Pearl Harbor*, and the blockbuster *Transformers* franchise. Renowned for his signature style of explosive set pieces, dynamic camera work, and groundbreaking visual effects, Bay's films have collectively grossed billions at the global box office. His work epitomizes the grandeur and appeal of big-budget, high-concept Hollywood filmmaking.[1]

In 2014, Samsung debuted their 105-inch UHD television, nicknamed "The Curve," at the Consumer Electronics Show in Las Vegas. To add star power to the launch, they enlisted Michael Bay, a master of cinematic spectacle, anticipating that his reputation would lend credibility and excitement to the event, generating buzz and boosting sales. However, the moment went viral—but for all the wrong reasons, leaving Samsung with a publicity spectacle they hadn't intended.

When Bay was introduced and took the stage, joining Joe Stinziano, Samsung's executive vice president, it was immediately apparent that the renowned director was uneasy. Fidgeting nervously and shifting his weight from side to side, Bay struggled to project confidence or credibility in his demeanor. Things quickly unraveled when a teleprompter malfunction left him flustered and unable to proceed without his scripted lines.

Stinziano attempted to salvage the moment by asking Bay a simple question about his work as a director, hoping to ease the tension. However, Bay's discomfort only deepened. His attempt to improvise faltered, leading to an awkward pause. Overwhelmed, he apologized, then abruptly walked off stage—bailing on the presentation just over a minute into his remarks. The incident left the audience and Stinziano stunned, with Bay's public meltdown soon becoming a widely shared viral video.

Shortly after the debacle, Bay took to his blog to apologize, writing, "Wow! I just embarrassed myself at CES . . . I guess live shows aren't my thing."[2] The Samsung episode has since become a prime example of how insufficient preparation, difficulty in thinking on one's feet, and overreliance on technology can jeopardize even the most high-profile presentations.

Signaling Theory and Congruence

First impressions are critical for a leader in establishing credibility, trust, and rapport. Similarly, when a character is introduced in a play, the audience immediately begins forming judgments: can they be trusted? Do they exude confidence or weakness? How do they interact with others? This same process—known as *signaling theory*—applies when a speaker begins a presentation or starts a meeting.[3] Every word, action, and interaction shapes how the audience perceives a speaker.

Researchers at the University of Toronto investigated how brief observations of an individual's behavior influence perceptions of charisma and judgments about leadership potential.[4] Their findings revealed that observers can assess a speaker's charisma and leadership suitability within just five seconds based on subtle behavioral cues. These "thin slices" are often reliable indicators of leadership qualities, supporting signaling theory and the psychology of first impressions. Furthermore, the study highlighted the accuracy of nonverbal behaviors in conveying a leader's traits and characteristics, even during brief observations.[5]

Social psychologist Amy Cuddy of Harvard Business School has studied first impressions and how we evaluate people we meet. "When we form a first impression of another person, it's not really a single impression. We're really forming two," says Cuddy, "We're judging how warm and trustworthy the person is, and that's trying to answer the question, 'What are this person's intentions toward me?' And we're also asking ourselves, 'How strong and competent is this person?' That's really about whether or not they're capable of enacting their intentions. Research shows that these two trait dimensions account for 80–90 percent of an overall first impression, and that holds true across cultures."[6]

One of the first things an actor learns when studying the craft of performance is that there is very little information in tension. The great acting teacher Lee Strasberg talked about the importance of relaxation for the actor and how, when tension overwhelms a speaker, the person cannot properly think, feel, or be present in the moment. "The elimination of tension is valuable, of course, for every human being, not just for the actor," Strasberg remarked. He added, "In the relaxation, we often see the possibilities of the human being. . . we see what he's capable of . . . . On the other hand, if he has difficulty in controlling his relaxation, then it means that he will never fully use his talent."[7]

Executive presence refers to the combination of qualities, behaviors, and skills that enable a person to project confidence, authority, and influence in a professional setting. To shape and influence an audience's first impression, a leader should approach every interaction with an actor's mindset. Actors understand that the moment they step onstage, the audience begins forming judgments—not just about them, but about the characters they portray. They recognize that their bodies serve as dynamic billboards, continuously broadcasting signals that the audience interprets to form perceptions. By consciously controlling these signals—known as *intention cues*—leaders can better manage, and even shape, how they are perceived. Intention cues are subtle indicators that reveal a person's underlying thoughts, feelings, or intentions. These cues can be verbal or nonverbal, including body language, facial expressions, tone of voice, eye movements, and word choices.

A speaker's effectiveness hinges not only on the message they convey but also on the clarity and congruence with which they deliver it. The noted Roman educator and rhetorician Quintilian emphasized this idea as far back as 75 AD when he remarked, "Words in themselves count for much and the voice adds a force of its own to the matter of which it speaks, while gesture and motion are full of significance, we may be sure of finding something like perfection when all these qualities are combined."[8]

The Three Channels: Verbal, Vocal, Visual

When presenting information or delivering a message, leaders should focus on three key communication channels: *verbal*, *vocal*, and *visual*. The verbal channel refers to the content of the message—the actual words chosen to convey meaning. The vocal channel encompasses tone, pitch, pace, and emphasis, which add emotion and nuance to the words. The visual channel includes body language, facial expressions, and overall appearance, all of which reinforce or detract from the spoken message. The most critical factor for a speaker is congruency—ensuring that all three channels are aligned. This means that what they say, how they say it, and how they present themselves visually all work together to convey the same message.

Neil deGrasse Tyson, the renowned astrophysicist and author, brings a unique perspective to communication. His background as a dancer gave him a deep appreciation for the expressive potential of the human body. Reflecting on this, Tyson emphasizes the power of nonverbal communication: "Words communicate, and yes, the spoken word does a very good job," he explains, "But you're not limited to that. You have facial expressions; you can smile, look sad, or tilt your head. You have hands for gestures and eyebrows to convey emotion. Why not let your body join in the act of communicating? It instantly doubles your effectiveness."[9]

Studies have shown that a speaker's use of gestures enhances a listener's comprehension and reinforces the overall meaning of the message being conveyed.[10] If you are passionate about the topic you are presenting, if you are speaking about something that matters to you, your body will want to help you express that. Conversely, when there is an absence of passion in your delivery—specifically less gestures or no gestures as all—we notice this. Drawing on his scientific rigor and artistic sensibility, Tyson underscores an important truth: communication is not confined to words alone. By engaging your entire body, you can amplify our message and connect with others on a deeper, more dynamic level.

The Verbal Channel

We'll start by exploring the verbal aspect of a leader's communication. Words possess immense power, capable of stirring deep emotional responses in an audience through their sheer impact. As renowned relationship expert John Gottman aptly points out, "Plays would not exist if words did not contain a great potential for communicating emotional information."[11] Just as actors and playwrights skillfully wield words to evoke connection and meaning, effective leaders must thoughtfully choose their language—both what to include and what to leave unsaid. This careful selection shapes how messages are perceived and drives the way others respond. A leader should avoid overusing corporate jargon or complex vocabulary in an effort to appear more authoritative. Studies show this approach can backfire,[12] with 58 percent of people admitting they've used a word to sound smarter—despite not knowing the word's meaning.[13]

In a series of experiments at University College London, Dr. Sophie Scott used brain imaging techniques to reveal that when we listen to someone speak, our brains process the message by dividing it into distinct parts, each stored in a different region. The words themselves are processed in the left temporal lobe, while the vocal dynamics—how the words are delivered—are processed in the right hemisphere, the area also associated with music and visual imagery. This dual processing highlights why words alone are insufficient; they must be delivered with congruent intentionality to engage both sides of the listener's brain effectively (more on this later).[14]

When aiming to project confidence and communicate assertively, the words you choose are crucial. As the feminist writer Rita Mae Brown put it, "Language exerts hidden power, like the moon on the tides."[15] A leader should avoid passive or tentative phrases such as "I think," "kind of," or "I mean." These are examples of *hedging language*—words or phrases that dilute the impact of your message by making it seem vague or noncommittal. While hedging may sometimes feel polite or cautious, it often undermines the strength of your argument and can make you appear less confident or unsure of your position.

Hedging also opens the door for others to challenge or dismiss your ideas more easily. Linguistically, a hedge signals uncertainty, framing your information as less convincing or authoritative. As one cognitive scientist explains, "Using a hedge marks the information as unreliable."[16] By eliminating unnecessary hedges, you enhance your credibility, communicate with greater clarity, and convey a stronger sense of conviction.

The Vocal Channel

To leverage the vocal channel of a leader's communication, it's essential to master the individual dynamics of the voice, including pace, volume, articulation, and pitch, to effectively engage and influence others. The way you use your voice plays a crucial role in engaging listeners. How quickly or slowly you speak, how loudly or softly, and the pitch you choose all contribute to your effectiveness. Is there a "music" to your voice, or do you fall into a monotone that lacks emotion and intentionality? A monotone delivery can make it challenging to captivate or engage an audience. And new research by Wharton marketing professor Jonah Berger found that speakers who vary the pace, pitch, and volume of their voices are more effective.[17] Take a moment to reflect on your communication style. How well do you use these vocal elements to engage listeners, convey authority, and ensure clarity during meetings or presentations? Are there aspects of your voice you can lean on more frequently to have greater impact?

Confident speakers understand the power of silence, and are not afraid to pause and let a thought or question hang in the air for a moment while an audience considers it. As Ralph Richardson, the legendary English actor, once remarked, "The most precious things in speech are the pauses."[18] Research indicates that conversational speech typically includes short (0.20 seconds), medium (0.60 seconds), and long (more than 1 second) pauses. Effective speakers, however, often pause for two to three seconds or more to enhance clarity and impact. Yet, studies reveal that the average speaker uses only 3.5 pauses per minute—far fewer than necessary to communicate effectively.[19] As a teaching in the Talmud, a primary source of Jewish theology, reminds us, "A word is worth one coin; silence is worth two."[20] Consider your communication style when presenting or leading a meeting. How comfortable are you with silence?

One common challenge for leaders is speaking too fast—a habit often driven by nerves or speech anxiety. This can lead to the use of *verbal viruses*, fillers such as "um," "ah," or similar disfluencies. Studies suggest these verbal viruses arise from our instinct to fill silence, even when we don't have anything meaningful to say. Research shows that the average speaker uses five verbal viruses per minute— roughly 1 every 12 seconds—which can undermine credibility and distract from their message.[21]

The first step in eliminating verbal viruses is cultivating self-awareness. Ask yourself, How frequently do you use these fillers? A simple yet effective strategy to reduce them is to record a presentation or Zoom meeting and carefully review the footage to identify recurring patterns in your speech. Pay close attention to moments where you insert unnecessary words or sounds. By consciously slowing down your pace and speaking with intention, you can eliminate the reliance on these habitual fillers, making your speech clearer and more impactful.

The Visual Channel

The final communication channel to consider is visual, which often plays an equally important—if not more significant—role in how an audience perceives a speaker. When someone steps onto the stage, the audience's first impression is shaped largely by what they see, which can dramatically influence how the message is received. These visual cues often establish the tone for the entire presentation and, in many cases, can speak louder than words. In this way, the visual aspect of communication doesn't just complement the message; it enhances or undermines the speaker's credibility and trustworthiness, often setting the stage for how the content will be perceived.

Psychology tells us that natural leaders are adept at communicating strength through their posture, gestures, and body language.[22]

Stanislavski was deeply committed to helping his actors understand that effective communication on stage goes beyond words. He taught them that body language, and the visual picture they create, was just as vital as speech in conveying meaning and emotion. There's one particular story, still recounted in acting classes today, that illustrates this principle.

Stanislavski devised a striking experiment during a work session with his actors in which he asked a student to step forward for an exercise. He then gradually bound the student's hands, feet, and torso, one after the other. Once the student's entire body was restrained, Stanislavski asked, "Which part would you like to have free first, so you can express yourself?" The student, initially unsure, hesitated and then realized that there was no easy answer. Without his hands, feet, or torso, he could not truly communicate. He quickly understood that each part of the body played a crucial role in the act of expression.

Among the most powerful visual tools a speaker or leader can use is a smile. A well-timed, genuine smile sends a clear message: it signals warmth, confidence, and approachability. Smiling shows that you feel at ease and in control, fostering trust and connection with your audience.

A smile is not just about appearances—though studies show that smiling can make you more attractive to others—it has a psychological impact as well.[23] Research shows that smiling can elevate your own mood and reduce stress, which makes you feel more comfortable in high-pressure situations. This positivity is contagious; as studies published in *Psychology Today* show, your smile can also lift the spirits of those around you, creating an environment that feels welcoming and engaging.[24]

Additionally, a smile can make you more relatable and likable. Audiences are naturally drawn to leaders and speakers who exude friendliness and authenticity. However, many of us are unaware of how often we forget to smile, especially when we're focused or nervous.

75

Elevating Your Leadership Impact

This is why it's essential to cultivate smiling as a habit—not just as an instinctive reaction when you are meeting someone for the first time but as an intentional part of your communication strategy.

Another essential tool for both an actor and a leader is the human face. Facial expressions reinforce a speaker's message and help convey emotions, as well as providing nonverbal cues that emphasize key points, clarify meaning, and keep an audience attentive. We first learn how to connect and communicate with others through facial expressions, starting as infants, by observing and mirroring the expressions of our parents or caregivers. These early interactions form the foundation of how we relate to the world around us.

Consider the brilliance of performers like Charlie Chaplin, Jim Carrey, or Rowan Atkinson in his role as Mr. Bean. They demonstrate the extraordinary storytelling power of the face, using expressions alone to communicate entire narratives without uttering a single word. Their work is a testament to the expressive potential of the human face, which can convey complex emotions and ideas with astonishing clarity. According to renowned psychologist Paul Ekman, "Facial expressions, even quickly passing, signal emotional expression. The face is the mind's involuntary messenger."[25] Our facial expressions are deeply tied to our emotions, often revealing what we're feeling before we even say a word.

As a speaker or leader, the more varied and intentional your facial expressions, the more engaging and relatable your communication will be. Expressive faces engage audiences, drawing them into the emotional and intellectual journey you're guiding them through. However, it's important that your expressions align with your intended message (again *congruency*). A mismatched expression— such as smiling when discussing a serious topic or scowling as you deliver good news—can confuse or alienate your audience.

Be mindful of situations where your facial expressions may falter. Nervousness or intense focus can sometimes lead to what we call *stone-face syndrome*, where all expression drains from your face. This can unintentionally communicate disinterest or discomfort, disconnecting you from your audience. As Ekman reminds us, "The face is the most powerful means of communication. It conveys feelings that words may hide."[26] To avoid communicating messages with the face that do not support your intention, practice staying present in the moment and consciously using facial expressions to reinforce your words.

Maintaining a solid, neutral posture is also important for a leader hoping to deliver a message with impact. Ideally, a leader conveys a relaxed, professional, and open demeanor—what we call a communicator's *home base position*. To achieve this, stand with your feet shoulder-width apart, knees unlocked, pelvis centered (to avoid swaying or shifting), arms hanging by your sides (when not in use), chest raised and open, shoulders relaxed, and head balanced naturally on your neck. This posture not only helps mask nervousness but also projects confidence—even in moments of uncertainty—solidifying a strong first impression.

Sigmund Freud once remarked, "No mortal can keep a secret if his lips are silent; he chatters with his fingertips, betrayal oozes out of him at every pore."[27] When nervousness or discomfort arises during a speech or presentation, it often manifests through *pacifiers*—subtle, unconscious gestures or behaviors used to self-soothe. Common examples include fidgeting with objects, touching one's face or hair, shifting your weight repeatedly, or rubbing your hands together. These actions, if unchecked, can undermine your confidence and distract your audience. To eliminate pacifiers, focus on intentionality in your movements and gestures.

Next, let's discuss movement for a speaker. *Spatiality*—the strategic use of physical space—plays a vital role in enhancing your message, presence, and connection with the audience. Moving toward your audience, when done thoughtfully and with respect for personal

77

Elevating Your Leadership Impact

space and cultural norms, conveys confidence and fosters a sense of engagement. Purposeful movement can also be used effectively to signal transitions between ideas or topics, adding clarity to your delivery, and making it easier for listeners to follow.

Another powerful communication tool for a leader or actor is the use of gestures. When using gestures in a speech or presentation, aim for precision and impact. Shakespeare gave us the best advice regarding gestures when he wrote in *Hamlet*, "Suit the action to the word; the word to the action." Expansive, natural, and well-timed gestures, performed above the waist, tend to make a speaker appear more confident and authoritative; they're also more interesting to watch. By contrast, gestures below the waist may inadvertently diminish presence, making the speaker seem smaller or less assured.

Research from the University of Vienna underscores the crucial role of gestures, revealing that they can convey important aspects of a speaker's personality, including traits like extraversion and dominance. Remarkably, gestures can even influence an audience's perception of the speaker's physical height, making them appear taller or shorter by a few inches. This illustrates how powerful nonverbal communication can be in shaping the way we are perceived, often in ways we might not even be consciously aware of.[28]

According to body language experts, one of the most science-backed gestures a leader can use to build trust involves the hands: specifically, displaying open palms, slightly tilted outward at a 45-degree angle. This gesture visually communicates openness, honesty, and a lack of hidden motives, helping the person appear more credible and trustworthy. Kasia and Patryk Wezowski, founders of the Center for Body Language, have extensively studied gestures and explain that "open palms are a sign of peaceful intentions . . . . it shows that you have nothing to hide, you're unarmed, and you're mentally open to what the other person is saying."[29] Conversely, the Wezowskis note that individuals who conceal their hands, keep their fists closed, or use overly restrictive gestures may inadvertently convey secrecy, defensiveness, or deception.

The final aspect of a leader's visual delivery channel is eye contact, a cornerstone of effective leadership and communication. Eye contact serves as a powerful tool to establish rapport and create meaningful connections with an audience. Research indicates that maintaining consistent eye contact during communication enhances your credibility, trustworthiness, and, most significantly, your likability.[30] Dr. Atsushi Senju, a cognitive neuroscientist at the Centre for Brain and Cognitive Development at Birkbeck, University of London, explains that the use of eye contact helps us appear more socially aware and empathetic.[31] Conversely, avoiding eye contact can diminish perceptions of your sociability and emotional intelligence, ultimately undermining your credibility.

When working with neurodivergent team members, it's essential to approach eye contact with flexibility and understanding. For some individuals, direct eye contact can feel uncomfortable or overwhelming, so it's important to be mindful of their preferences and avoid prolonged or intense staring. If they look away, gently adjust your gaze to match theirs, creating a more inclusive and respectful atmosphere. By being attuned to these subtle cues, you help create a space where all team members feel valued and at ease.

When addressing a large crowd, aim to scan the room and make eye contact with as many individuals as possible, ideally staying with one person for at least two to three seconds before moving on. This simple gesture conveys authenticity and inclusiveness, making your audience feel seen and valued. In virtual settings, the equivalent of this is looking directly at the camera. Although it might feel counterintuitive, maintaining your gaze on the camera lens gives viewers the impression that you're speaking directly to them, fostering a sense of personal connection even through a screen.

79

Elevating Your Leadership Impact

Beyond building connection, eye contact provides real-time feedback on how your message is landing. Think of it as your instant performance scorecard. The facial expressions and body language displayed by your audience can reveal a wealth of information: are they nodding in agreement? Smiling? Leaning in with interest? Or do they appear distracted, disengaged, or worse—on the verge of nodding off? These nonverbal cues offer crucial insights into their level of engagement. As a leader, it's your responsibility to remain attuned to these signals and adapt your tactics and delivery accordingly.

By mastering the art of purposeful eye contact, you demonstrate not only confidence and presence but also empathy and awareness—qualities that distinguish exceptional leaders from the rest.

Next, we'll discuss the importance of authenticity in leadership and how it relates to building trust and fostering genuine connections with others. We'll explore how embracing your true self can enhance your charisma and make you a more effective, influential leader.

Chapter 6

Why Authenticity Matters

Be yourself; everyone else is already taken.

—Oscar Wilde

Crafting Connections: Transforming Chicago's Fine Dining Scene

Christopher Gerber's journey through the high-end hospitality industry in Chicago is a story of transformation, skill, and a profound understanding of the emotional connection that makes a dining experience extraordinary. Originally moving to Chicago in 1993 to pursue a career as a professional actor, Gerber began waiting tables at various restaurants to make ends meet. At the time, his approach to the job was transactional—he saw it merely as a paycheck, not fully understanding the pivotal role he played in shaping how guests experienced the restaurant.

Over time, however, Gerber began to understand the significant impact of the customer experience. He realized that fine dining wasn't just about serving a meal; it was about creating a memorable, emotional connection with each guest. This epiphany marked the beginning of his transformation from an average waiter into a rising star in the hospitality world.

Gerber's career soared when he joined Alinea, one of Chicago's most acclaimed restaurants, as general manager, helping to open its doors under the leadership of executive chef Grant Achatz. There, he crafted the restaurant's original service handbook, establishing the foundation for a guest experience that would later be recognized as world-class. Thanks to the groundbreaking foundation he established, Alinea earned an extraordinary three Michelin stars and was honored as the "Best Restaurant in the World" by *Elite Traveler*. This recognition underscored Gerber's unwavering commitment to excellence and his extraordinary ability to elevate every detail of the restaurant, creating an unparalleled dining experience.

Always striving for new challenges, Gerber pushed his limits further as the general manager of Smyth, a newly launched restaurant in Chicago, the brainchild of executive chefs John Shields and Karen Urie Shields. At Smyth, Gerber applied his meticulous standards of quality and his relentless focus on the guest experience. He understood that exceptional service went beyond just the food; it was about crafting an environment where every detail—from the ambiance to the table service to the presentation of drinks and dishes—was meticulously calibrated to elevate the entire experience. His dedication paid off in 2023 when Smyth became only the second Chicago restaurant (alongside Alinea) and one of just 14 in the United States to earn three Michelin Stars—an exceptional and rare accomplishment.

I spoke with Gerber, a friend and fellow alumnus of my drama school, about how his acting background and training have influenced his celebrated work in hospitality. "All of those techniques I learned as an actor—being in the moment, listening, saying 'yes,' 'finding a way in,' connecting—they inform me probably every day," he explained.

Gerber's leadership in the hospitality industry is distinguished by his technical expertise and his exceptional ability to forge genuine emotional connections with people from the very first impression. He believes even the smallest interactions, like taking a guest's coat or pouring water, can transform an ordinary process into a meaningful moment. This focus on emotional intelligence and intentional connection elevates the dining experience and sets a new standard for leadership in the industry. By recognizing that every moment is an opportunity for deeper connection, Gerber has not only reshaped fine dining in Chicago but also demonstrated how great leaders can create meaningful experiences that leave a lasting impact.[1]

Charisma as a Catalyst

In 2023, both Merriam-Webster and Oxford University Press selected "words of the year" that reflected societal preoccupations with authenticity and personal charm. Merriam-Webster chose the word *authentic*, driven by stories and conversations about celebrity culture, identity, and social media.[2] Oxford University Press selected the word *rizz*—a colloquial term for style or charm, underscoring the cultural emphasis on personal charisma.[3] Together, these choices illustrate a societal focus on distinguishing genuine qualities from phony ones, emphasizing the value placed on authenticity and personal appeal in contemporary communication.

While many people have a general sense of what charisma entails, the concept is far more complex than it may initially appear. In *The Bullseye Principle*, we described charisma as that almost magical, hard-to-define quality we instinctively seek in leaders—a blend of passion and confidence that captivates and inspires. But charisma goes beyond just those two traits. It's a multifaceted quality that also includes authenticity—the ability to stay true to oneself while connecting deeply with others. Additionally, it reflects one's attitude and mindset—the way they face challenges and seize opportunities with resilience and determination. Charisma thrives on exuberance, that contagious energy that lights up a room, as well as optimism, which sparks hope and motivates action. Recently, younger generations have coined the term *main character energy*, referring to people who carry themselves as though they're the protagonist in their own life story. This concept closely aligns with charisma, as both involve a strong, magnetic presence that naturally draws others in.

The word *charisma* originates from the Greek term meaning "favor" or "gift."[4] We all know leaders and public figures who radiate charisma—individuals who captivate us with their energy, authenticity, and magnetism. Icons like Dwayne "The Rock" Johnson, Beyoncé, Taylor Swift, and even polarizing figures like Donald Trump and Vladimir Putin, demonstrate how charisma can inspire admiration, loyalty, and a profound connection with others. Their presence elevates their communication and influence, drawing people to them almost effortlessly. As you reflect on your leadership and communication style, how would you rate your level of charisma?

Bob Lambert, a marketing executive you'll meet in Chapter 18, once shared with me a remarkable experience his team had with the legendary boxer Muhammad Ali.[5] At the time, Lambert's marketing firm was working with Ali's Worldwide Fan Club. One day, as the story goes, Lambert's team was riding in a car with Ali, crawling through traffic on Madison Avenue in New York City. From the car, they watched the bustling crowds, each person weaving through the chaos with a sense of purpose and unwavering focus.

Ali suddenly turned to one of the team members and said, "I have stopping power." Puzzled, the person asked what he meant. With a mischievous sparkle in his eye, Ali simply replied, "Watch, I'll show you," and asked the driver to pull over. Opening his car door, Ali stepped out onto the busy street and, almost instantly, the hurried, distracted New Yorkers came to a standstill. Immediately recognizing Ali, people stopped what they were doing and flocked to him—some clamoring for autographs, others snapping photos, and many just wanting to bask in the presence of his greatness.

After a few minutes, Ali climbed back into the car. Smiling as the driver pulled away, Ali turned to the rest of the team and said, "See what I mean? *Stopping* power."

Charismatic figures like Muhammad Ali possess a rare ability to captivate and inspire, effortlessly drawing others in and eliciting trust, support, and attention. I experienced this firsthand in the 1990s when I had the opportunity to appear alongside basketball legend Michael Jordan in a commercial for his clothing brand. Some individuals simply radiate presence and charisma—and Jordan is one of them. When he walks into a room, it's as if the energy shifts; it's nearly impossible to focus on anyone—or anything—else.

This kind of personal magnetism enables leaders and public figures to forge emotional connections, and their ability to move others on a deeper level is a powerful asset. It enables them to unite people around a vision, spark a sense of shared purpose, and leave an impression that goes far beyond words. This emotional resonance creates a lasting impact and enduring influence—a quality shared not only by traditional leaders but also by the most prominent figures of the digital age: influencers.

Consider, for a moment, the meteoric rise of YouTube and social media influencers, a profession that barely existed a decade ago. Their primary job? To attract attention, command eyeballs, and drive engagement on platforms like YouTube, Instagram, and TikTok. Unlike traditional celebrities, influencers often build their empires from the ground up, crafting an authentic personal brand that resonates deeply with their followers. Influencers today undeniably hold significant sway; Pew Research revealed that one in five Americans now turn to them for news—a figure that jumps to 40 percent among those under 30.[6] Reflecting this shift in cultural aspiration, a 2023 Morning Consult survey found that 57 percent of Gen Zers and 41 percent of adults overall would choose "influencer" as a profession, underscoring the growing appeal and perceived legitimacy of this modern career path.[7]

Consider Jake Paul, for example, one of the most notable influencers who successfully transitioned into entrepreneurship. Starting as a

85

Why Authenticity Matters

content creator goofing off on YouTube before becoming an actor on the Disney Channel, Paul leveraged his charisma, controversial antics, and innate understanding of audience engagement to build a loyal fan base. He didn't just entertain; he captivated millions by blending humor, drama, and relatability in ways that kept viewers coming back. This attention translated into immense financial success—Paul has made millions through ad revenue, merchandise sales, sponsorships, television shows, and has even pivoted into professional boxing, where he's generated tens of millions more by marketing his fights as must-watch events. In 2024, Jake Paul's reported net worth was more than $120 million, demonstrating how a magnetic online presence can evolve into a lucrative business empire.[8]

Influencers like Jake Paul, as well as politicians like Barack Obama and Donald Trump, prove that charisma in the digital age isn't just about leading people, it's about captivating them. Their ability to move audiences emotionally, whether through excitement, controversy, or relatability, drives their success and, in turn, enormous wealth and power. Attention, in this context, becomes currency, and those who know how to attract and sustain it hold the keys to unparalleled influence and financial reward.

The good news about charisma is that it's not an innate trait— it's a skill that can be developed. It's a powerful mix of behaviors, mindset, and techniques that anyone can hone and refine with consistent practice. By understanding its many layers, we can demystify charisma and begin to nurture it within ourselves and others. We've already covered some of the traits needed to develop one's personal charisma, such as confident body language, expansive gestures, and a strong speaking voice. In upcoming chapters we'll be detailing others such as storytelling and anecdotes, metaphors, and the use of rhetorical questions. But other aspects of leadership, such as relatability, self-disclosure, and a leader's personal values and integrity, all play a part as well.

86

Synergy and Sparks

Extensive large-scale studies have demonstrated that charisma is an invaluable asset across various work contexts—whether in small or large organizations, public or private sectors, and in both Western and Asian cultural settings.[9] And research confirms that by honing the key components of charisma and intentionally developing them, anyone can enhance their influence, build trust, and project a stronger leadership presence.[10]

Charisma, at its core, is neither inherently good nor bad—it's a neutral tool that leaders use to influence others. Its impact largely depends on the values and convictions of the leader wielding it. In the hands of narcissistic or unscrupulous leaders, or when misused, charisma can become a double-edged sword. It has the potential to foster toxic work environments, erode trust, and create challenges like diminished morale, burnout, or even manipulation. Understanding the power of charisma is crucial to ensure it's used responsibly and ethically.

The Dark Side of Magnetism

A perfect example of the public being hoodwinked by a leader's charisma occurred in 2004, when Elizabeth Holmes, a sophomore at Stanford University, dropped out of school to launch her startup, Theranos. The company promised to revolutionize health care by providing rapid, accurate blood tests with just a few drops of blood. Holmes soon partnered with Ramesh "Sunny" Balwani, a businessman she had met during a Stanford-sponsored trip to China, and together, they built the foundation for what would become one of Silicon Valley's most notorious scandals.

By 2014, a decade into her journey, Holmes had mastered the art of self-presentation, leveraging her charisma and media savvy to command attention and shape her public persona. To bolster her authority, she notably deepened her voice and adopted a signature

87

Why Authenticity Matters

all-black wardrobe, drawing comparisons to Steve Jobs during Apple's meteoric rise. Her efforts were highly effective. Holmes captured the collective imagination of Silicon Valley and beyond, gracing the covers of *Inc.*, *Fortune*, and *Forbes*, with headlines heralding her as—you guessed it—"The Next Steve Jobs." By the end of that year, she had raised $400 million from investors and was ranked among America's richest women, with a net worth estimated at $4.5 billion. She seemed unstoppable.

But there was one major problem: Theranos's technology did not work as advertised. The company's much-touted device, which claimed to run 240 tests on a single drop of blood, could not deliver on its promises. In truth, the tests relied on traditional blood-drawing methods and outsourced equipment, contrary to the revolutionary claims Holmes had made. The carefully crafted persona of Elizabeth Holmes—driven, visionary, and infallible—began to crack.

In 2015, Holmes faced her first major challenge when the *Wall Street Journal* published an investigative report questioning the accuracy and reliability of Theranos's blood-testing technology. The report revealed that the company had been using standard machines to conduct tests, not its proprietary devices. This revelation marked the beginning of the end for Theranos. By 2016, federal regulators were scrutinizing the company, forcing Holmes to void two years' worth of blood test results. *Forbes* adjusted her net worth to $0, and the once-celebrated entrepreneur became a pariah in Silicon Valley.

By 2018, amid mounting lawsuits and failed lab inspections, Holmes and Balwani were charged with "massive fraud." Federal prosecutors alleged that the pair had defrauded investors of more than $700 million by exaggerating—or outright fabricating—claims about the company's technology, financial performance, and future potential. The scandal shocked the business world, not only because of its scale but also because so many prominent figures had been deceived. High-profile investors and board members included former

88

Synergy and Sparks

US Secretaries of State George Schultz and Henry Kissinger, media tycoon Rupert Murdoch, and Oracle cofounder Larry Ellison, all of whom were captivated by Holmes's vision and charisma.[11]

In June 2018, Holmes and Balwani were indicted on federal wire fraud charges. The COVID pandemic delayed legal proceedings, but in January 2022, Holmes was found guilty on four counts of federal fraud and sentenced to more than 11 years in prison.[12] Six months later, Balwani—who had also been revealed as Holmes's secret romantic partner—was convicted on similar charges and received a 12-year sentence.[13]

The meteoric rise and dramatic fall of Holmes underscore the power of charisma and storytelling. Her ability to weave an inspiring, albeit fictional, narrative convinced investors, the media, and even seasoned business leaders to overlook warning signs. Holmes's story serves as a cautionary tale of how charisma, when wielded irresponsibly, can blind people to the truth and enable deception on an unprecedented scale.

When working with a charismatic leader, it's essential to remain vigilant and assess two critical factors: intentionality and ego. These elements can help you gauge whether the leader's influence is genuinely constructive or potentially manipulative. Charismatic leadership, while often inspiring, can also harbor a darker side, making it important to recognize the difference between charm and authenticity. "The human tendency is to judge people on their appearances. The brain likes to make shortcuts so that we don't have to process too much," notes psychologist Robert Greene, warning, "so we judge people by appearances . . . a person who seems charming or who seems intelligent, we make the assumption that that's who they are. And boy, do we pay a price . . . . People who are devilish or aggressive don't wear horns on their head. Or fools don't have a cap and bells. They learn to disguise it from very early on, and you're mistaking the mask for reality."[14]

89

Why Authenticity Matters

Manipulative leaders, though often charismatic, frequently display a lack of genuine concern for others' needs, focusing instead on their personal gain or recognition. They may resist criticism or feedback, creating an environment where dissenting voices are silenced or ignored. Another troubling sign is the development of a "cult-like" following, where individuals feel pressured to conform and independent thinking is discouraged. Such leaders may also foster an "us versus them" mentality, positioning themselves as the only solution or authority figure able to solve your problems. In doing so, they often dismiss opposing viewpoints or rational thought, framing any dissent as a threat to their vision or leadership.

These behaviors are red flags that suggest a leader may not have your best interests at heart. They indicate a relationship where trust must be approached cautiously. By staying mindful of these warning signs, you can navigate such dynamics with greater awareness. This not only protects you from undue influence but also helps you discern whether the charisma you're drawn to is genuine or a manipulative tactic.

Style-Flexing: Communicating with Agility

Effective leadership in today's dynamic world demands a high level of adaptability. In every interaction, we unconsciously signal our power and status to others. The more consistently we send these signals, the more distinct and recognizable our personal style becomes. One tool for achieving this is *style flexing*—the intentional adaptation of one's communication, behavior, or leadership style, to better connect with and motivate different individuals or groups. Style flexing, rooted in emotional intelligence and situational awareness, enables leaders to remain adaptable and effective across a wide range of contexts. As noted in Chapter 1, the Pinnacle Method's third step for influential communication emphasizes modifying your delivery. When executed effectively, these "modifications" result in successful style flexing.

Style flexing enables leaders to adapt their approach to suit the unique demands of a situation, the needs of their team, or the broader organizational context. Rather than relying on a single, fixed leadership style, leaders who practice style flexing adjust their strategies to navigate changing circumstances and diverse team dynamics. This flexibility enhances communication, strengthens relationships, and builds trust within teams. For example, a CEO might use formal, data-driven language when presenting to investors and then switch to a more casual tone for a company town hall. Similarly, a project manager might take a hands-on approach with a junior team while offering greater autonomy to a more experienced one, fostering trust and ensuring productivity across both groups.

In meetings, a leader adept at style flexing knows when to step back and listen, as well as when to assert themself with ideas or insights. Similarly, a speaker addressing a large audience at a conference might use expansive gestures, a powerful voice, and dynamic energy to engage and inspire the crowd. By contrast, during a one-on-one mentoring session later that day, they might shift to a more conversational tone and subdued body language to foster intimacy and deepen their connection with the mentee.

Ultimately, style flexing in leadership communication is about fostering flexibility, adaptability, and responsiveness. This skill empowers leaders to navigate the evolving challenges of the modern workplace with agility, ensuring their approach stays relevant, impactful, and effective across diverse situations and audiences.

Personal Branding: Where Identity Meets Impact

Personal branding is the intersection of who you are and how others perceive you. It reflects your values, personality, work ethic, and expertise, forming the core of your professional reputation.

Every interaction—whether in person or online—shapes that reputation, influencing others' perceptions. From workplace conversations and presentations to social media posts and email responses, your personal brand is defined by both what you say and how you show up consistently.

The concept of personal branding first gained prominence in 1997 when Tom Peters, a corporate branding expert, published an article in *Fast Company* asserting that individuals can be as much a brand as companies like Nike or Coca-Cola. Peters wrote, "Everyone has a chance to stand out . . . to be a brand worthy of remark."[15] By clearly defining your personal brand, you have the opportunity to distinguish yourself and make a lasting impact. Your personal brand encompasses your background, experiences, values, and aspirations, as well as how others perceive you.

Rosalind Brewer, the former CEO of both Sam's Club and Walgreens Boots Alliance, began her journey as the daughter of General Motors assembly line workers. She started her career as a chemist and climbed the corporate ladder, ultimately becoming the second Black woman to ever helm an S&P 500 company. During an interview on the *Today* show, Brewer shared a pivotal experience at a meeting with fellow CEOs.[16] The encounter challenged her confidence and pushed her to adapt her style and assertiveness on the spot.

In 2017, Brewer was invited to a private gathering composed entirely of CEOs. "I'm not a person who will walk in a room and tell you my title," admitted Brewer, "But when I'm in a room with like-minded people, I would just assume that you would think that I should be there."

Brewer recalled how one of the male CEOs at the event repeatedly asked her what she did for a living, wondering if she was in sales or marketing. At the time, Brewer was the CEO of Sam's Club, a company valued at more than $16 billion. She was taken aback by his confusion or apparent skepticism about the idea that she could be a CEO. "He just couldn't understand," Brewer said. "He must have asked me 20 questions."

Finally, Brewer decided it was time to assert herself in the moment and take control. She turned to the man and said, "This is a CEO function. I'm the CEO of Sam's Club." The man's reaction revealed a deep bias that had lingered unspoken. In that instant, Brewer had not only claimed her rightful place but also shone a light on the assumptions that often obscure the paths of women leaders.

Brewer's story is a compelling reminder of the critical role confidence and self-advocacy play in environments where one's authority or belonging is questioned. It underscores the importance of standing firm—not just for personal validation but also to challenge outdated assumptions and create a path for others to be seen and recognized for their true potential. One can imagine that the next time that particular gentleman encountered Brewer, he won't just remember her title—he'll also carry with him a newfound respect for her gravitas and credibility.

As Rosalind Brewer demonstrated, your personal brand shapes how others perceive you, based on their past experiences and interactions with you. Building a personal brand isn't about self-promotion or being inauthentic—in fact, authenticity and consistency are key to establishing trust and credibility. One study found that 98 percent of employers research potential candidates online, and 80 percent say the personal branding they encounter plays a significant role in their hiring decisions.[17] Protecting and enhancing your brand requires intentional effort, aligning your actions with your core values to build a strong, trustworthy reputation. As Carl Jung, the father of analytical psychology, once said, "The world will ask you who you are. And if you don't know, the world will tell you."[18]

Here's a simple exercise to gain insight into your personal brand: write down three words you would use to describe yourself as a leader—don't overthink it, just go with the first words that come to mind. Next, ask a trusted colleague, friend, or family member to share the three words they'd use to describe you. Compare the two lists. Do they align, or are there gaps? If you notice any inconsistencies, it might be time to refine your brand to ensure others perceive you the way you intend.

Your personal brand is a powerful leadership asset, shaped by consistent, authentic behavior. Just as authenticity is crucial for an actor embodying a character, it's equally vital for a leader guiding a team. As actress Maggie Smith once said, "The time onstage is easier than the rest of one's existence. At least for those two and a half hours, you can be quite sure who you are."[19] This insight speaks to the universal challenge of staying true to oneself, whether on stage or in a leadership role. By consciously defining and managing your brand, you can build trust, differentiate yourself, and leave a lasting impact in every interaction.

Yet, even with a strong personal brand, leadership remains a complex and demanding endeavor. In Part III, we'll explore strategies for keeping your team engaged and productive, while managing the ongoing challenges of maintaining alignment and focus.

Part III

Influence

Chapter 7

Unlocking the Science of Engagement

What comes out of your mouth comes into your life.

—Jen Sincero

How the iPhone Almost Didn't Happen: A Lesson in Persuasion

When Steve Jobs first introduced the iPhone in 2007, he called it a "revolutionary product" in a category desperate for reinvention. Fast-forward to today, and Apple is the world's leading smartphone brand, selling more than 2.3 billion iPhones, and generating more than $1.65 trillion in revenue since the mid-2010s.[1] By nearly every measure, the iPhone stands as Apple's most successful product. However, the meteoric success of this groundbreaking device was far from guaranteed. In fact, the very person often credited with the iPhone's invention once nearly derailed its development.[2]

The iPhone began as an experimental project, undertaken without Steve Jobs's knowledge, by Apple's executive staff and their technical teams. For years, Jobs insisted Apple would never make a phone. Even when the company secretly began developing one—under the codename "Project Purple"—Jobs remained skeptical about its value and unsure whether the emerging smartphone market was worth Apple's time and investment.[3] At the time, cell phones like the BlackBerry were seen as "geeky-looking" and aimed mostly at the email-obsessed, "pocket protector crowd."[4]

To persuade Steve Jobs to embrace the idea of developing an Apple phone—something he had been adamantly against—Apple's engineers had to deeply understand what motivated him to get him to reconsider. Jobs had strong reservations, bringing a list of reasons why an Apple phone was a bad idea. Chief among these was his belief that cell phones were clunky and inelegant—everything Apple's products were not.

Instead of dismissing his concerns, the engineers acknowledged them. But they also challenged Jobs to imagine how beautiful, intuitive, and groundbreaking a phone designed by Apple could be. They also, wisely, appealed to his ego and competitive spirit, pointing out that Microsoft was likely to enter the mobile phone market at some point and did Apple really want to surrender such a critical market to their biggest rival?

Over the following months, the engineers chipped away at Jobs's resistance. They built early prototypes in secret, demonstrated potential designs, and refined their concepts. Slowly, as they shared their progress, Jobs began to see the value of the idea and eventually became one of the iPhone's most passionate champions.

The key takeaway is this: visionary leaders like Steve Jobs are essential for driving innovation and success. However, organizations also need stakeholders, like Apple's engineers, who have the courage and skill to challenge and influence even the most determined leaders. Without a team willing to persistently and strategically shift Jobs's perspective, the iPhone might never have been created. By combining professional persistence with creative foresight, the Apple engineers transformed an initial no into one of the most groundbreaking innovations in modern history.[5]

The Neuroscience of Influence

The human brain, with its 86 billion neurons, is an incredibly complex network of connections that are constantly firing off signals and processing information. Every day, we navigate an endless stream of decisions and interactions, balancing speed and efficiency in everything from social dynamics to simple tasks.

As we move through life, our brains are continually sorting and prioritizing information, making snap judgments about what to focus on and what to ignore. *Is my boss trustworthy? Should I implement that feedback or disregard it? Should I cross the street to avoid this growling dog?* One of the most remarkable abilities of the adult brain is its capacity to focus on a specific task or detail while tuning out other, less relevant stimuli. This ability comes from the brain's network of smaller communities of neurons, each specializing in different functions. Some of these communities are wired to pay attention to particular details, while others filter out what's deemed unnecessary or irrelevant.

What's especially fascinating is how this process of attention management can be influenced—both in ourselves and in others. Because much of this focus happens automatically and unconsciously, we can learn to shape or direct attention by carefully selecting the information we present to others. According to Harvard Business School Professor Gerald Zaltman, 95 percent of purchasing decisions are made in the subconscious, in the feeling mind.[6] Understanding that people's brains are wired to focus on specific details means we can guide their attention to what matters most, whether we're in a leadership position, trying to persuade someone, or simply navigating a social interaction.

For example, when we aim to influence others, we can present information in a way that taps into the brain's natural tendency to prioritize certain details. By highlighting key points or framing an argument to align with the listener's existing mental filters, we can effectively spotlight what we want them to focus on. This might involve appealing to their emotions, values, or past experiences—anything that activates the brain's automatic response to certain types

99

Unlocking the Science of Engagement

of information. Similarly, when we want to minimize distractions or help someone stay focused, we can simplify the environment or reduce cognitive load by removing irrelevant details or distractions. By structuring both our communication and surroundings with this in mind, we make it easier for others to engage with and act on the most important points.

Ultimately, the brain's ability to continually adjust its focus enables us to respond quickly and effectively to the world around us; it also opens up opportunities for influence. By understanding how the brain prioritizes information, we can better guide attention, shape decisions, and influence behaviors in ways that are subtle yet powerful. In this sense, the brain's spotlight mechanism is not just about managing what we pay attention to but also about harnessing that knowledge to steer the focus and actions of others.

According to an article in *Harvard Business Review*, economists estimate that persuasion accounts for up to a quarter of America's national income, underscoring its immense economic influence. This highlights persuasion's central role in driving the success and growth of entire industries. For instance, advertising campaigns, such as those by DraftKings, Mercedes-Benz, or McDonald's, rely heavily on persuasive techniques to shape consumer behavior, ultimately boosting sales and market dominance. Similarly, persuasive communication and leadership in the business world often determines the long-term success of companies by influencing investor confidence, employee productivity, and customer loyalty.[7] According to Marena Costa, a former principal user experience designer at Amazon, corporations' efforts to capture and influence consumer's attention are no accident: "It's a science—an intentional, complex, and highly refined science."[8]

In today's world, information and influence have become vital forms of currency for leaders, and the ability to effectively persuade others—whether to shift their thinking, change their perspective, or alter their actions—can provide a significant competitive edge, both on a personal level and for the organization as a whole. The capacity to influence isn't just about presenting facts but also about shaping decisions, building trust, and driving meaningful outcomes. Reflect on the work you did last week: can you identify a moment when you needed to influence someone? What strategies did you use? How successful were you in that situation?

Professional actors and business leaders both harness the power of influence to inspire, connect, and persuade. At the heart of their work is the ability to connect emotionally with their audience and arouse what Dale Carnegie referred to as an *eager want*—a desire to take action, embrace new ideas, or achieve a meaningful goal.[9] Both professions demand vulnerability and empathy—actors must channel authentic emotions into their performances, while leaders must demonstrate genuine care for their teams and stakeholders.

In any business setting, no matter your role or industry, a significant portion of your work involves influencing others. If you're in sales, you might need to persuade a potential client to purchase your product or service. As a manager, you may find yourself convincing senior leadership to allocate additional resources to a project that needs revitalization. Or perhaps you're in a job interview, striving to highlight your unique skills and experiences to secure a position.

However, the art of influence isn't limited to professional settings—it extends to our personal lives as well. After leaving the office, you might find yourself negotiating with a neighbor to lower the volume of their music during quiet hours. Or, you could be encouraging your child to clean their room by explaining the benefits of organization. Even in broader community settings, like a local meeting, you may engage in a debate over the advantages of funding additional after-school programs for the neighborhood's youth. All of these examples involve influencing others in the pursuit of a given objective.

Unlocking the Science of Engagement

To influence effectively, actors and business leaders focus on understanding the desires, motivations, and challenges of their audience. For actors, this means interpreting the requirements of their role and the emotions and actions they need to evoke in their scene partners. For leaders, it involves identifying the goals of their team, clients, or organization and crafting solutions that address those needs and answer the questions, *What benefit or value can I provide them?* and *Why should they care?* Both actors and leaders seek to align their message and delivery with the values and priorities of their audience. By delivering solutions that resonate on a personal level—as the Apple team did with Steve Jobs—people can use their influence to spark action and leave a lasting impact. A shared mastery of emotional intelligence, adaptability, and communication is what elevates a person's ability to move people and create change.

In corporate settings, it's common to assume that facts, statistics, and data will speak for themselves and influence without additional effort. Subject matter experts—such as engineers, scientists, and analysts—often believe that the delivery of their message is secondary to the content itself. They might present cluttered slides, overloaded with charts and figures, delivered in a monotone voice, assuming their audience will see the merit in the information alone. However, neuroscience tells a very different story.

Studies show that our brains are wired to prioritize emotional connection, context, and storytelling over raw data.[10] While data appeals to the logical part of the brain, it's often the emotional and narrative framing that captures attention, builds trust, and drives decision-making. Even the most accurate or insightful information can lose its impact if it's not communicated in a way that engages the audience. Presentation matters, and the most influential professionals are those who balance clarity and substance with the ability to connect and inspire.

102

Synergy and Sparks

Defusing Resistance

Captivating others may seem straightforward in theory, but real-world challenges—such as shrinking attention spans, constant multitasking, and growing workloads—often leave audiences feeling distracted, disengaged, and overwhelmed. To complicate matters further, there is the concept of *reactance*, a psychological phenomenon where people resist when they perceive their freedom to choose is being threatened. As Jonah Berger, the marketing professor at Wharton, explains, "When we try to push someone to do something, ask them to do something, or persuade them to do something, they often don't do what we want. They often do the opposite. They push back." He likens reactance to an "anti-persuasion radar" that detects perceived threats and actively deflects them.[11]

For example, when an employee feels micromanaged, their autonomy feels threatened, and they may resist out of a desire to maintain control. Similarly, a company that mandates a full-time, return-to-office policy may face pushback from employees who value the flexibility of remote work. In sales, reactance can arise if a client feels pressured to make a quick decision or adopt a solution they're not entirely comfortable with. In all these cases, when individuals feel their freedom or choices are being restricted, their natural reaction may be resistance—sometimes leading them to do the opposite of what's intended.

Reactance theory, introduced by American social psychologist Jack Brehm in 1966, explores how individuals resist external social influence and take action to restore their sense of autonomy when they perceive their freedoms are being restricted.[12] Since its inception, the theory has sparked extensive research into how people respond to limitations on their choices. For leaders, understanding and effectively addressing this resistance is essential for inspiring teams and motivating clients toward meaningful outcomes.

103

Unlocking the Science of Engagement

As we explored in Chapter 5, the words you choose have a profound impact on your audience or listener, especially when it comes to reactance. Research consistently shows that language plays a crucial role in influencing others—whether you're addressing a team member, a peer, or a loved one, and the language you use can either build rapport and cooperation or create resistance and conflict.[13]

Forceful, controlling language—using words such as *should*, *must*, *need*, and *ought*—can trigger reactance, as this type of language tends to alienate rather than persuade. It can sound threatening and coercive, and instead of bringing the listener closer to your point of view, it pushes them further away. By contrast, noncontrolling language—words like *consider*, *can*, *could*, and *may*—are perceived as more inviting and less imposing, leading to greater openness and receptivity.[14]

One compelling study on reactance illustrates this dynamic effectively. Researchers sought to persuade members of a fitness club to try a new set of exercises. They started by dividing the members into two groups. The group that received a forceful message, using language like "you have to do this" or "this is mandatory," reacted with stronger feelings of anger and resistance. They were also significantly less willing to participate. By contrast, those who were simply invited to consider the exercises, with a softer, more neutral request, exhibited far less reactance. This group was not only less defensive but also more open and receptive to the idea of trying the new exercises. The study highlights how the manner in which a request is framed can significantly influence people's willingness to comply, with more autonomy and less coercion often leading to greater cooperation.[15]

Watch Your Words: Why Language Matters

The impact of language on a listener extends far beyond mere emotions—it can even influence a person's biology. The brain regions responsible for processing language are closely connected to those that regulate bodily systems, such as heart rate, digestion, and respiration. This interconnected network, known as the *language network*, means that the words you speak can affect not only how people feel emotionally but also how their bodies physically respond to your message. For example, calming language can lower someone's stress levels and heart rate, while charged or aggressive messages might trigger a fight-or-flight response.[16]

For leaders, the implications of language are profound and far-reaching. Dismissive, condescending, or hostile language can trigger a physiological stress response in a listener, provoking a spike in heart rate, shallow breathing, and physical tension. As a result, the person may shut down emotionally and mentally, effectively tuning out the remainder of your message. A single harsh word, unfair generalization, or biased remark can inflict lasting emotional harm, intensifying feelings of defensiveness and eroding trust. This not only damages relationships but also undermines your ability to communicate effectively. Sadly, negative comments intended to upset or provoke others have become all too common, especially in today's digital age.

Modern research underscores the potency of negative language in capturing attention. A major study conducted by New York University found that each additional word of moral outrage you include in a tweet increases its retweet rate by 20 percent, a result of what's known as *negativity bias*.[17] This bias leads us to give more weight to negative stimuli while overlooking positive ones. Similarly, a study by the Pew Research Center discovered that Facebook posts filled with combative messages or indignant disagreement are more likely to be liked, shared, and commented on—sometimes doubling engagement.[18] As the adage goes, "If you want to draw a crowd, pick a fight."

Language has a profound impact on relationships, trust, and engagement. Thoughtful words, like compliments or empathetic statements, can reduce stress, build trust, and strengthen connections. When delivered authentically, they make audiences more receptive and foster collaboration. As a leader, being mindful of your language can significantly influence, motivate, and engage others, shaping both emotional and physiological responses.

When a leader attempts to influence a stakeholder, it's crucial they cultivate a deep and thorough understanding of that person's motivations. This involves not only recognizing their wants and needs but also identifying any pain points or obstacles they may be facing at the moment. Once this understanding is established, the leader must then align their proposed solutions in a way that directly addresses those needs and concerns. This approach creates a foundation of trust and relevance, ensuring that the leader's contributions are seen as both valuable and meaningful in the context of the stakeholder's situation. When a leader's message resonates with their intended audience, hitting the mark with precision, it achieves conveyance.

In psychology, *conveyance* is the process of transmitting ideas, emotions, or information from one person to another. It's not just about delivering words but ensuring the message is understood and accepted. Effective conveyance involves not only language but also tone, body language, emotional resonance, and context, aiming for the receiver to grasp both the meaning and intent behind the message.

To capture and keep the attention of an audience, delivery is just as important as the content itself. A presentation should never be purely informational; if that's the goal, an email would usually suffice. Instead, every message should aim to influence how listeners think, feel, or act. To make an impact, two critical elements are essential: engagement, which grabs and maintains the audience's attention, and memory, ensuring that the information is not only heard but also retained. Without these elements, even the most well-crafted message can fail to leave a lasting impression.

106

Synergy and Sparks

In both the 2016 and 2024 elections, engagement played a key role in Donald Trump's appeal. His unscripted, often shocking behavior on the campaign trail broke away from the carefully curated personas typical of modern presidential candidates. "In an era when there's this enormous competition for eyeballs and for attention, if you're outrageous enough and if you're audacious enough, you could always capture the coverage," observed Democratic political strategist David Axelrod. "Donald Trump has changed the rules of politics by showing up at every media outlet that would have him. They all wanted him because they never knew what he was going to say."[19]

Trump's lack of a verbal filter made him both compelling and polarizing—audiences tuned in whether they found his remarks thrilling or offensive. His unpredictability—a trademark part of his brand as a businessman and politician—ranged from juvenile name-calling to spreading inflammatory and false claims, such as accusing Haitian migrants in Ohio of eating cats and dogs, to his unconventional dance moves at rallies. Trump's brash, unfiltered style provided a steady stream of material that dominated news cycles and kept him in the public eye long after the events themselves had ended.

However, the shock tactics that fueled Trump's campaign success proved less effective during his first term as president, where Americans expected steadier leadership. The COVID crisis of 2020 was a turning point, as Trump's impulsive style and improvised statements fell short of providing the clarity and reassurance Americans needed during a global health emergency. During one memorable press conference, Trump made an off-the-cuff comment suggesting that COVID could perhaps be treated by injecting disinfectant or using light inside the body. "So, supposing we hit the body with a tremendous—whether it's ultraviolet or just very powerful light . . . supposing you brought the light inside the body," he mused, adding, "And then I see the disinfectant, where it knocks it out in a minute . . . is there a way we can do something like that, by injection inside or almost a cleaning?" These untested remarks created a media firestorm and prompted immediate warnings from medical experts, including the CDC, cautioning Americans against the dangerous idea of injecting bleach. This incident highlighted the downside of improvisation in a role that demands credibility, transparency, and informed leadership.[20]

Incorporating Intrigue

Steve Jobs masterfully harnessed intrigue during Apple product launches, famously using the phrase "one more thing" to create anticipation and keep audiences on the edge of their seats. Apple is known for its secretive approach, withholding information about upcoming products to build excitement and fuel speculation. This approach heightens curiosity and creates an air of mystery around each event, leading fans and the media to eagerly speculate on what would be unveiled. By strategically revealing only select details and saving major announcements for the very end, Jobs ensured that audiences were fully engaged and primed for each revelation. This careful orchestration amplified the impact of each announcement, turning Apple's product launches into memorable events that reinforced the brand's reputation for innovation and intrigue.

A powerful tool for engaging an audience during a speech or presentation is the use of a *teaser*—a brief preview designed to spark curiosity and build anticipation. It gives the audience a sneak peek of what's coming, encouraging them to stay attentive. TikTok data shows that 63 percent of the platform's top-performing videos deliver their main message within the first three seconds; research on successful Instagram Reels shows a similar trend.[21] Like a movie trailer, a teaser offers just enough to intrigue the audience without giving away the whole story. For example, effective teasers might include lines like, "What's the most common mistake people make when trying to improve productivity? I'll reveal the surprising answer in a moment," or "I'm going to show you a photo shortly, and you won't believe what it reveals about human behavior."

Intrigue jolts us out of complacency and demands our focus and attention. It challenges our assumptions. Intrigue can be used to draw people in and guide them toward the point of view that aligns with the objective you are trying to accomplish. Just as audiences enjoy twists and turns in the plots of movies and plays, incorporating a sense of intrigue into a presentation or meeting can help build excitement and generate interest with an audience. Storytellers build suspense by withholding key facts or details as long as they can, revealing information only when absolutely necessary. According to anthropologist Dr. Helen Fisher, this teasing of information and the mystery it creates in the mind of a listener actually triggers the flow of dopamine, the chemical in the brain mentioned in Chapter 2 that provides a natural high.[22]

Long before neuroscience shed light on the mechanisms of influence and engagement, Constantin Stanislavski reflected on the enigmatic bond that forms between a speaker and their audience. "Haven't you felt in real life or on the stage, in the course of mutual communion . . . that something streamed out of you, some current from your eyes, from the ends of your fingers?" the renowned acting teacher once mused. "What name can we give to these invisible currents which we use to communicate with one another? Someday this phenomenon will be the subject of scientific research."[23]

Research has now been conducted, and findings demonstrate that our brains are inherently wired to bypass anything boring and prioritize emotional connections and contextual understanding.[24] True engagement occurs when a speaker's message resonates with the audience on two levels simultaneously: influencing logic, which is processed in the neocortex, and emotion, governed by the limbic system. These brain regions work in tandem to help us interpret and

109

Unlocking the Science of Engagement

respond to social and environmental cues, highlighting how crucial emotional and contextual information is in shaping our reactions. This dual processing underscores the importance of addressing both the logical and emotional aspects of communication to create deeper connections and more effective engagement.

When both regions of the brain are activated, *neural entrainment* occurs, synchronizing the brainwaves of the speaker and listener. This alignment fosters a deeper connection, amplifying the speaker's influence and creating a more impactful, resonant communication experience.[25] As this alignment deepens, the next step is mastering the ability to ask effective questions.

In Chapter 8, we'll explore how mastering the art of questioning can significantly enhance your communication skills, deepen your connections with others, and increase your influence in both personal and professional settings.

Chapter 8

Creating Outcomes by Design

Curiosity is a superpower—if you have the courage to use it.
—Brian Grazer

Shaping Success by Asking the Right Questions

In the mid-20th century, Taiichi Ohno, an industrial engineer at Toyota and a pioneer of the Toyota Production System (TPS), introduced the Five Whys as a method to identify the root cause of problems.[1] The technique is straightforward: when a problem arises, you ask why repeatedly—typically five times—to peel back the layers of symptoms and get to the underlying cause. Each why uncovers a deeper layer of understanding, helping to avoid superficial solutions by pinpointing the root cause of the problem and fostering long-term resolutions. Over time, the five whys evolved into a cornerstone of Toyota's operational philosophy, yielding transformative benefits such as streamlined problem-solving, greater efficiency, superior quality control, and significant cost savings. Beyond these tangible outcomes, the method also fostered a culture of employee empowerment and continuous improvement. This approach was instrumental in establishing Toyota's global reputation for excellence and innovation. Harnessing the power of why with your teams can similarly drive success and unlock their full potential.

Research indicates that asking thoughtful questions, rather than offering direct answers, can help reduce defensiveness, manage uncertainty, and foster more collaborative dialogue among teams.[2] By posing questions, you're not dictating what someone should think or do but instead giving them a sense of control and inviting their perspective. Questions like "What if?" or "Could we?" are especially effective in sparking creativity, as they open the door to curiosity and the exploration of possibilities. This approach can transform a conversation or meeting into a shared problem-solving effort, influencing thinking and encouraging deeper engagement. As Maggie Jackson, author of *Uncertain: The Wisdom and Wonder of Being Unsure*, reminds us, "One of the most important facets of our curiosity is the ability to tolerate the stress of the unknown."[3]

Behind every question lies an opportunity for discovery and insight. For leaders, the questions you ask and when you ask them—your *question design*—are critical tools for fostering trust, gaining clarity, and unlocking outcomes. Thoughtful questioning can inspire your team, uncover challenges, and align efforts toward shared goals. In an interview on *The Tim Ferriss Show*, Spotify CEO Daniel Ek emphasized the importance of asking the right questions, specifically for leaders, stating, "It's almost always back to purpose—like, why are we doing things? Why does it matter? How does this ladder up to the mission?"[4] To employ questions effectively, it's essential to understand their intent and timing. Good questions should be concise, should build on something that has been previously said, and should be specific. The three core types of questions leaders can employ are *data*, *insight*, and *rapport building*.

Data questions are closed-ended and designed to gather specific information: facts, figures, or a simple yes or no. They help you quickly establish a clear understanding of the situation and inform your decisions. For example, you might ask, "What date would you like this program to be initiated?" or "Who else needs to be involved in this process?" These questions are practical tools for ensuring you have the foundational details needed to move forward effectively.

Insight questions, by contrast, are open-ended and encourage deeper thinking. This type of question casts a wider net and helps you understand the thought processes, motivations, and challenges your team members face. It provides an opportunity to uncover underlying concerns and prioritize actions. Asking "How do you think this challenge is affecting team morale?" or "What do you believe is the root cause of this issue?" allows you to explore perspectives that might not surface otherwise, driving a more nuanced understanding of complex situations.

Rapport-building questions focus on connection and trust. These questions demonstrate empathy and genuine interest in your team's well-being and experiences. They create an environment where individuals feel valued and heard, fostering stronger relationships. For example, you might ask, "Are you looking forward to your vacation to Barcelona?" or "How are you navigating your workload with everything else going on?" These questions not only deepen connections but also provide insight into personal or team dynamics.

As a leader, it's important to recognize that your team members have both *stated* needs (the concerns and priorities they explicitly express) and *unstated* needs, which may require more thoughtful questioning to uncover. Stated needs from your team members might include requests like "We need more resources to complete this project on time" or "I need clarity on the priorities for this quarter." These are relatively straightforward and can often be addressed directly.

Unstated needs, however, can be more complex. For example, a team member might consistently request deadline extensions, but their real need could stem from feeling overwhelmed by unclear expectations or inadequate training. Similarly, a team's request for new tools

113

Creating Outcomes by Design

may mask an underlying need for better collaboration or communication practices. These deeper needs often remain unspoken unless uncovered through thoughtfully asked, open-ended questions.

To address both stated and unstated needs, leaders can ask targeted, exploratory questions. For instance, if a team member raises a concern about a tight timeline, you might follow up with "What do you feel is the biggest barrier to meeting the deadline?" or "What support would help you feel more confident in achieving this goal?" These types of questions not only provide clarity but also demonstrate that you value their input.

When a negotiation or conversation hits a brick wall, two simple yet powerful phrases can be employed to help uncover information that remains stubbornly unspoken. The first is "Tell me more." These three words, though deceptively simple, are remarkably effective. They invite the other person to share additional details or context that might not have surfaced yet. This open-ended approach encourages them to elaborate, often revealing insights into their challenges, concerns, or pain points. For instance, you might say, "Tell me more about the challenges your team is experiencing with their global counterparts" or "You mentioned there's been an issue with attrition lately. Tell me more about that."

The second phrase, "If you had a magic wand," allows someone to bypass objections or excuses by removing perceived barriers. It encourages the other person to imagine an ideal scenario, and offers you valuable insights into what they truly want or need. For example, you might ask, "If you had a magic wand, how many people would you hire for this project?" or "If you had a magic wand, what would the perfect solution to this problem look like?"

These two phrases work because they foster curiosity and creativity, helping to unlock hidden insights and move the conversation forward. By asking the right questions—questions that go beyond surface-level concerns—you create a safe space for your team to

114

Synergy and Sparks

share their challenges and perspectives. This approach enables you to address potential obstacles proactively and ensures that your team feels both supported and understood.

Before any conversation, take the time to prepare by organizing your thoughts and identifying the areas where you need more clarity. Jot down questions that will help you gain insights or clarify key details. Ensure your questions are clear, concise, and purposeful, blending data, insight, and rapport-building approaches. Thoughtful preparation ensures each question you ask contributes meaningfully to the conversation, rather than feeling superficial or redundant.

By using strategic questioning in your leadership conversations, you can unlock crucial information, overcome barriers, and build alignment. This intentional approach to asking questions not only strengthens relationships with your team but also empowers them to achieve their best, creating a culture of trust and collaboration.

On the Spot: Fielding Questions in the Moment

For most people, the thought of speaking without preparation or answering difficult questions is a source of fear and anxiety. Think back to times when you've stumbled over your words—whether it was fumbling an answer in high school, misspeaking during a meeting, or losing your train of thought while sharing an idea over Zoom. Impromptu speaking—delivering a speech or response with little to no preparation—is one of the most challenging forms of communication to master. And yet, it's arguably the most important and certainly the most common. Impromptu speaking demands quick thinking, mental agility, and happens in real time, on the spot, with no rehearsal. Whether it's answering questions during a conference call, offering ideas in a brainstorming session, or chatting with colleagues in the elevator, we're constantly presented with opportunities to speak in the moment.

115

Creating Outcomes by Design

One of the most striking recent examples of the high stakes and risks of impromptu speaking occurred on a stage in Atlanta. A poorly executed response to a question stunned millions of viewers, sent shockwaves around the world, and marked the dramatic end of a powerful leader's career. This leader, who had enjoyed more than 50 years of distinguished public service, saw his legacy irrevocably altered in just a matter of seconds.

Joe Biden: Stumble in the Spotlight

Joe Biden began his political career at the age of 29, becoming one of the youngest Americans ever elected to the United States Senate. He served for more than 36 years as a senator before being selected by Barack Obama to be his running mate. Biden went on to serve as vice president for two terms, from 2009 to 2017. In 2020, Biden ran for president against the incumbent, Donald Trump, and won a fiercely contested election—one that ultimately saw Trump's supporters storm the US Capitol in an unprecedented attack on American democracy.

In 2024, Joe Biden faced off against Donald Trump in a rematch for the presidency. At the time, Biden, at 81, was the oldest sitting president in US history. As the campaign unfolded, a troubling narrative began to take shape in the media and online: whispers—and sometimes outright claims—that Biden was too old, too confused, or too mentally diminished to serve another four years. The growing concerns about his age and fitness for office put Biden's team on the defensive. In response, his advisors made a bold move: they proposed shifting the first presidential debate from its traditional September date to June, with the goal of showcasing Biden's mental acuity and leadership abilities in an effort to counteract and regain control of the narrative.

Biden and his team spent weeks preparing for the high-stakes debate, with 51 million viewers tuning in to watch the two political heavyweights clash for the first time in four years. Biden's performance was rocky from the start. As he stepped onto the stage, his movements appeared slow and his gait unsteady, as though each step required more effort than the last. There was a noticeable hesitation in his posture, as if the weight of the moment—and perhaps the years—was pressing down on him.

As the debate began, things quickly spiraled for Biden. His responses were increasingly disjointed, mumbled, and difficult to follow, with fragmented sentences that left many of his points and assertions unclear or incomplete. The situation reached a breaking point when one particular exchange, now viral, crystallized the public's growing doubts about Biden's mental acuity, deepening concerns rather than offering reassurance. It happened a mere 12 minutes into the debate, when the CNN moderator posed a question to Biden about the national debt. His response began confidently but quickly unraveled into a jumbled, incoherent mess, as the sitting president seemed to get tangled up in his own thoughts.

"I should say in a 10-year period we'd be able to wipe out his debt," Biden began forcefully, but then faltered, trailing off: "We'd be able to help make sure that all those things we need to do—child care, elder care, making sure that we continue to strengthen our health care system, making sure that we're able to make every single solitary person eligible for what I've been able to do with the, with the COVID, excuse me, with, um, dealing with everything we have to do with, uh, look, if . . . we finally beat Medicare."[5]

The millions watching at home, along with the moderators and even Donald Trump, were stunned by this incoherent response. As the debate wore on, Biden's answers continued to lack clarity and coherence. At one point, after a meandering response about the border, Trump—wearing an expression of mock pity—shook his head and remarked, "I really don't know what he said at the end of that sentence. And I don't think he knows either."[6]

117

Creating Outcomes by Design

The debate was a disaster for Biden. Viewers across America watched as his age and cognitive struggles became painfully evident, making it increasingly difficult for him to communicate with clarity or conviction. Already facing a fiercely competitive race against Trump, Biden's performance cast serious doubt on his ability to secure a second term.

In the weeks that followed, as support for his reelection campaign dwindled, it became clear that his path to victory had all but evaporated. Less than a month later, Biden dropped out of the race and publicly endorsed Vice President Kamala Harris as his successor.

While few of us will ever face the high-stakes pressure of communicating as presidential candidates, we all find ourselves speaking impromptu in everyday situations. Consider how much of your daily communication happens without any preparation. At breakfast, you explain to your spouse why you won't be able to pick your daughter up from school—impromptu speaking. At a restaurant, you find out your server is from the same city as your immigrant grandparents—impromptu speaking. On a plane, the person sitting next to you asks about your job—impromptu speaking.

The Dilution Effect

Joe Biden's subpar debate performance underscored a key truth about impromptu speaking: it can carry significant risks. Once words are spoken, they cannot be taken back, and they often linger in the minds of the audience long after the conversation ends. Like a defendant in court, you're held accountable for every word you say. That's why, in many situations, it's often wiser to say less than risk saying something you might regret. The more you speak, the greater the chance of misspeaking, confusing or boring your audience, or inadvertently making a statement you'd rather take back. In short, being concise isn't just a matter of efficiency—it's a strategy to protect your credibility and avoid unnecessary pitfalls. Additionally, when we are overwhelmed with too much information at once, it impairs our ability to process it—a phenomenon in social psychology known as the *dilution effect.*

The term *dilution effect* was first introduced by psychologists Richard Nisbett, Henry Zukier, and Ronald Lemley in 1981.[7] They discovered that when participants in a study were presented with both relevant (diagnostic) and irrelevant (nondiagnostic) information, they tended to give less weight to the important, diagnostic details. In other words, the presence of unnecessary information "diluted" the impact of the relevant information. For example, when you're answering a question or telling a story, the more extraneous or unrelated details you include, the weaker and less effective your response or story becomes. The dilution effect demonstrates how irrelevant information can interfere with decision-making and judgment, ultimately reducing the clarity and effectiveness of the conclusions we draw.

Steve Bannon, the former chief strategist for Donald Trump and a prominent figure within the conservative movement, frequently employed the dilution effect in a deliberately calculated and cynical manner, a strategy he described as "flood[ing] the zone with shit." That particular phrase encapsulated Bannon's approach to political communication and media manipulation.[8]

Bannon's tactics—aggressively adopted by Donald Trump during the early months of his second presidential term—involved flooding the public with a relentless stream of information, much of it false, misleading, or irrelevant, designed to confuse, distract, and ultimately wear people down.[9] By flooding the media landscape with chaotic and contradictory narratives, Bannon and Trump aimed to create an environment where it became difficult for individuals to discern fact from fiction. In such an atmosphere, it is then easier to manipulate public opinion, sow doubt, and advance a specific political agenda.

119

Creating Outcomes by Design

As journalist Jonathan Rauch pointed out, the goal for doing this was clear: "This is not about persuasion: This is about disorientation."[10]

Mastering Spontaneous Communication

For any leader, excelling at impromptu speaking can be challenging, but it is entirely within reach with the right skills and practice. The key to responding effectively in the moment is to pause before you speak. When you're asked a question or need to react quickly, you typically have one or two seconds to gather your thoughts. That brief pause can be the difference between a thoughtful response and a rushed one, so make sure to use it wisely.

Another helpful strategy is to slow your speaking rate. When speaking off the cuff—especially in a second language—taking the time to articulate your words clearly helps you maintain control of your message and avoid rushing. A deliberate pace not only gives you more time to think but also helps you frame and deliver your thoughts more clearly and persuasively. Remember, once the words are out, you can't take them back, so it's worth investing those extra moments to speak with intention and confidence. Additionally, it can be helpful to "package" your answer using a connector statement at the top and a checkback at the end.

A *connector statement* is a brief phrase or remark you can use to link your response to the question you've been asked, while giving yourself a moment to gather your thoughts and consider your answer. It's particularly helpful when you're faced with a surprising or challenging question. For example, you might say, "That's a fair question—I'm happy to answer it" or "I can see why you'd ask that—let me explain." Other options include "This is definitely an important topic for us at [company] . . ." or "Thanks for raising that—I'm happy to address it." These connector statements act as a useful tool, offering a brief pause to collect your thoughts and formulate an appropriate response to maintain both your credibility and composure, even in unexpected or tough situations.

After using a connector statement and delivering a clear, concise answer, it's important to conclude with a *checkback*—a technique that enables someone to confirm their response has been understood by the questioner. A checkback can be verbal, such as asking, "Did I answer your question, Rami?" or nonverbal, like observing Rami nodding in agreement. Regardless of the approach, the goal is the same: to ensure your response has fully addressed the question and met the questioner's needs. This not only helps to clarify any potential misunderstandings but also demonstrates your attentiveness and commitment to providing a thorough, thoughtful answer.

In the heat of the moment, it's not uncommon to be asked a question you're unprepared for or unable to answer. Whether it's a surprise inquiry or one that catches you off guard, revealing confidential information or diving into a topic you're not fully equipped to discuss can be risky and potentially damaging. The good news is that there are four highly effective techniques to help you navigate these situations: *bridging, spotlighting, repetition*, and *reframing*. Each of these strategies can help you stay in control, protect your message, and steer the conversation in a direction that suits your objectives.

Bridging For leaders, it is crucial to maintain control of conversations and guide discussions toward productive outcomes. Bridging is a technique that enables you to steer a conversation away from difficult, uncomfortable, or off-limits topics and redirect it back to the key message you wish to communicate. It's a way to deflect questions or interruptions without dismissing them outright. A simple bridging phrase is "I can't speak to [topic you don't want to discuss], but what I can tell you is [relevant information you want to share]." By using a bridge, you subtly shift the focus to a topic you're more comfortable addressing, while maintaining your credibility and making the questioner feel heard.

Spotlighting Spotlighting is an incredibly effective technique for managing tough questions, as it helps you center your response on the most crucial points. When faced with a challenging inquiry, you can begin by highlighting the key takeaway: "The most important thing to remember here is . . . . " or "If there's only one thing you take away from my speech today . . . ." This approach keeps your answer focused and ensures that the core message you want to convey stands out clearly. It also helps guide the audience's attention to what really matters, even if the question itself is complex or tangential.

Repetition Repetition is another powerful tool that works seamlessly with spotlighting. By restating a key point, you reinforce its importance and ensure it sticks with your audience. For instance, "Last year, we doubled our productivity in the first three months—I'm serious—our productivity literally doubled." Repeating the core message not only underscores its significance but also makes it more memorable, ensuring that it resonates with your audience long after the conversation ends.

Reframing Reframing is a powerful rhetorical tool when you need to address a legitimate question but want to shift the focus to better align with your message. Reframing enables you to rephrase the question or issue in a way that highlights a more positive or constructive perspective, giving you control over the direction of the conversation. For example, if a salesperson is asked why their proposal is so expensive, they might first acknowledge the concern: "I understand your hesitation about the price," but can then reframe by shifting the focus: "Let's take a moment though to consider the value this proposal will bring in terms of boosting your team's productivity." This approach enables the responder to address the core issue while guiding the conversation toward a more favorable perspective.

For leaders facing tough questions in the moment, developing comfort with the discomfort that often comes with impromptu speaking is crucial. While it may seem impossible to prepare for a high-stakes question and answer session, given that you can't predict the questions ahead of time, there is a proven preparation technique that can help you succeed. Though its name may sound a bit intimidating, it's one of the most effective tools a leader can use. In fact, it's been a secret weapon for military officers, business titans, and world leaders for decades.

Creating a Murder Board

The term *murder board* (sometimes called a *scrub-down*) refers to a group of questioners assembled to critically evaluate a proposal or to help someone prepare for a challenging oral examination. Originally developed in the US military, the concept of the murder board as a preparation tool has since spread to academic, governmental, and business environments. Its primary purpose is to identify potential vulnerabilities, weaknesses, and overlooked issues in a leader's presentation or pitch, helping to refine the content and delivery before facing a broader or more challenging audience.[11] If you've ever watched an episode of *Shark Tank* or *Dragon's Den*, you've likely imagined what it would be like to face a panel of tough investors, fielding their relentless questions and challenges. This is exactly why creating a murder board *before* a high-stakes meeting or presentation is so essential—so you can be thoroughly prepared for the intense scrutiny you may face.

A murder board involves colleagues or team members role-playing as the actual audience, simulating a real-world environment—much like actors rehearsing a performance. Participants ask tough, "gotcha" questions to challenge assumptions, expose flaws, and prepare the presenter for difficult scenarios. The key idea of a murder board is simple: it's better to stumble in a low-stakes environment, where you can refine your response, than to falter in front of a client or senior leader, where the stakes are much higher.

To create a murder board before your next presentation or meeting, assemble a small group of trusted colleagues or team members familiar with the subject. Their role is to simulate tough questions and challenges you might face, so encourage them to adopt the perspectives of skeptical audience members, clients, or stakeholders. Start by presenting your key points or strategy, then have the group probe with difficult questions—such as "What if this doesn't work?," "How does this benefit our bottom line?," or "What risks are we overlooking?"

The person presenting should practice delivering their answers on the spot, while the group provides feedback, pointing out weak spots in their narrative or argument, and suggesting stronger responses. The murder board should be a safe space for constructive criticism, enabling the leader to refine their messaging and anticipate potential challenges so they're fully prepared when facing the real audience.

In Chapter 9, we'll dive into the power of passion and how it can ignite others, exploring how genuine enthusiasm is contagious and can inspire action. Plus, we'll reveal two time-tested formulas for crafting the perfect pep talk or motivational message that resonates and drives change.

Chapter 9

How Leaders Drive Passion and Purpose

No alarm clock needed. My passion wakes me.

—Eric Thomas

The Spark That Created Spanx

Sara Blakely, the charismatic, self-made billionaire founder of Spanx, the global hosiery and shapewear brand, has often shared how crucial passion was to her success as an entrepreneur. Blakely's unconventional journey began with a failed attempt to land the role of Goofy at Disney World, followed by a challenging stint selling fax machines door-to-door.[1]

Blakely came up with the idea for Spanx while getting ready for a party. Frustrated by the lack of comfortable hosiery options, Blakely cut the feet off a pair of pantyhose and the concept for Spanx was born. "Having purpose gives you courage," said Blakely, "When I think about my purpose, I think about my grandma and my mom, and all the other women who came before me, and all the women who will come after."[2]

After designing an initial prototype, Blakely faced a series of rejections and closed doors, as manufacturers and fabric suppliers—most of whom were men—failed to grasp the value of her product. It was in these challenging moments that Blakely's passion and sense of purpose truly came to the forefront. "When I started Spanx I had no idea what I was doing," said Blakely. "My knowledge in this industry was little to none. What always fueled me, even in times of extreme self-doubt, was how much I cared. When you stay connected to your purpose, you find the courage you never knew you had."[3]

After reaching out to various potential partners and distributors, Blakely managed to secure a brief 10-minute appointment with the buyer at her local Neiman Marcus, a well-known retailer. During the meeting, Blakely took a bold step by inviting the buyer to the ladies' restroom to personally model the Spanx and demonstrate how the product worked. Impressed, the buyer placed a test order to assess consumer interest in the product—and the rest is history. As of 2021, Spanx was valued at approximately $1.2 billion.[4]

Despite facing numerous early setbacks, Blakely's passion and unwavering determination ultimately fueled her entrepreneurial journey, leading to the creation of one of the most successful companies in the fashion industry. For Blakely, the key to effective leadership lies in understanding and embracing personal passion: "What breaks your heart, or what fires you up? Whatever that is, there's your passion. Pay attention."[5]

The Fuel Behind Achievement

Being a leader today comes with unique challenges, shaped by ever-evolving global dynamics, technological advancements, and shifting societal expectations. Gallup's latest annual report on US workplace engagement shows a concerning decline, with employee engagement hitting its lowest level in a decade. Only 31 percent of US employees say they feel engaged at work—and in Europe, that number drops even further to just 13 percent. Gallup attributes this increasing sense of detachment among employees to several key factors. These include rapid organizational changes, the challenges arising from the transition to hybrid and remote work models, shifting customer and employee expectations, and broken performance management practices that no longer meet the needs of the modern workforce.[6]

While leadership can be exciting and rewarding, it can also be isolating, as leaders are often required to make difficult or unpopular decisions. Today's leaders are not only responsible for setting a clear vision and driving results but also for motivating and supporting their teams through this complex and fast-changing new landscape. Success in leadership increasingly hinges on a leader's ability to communicate effectively and build strong relationships with their teams. And the manner in which someone leads can have a huge impact on the morale of their team members.

Studies show that more than 70 percent of an employee's perception of their organization—and, by extension, their job—is influenced by their manager's morale and behavior.[7] In fact, a manager's impact on an employee's mental health can be as significant as that of a spouse.[8] This phenomenon, known as *emotional contagion*, underscores how a leader's emotions can profoundly affect their team's mindset, performance, and the overall tone and outcome of interactions.

Emotions transmit through a kind of wireless network of mirror neurons—small brain cells that help us empathize with others and grasp their emotions.[9] For example, when you see someone yawn, these neurons can trigger a response in your own brain, causing you to yawn as well; if someone tells you a heartbreaking story, you feel the essence of that heartbreak as well. Human neurobiology links the emotional experiences of one person to another, meaning that every social interaction—whether personal or professional—creates behavioral synchrony between individuals. This synchrony has the power to shape or shift emotional states.

Acting guru Sanford Meisner once remarked, "If you have the emotion, it infects you and the audience. If you don't have it, don't bother."[10] Much like actors on stage who aim to evoke genuine emotional responses from their scene partners to make the performance feel honest and authentic, employees also respond to the emotional cues of their boss or manager, which in turn affects their own emotional engagement and performance. Unfortunately, only 3 in 10 managers worldwide feel truly engaged in their roles.[11] And, as anyone who's worked on a team knows, just as passion is contagious—so too is apathy.

A leader who demonstrates passion can be a powerful source of inspiration for their team. Passionate leaders are driven by curiosity, a desire to explore new possibilities, and a willingness to take bold risks, which in turn sparks excitement within the team. For example, a tech startup CEO who passionately talks about the potential impact of their new product can ignite the same excitement in their team, pushing them to think outside the box and approach problems with renewed creativity. Their enthusiasm is contagious—when the leader genuinely believes in the mission, it encourages team members to engage more deeply, show initiative, and contribute to the shared vision with greater commitment and creativity. A passionate leader sets a high standard of dedication, motivating others to push beyond their comfort zones and invest in the collective outcome.

When leading a team, inspiring them to pursue a shared vision is essential for success. A leader's ability to communicate this vision in a compelling and meaningful way makes all the difference. Consider a coach who, through both words and actions, helps players see the broader goal of a championship not just as a win but as a culmination of personal growth, teamwork, and perseverance. This sense of purpose fosters resilience and a deeper connection to the task at hand.

However, it's important to recognize that not all forms of motivation are equally effective. While passion can certainly fuel high performance, it needs to be coupled with an understanding of what truly drives each individual on the team. For instance, while some team members may be motivated by the challenge and excitement of big risks, others may find more value in steady progress and stability. A leader who takes the time to understand the diverse motivational factors that drive their team is more likely to cultivate an environment where everyone feels empowered, valued, and engaged. To do this effectively, it's crucial for a leader to recognize the two primary types of motivation that influence human behavior: intrinsic and extrinsic motivation.

- *Intrinsic motivation* stems from within yourself, driven by a genuine interest, enjoyment, or personal satisfaction derived from the activity itself. When you are intrinsically motivated, you engage in tasks because you find them inherently fulfilling, not because of any external reward or recognition. You do it because you want to do it.

- By contrast, *extrinsic motivation* is fueled by external factors, such as tangible rewards or external pressures. This type of motivation often involves working toward a specific goal—like earning a higher salary, receiving a promotion, or meeting a required deadline—where the primary incentive is the external benefit or outcome, rather than the activity itself.

The core idea is simple: incentives shape behavior. Change the incentive, and you change the way people act. However, research consistently reveals that intrinsic motivation tends to lead to greater long-term benefits than extrinsic motivation. While external rewards like bonuses or recognition can encourage short-term performance, intrinsic motivation fosters deeper engagement, creativity, and sustained effort over time. When people find joy or purpose in what they're doing, they're more likely to persist, innovate, and take ownership of their work.[12]

The boxer Muhammad Ali once declared, "I'm happy because I'm fulfilling my purpose in life. See, everything was created for a purpose.

Trees have a purpose. The moon has a purpose. Rats have a purpose." Ali went on to emphasize the point even further, stating, "Ten men with the knowledge of their purpose are more powerful than a thousand men working from morning until evening without understanding theirs." In other words, having a clear sense of purpose makes individuals far more effective and driven than those who work without understanding the deeper meaning behind their actions.[13]

Pat Riley has won nine NBA championships as a player, coach, and executive, establishing himself as one of the most legendary figures in professional sports. Throughout his career, Riley demonstrated an exceptional ability to coach and manage players with diverse styles and personalities, skillfully adjusting his communication to be able to effectively develop each individual. He also understood how to capture attention and inspire action. One iconic moment from the 2006 NBA Finals illustrates this point perfectly.[14]

In that series, Riley's Miami Heat were trailing the Dallas Mavericks two games to none. Facing a challenging situation, Riley delivered what was later described as one of his "best motivational messages ever." In the locker room before the third game, Riley placed a large bucket of ice water in front of his team and began speaking: "If you want to win a championship, you have to want it—" He abruptly paused, then, to the surprise of his players, plunged his head into the bucket of ice water and held it there for over a minute. The players watched in stunned silence until Riley finally emerged, gasping for air, and completed his sentence: "—like it's your last breath."

The Heat went on to win that game, the next three in a row, and ultimately the 2006 NBA Championship—a victory that stood as a testament to Riley's unique ability to motivate and inspire.

For leaders, bringing passion to your work provides many benefits. When people feel passionate about their efforts they are more willing to invest their time and energy, to go above and beyond. Research has shown that when employees are inspired by a clear sense of purpose, they are willing to dedicate up to 40 percent of their discretionary time to their company.[15] Work passion has also been proven to improve individual performance as well as personal well-being, and research shows that when workers interact with a passionate leader, there is a "trickle-down" effect whereby that leader's work passion is transferred to those team members.[16] As Virgin Group Founder Richard Branson once observed, "Passion, like a smile, is contagious. It rubs off on everyone around you and attracts enthusiastic people into your orbit."[17]

To inspire passion and purpose within a team, a leader has to be attentive and engaged, demonstrating enthusiasm and curiosity in a way that motivates others to do the same. Passionate leaders empower their team members by granting autonomy, offering opportunities for growth, and encouraging them to take on challenges in pursuit of a clearly defined goal.

Decades of research have consistently shown that high engagement—where individuals feel a strong connection to their work, their colleagues, and the broader goals of the team—leads to positive outcomes for both the individual and the organization. When people believe their contributions are meaningful and directly affect the team's success, engagement thrives, driving performance and satisfaction.[18] In one Harvard Business School study, 76 percent of people reported that their best days at work involved making progress toward a goal—reinforcing the idea that purpose can be a powerful motivator.[19]

One often overlooked yet crucial element of a positive and engaging work environment is fun. The human brain is naturally wired to respond to enjoyment, releasing dopamine—the neurotransmitter linked to pleasure, motivation, and learning—whenever we experience fun. This biochemical response reinforces behaviors that promote well-being and encourages us to repeat them. Research suggests that incorporating fun into the workplace can be a powerful tool for boosting both employee performance and overall well-being.[20] Not only does it make us feel good but it also enhances our capacity to learn, problem-solve, and think creatively.

After acting school, I had the great fortune to work with Academy Award–winning director Miloš Forman (*One Flew Over the Cuckoo's Nest, Amadeus*). Meeting him at his Ritz-Carlton suite, I was nervous, but the legendary filmmaker immediately put me at ease. Far from intimidating, he was warm, playful, and full of energy.

For two days, we rehearsed scenes from the film, transforming hotel furniture into makeshift sets and cars—just playing—much like I did as a boy, building forts with my friends in the backyard. It was an eye-opening experience, reminding me of the freedom that comes from letting go of expectations and embracing a sense of play. Ultimately, the film was never financed, but Forman left me with a lasting lesson: no matter your status or career, creativity thrives on a spirit of fun and imagination.

In fact, a recent survey found that 79 percent of employees believe fun at work leads to greater productivity. Gallup research shows that employees who report having fun at work are more likely to be engaged, leading to 21 percent higher productivity for their companies.[21] Consider how managers or bosses lead within your organization—how does the concept of fun factor into their approach? Do they encourage moments of lightheartedness or team-bonding activities that build camaraderie? Or is the workplace more focused on strictly meeting deadlines and hitting targets, with little room for enjoyment?

The Downside of Passionate Leaders

Passion is a trait highly valued by organizations, especially in leaders, as it drives motivation and helps maintain focus on goals. While research frequently highlights its positive impact, there is a darker side to passion that can foster negative behaviors and harm others. One study found that leaders who tied their work performance to their identity and self-esteem were more likely to experience higher levels of obsessive passion.[22] As Harvard Business School assistant professor Jon M. Jachimowicz notes, "You can't just express passion and expect it will be jolly good. It isn't always the way to get people on board with you. There's a time and place for it." If not expressed thoughtfully, passion can even be dangerous, depending on when, how, and to whom it is directed.[23]

New research suggests that if leaders aren't mindful of how and when they express their passion for work, it can alienate colleagues or even make them feel threatened. Furthermore, leaders who become overly consumed by their passion may start to define themselves by their work, which can lead to exhaustion, burnout, and an increased likelihood of exhibiting abusive behaviors toward others.[24] Reflect on the leaders you've worked with throughout your career. In what ways did they express their passion, and what impact did it have on their teams and overall success?

To harness passion as a positive force in leadership, begin by acknowledging that passion is not inherently a virtue—it can be both constructive and destructive. Recognize when passion enhances performance and when it becomes counterproductive. Encourage your team to separate their work from their identity and self-esteem, and lead by example, focusing on self-growth and personal development. Additionally, support passionate team members by providing tools and resources—such as training, workshops, or team-building activities—that help them self-monitor and prevent burnout.[25]

As an organization, it's not enough to simply hire individuals based on their passion. Leaders must also develop the skills to manage and channel that passion effectively. This involves recognizing when passion is driving positive outcomes and when it may be pushing individuals toward burnout or unhealthy behavior. By learning

133

How Leaders Drive Passion and Purpose

how to cultivate and direct passion in a balanced way, leaders can ensure that it becomes a powerful tool for productivity and engagement, rather than a source of stress or conflict.

Fueling Team Drive: Motivating Language and Mental Contrasting

A key responsibility of leadership is to inspire and empower teams—helping individuals feel valued, fostering career development, and driving the achievement of goals. By cultivating an environment where people are passionate and motivated, leaders can help their teams see the impact of their work and how it aligns with the broader mission of the organization. Effective leaders build the capacity for growth and innovation by creating a purposeful, energized workplace that fuels creativity and commitment. To do this successfully, let's explore two powerful frameworks for delivering a compelling pep talk or motivational message that will inspire and drive meaningful action: motivating language and mental contrasting.

Motivating Language Theory

Jacqueline and Milton Mayfield, a husband-and-wife team at Texas A&M University, have spent nearly three decades researching motivating language theory and its application in the business world. The theory, originally proposed by Jeremiah Sullivan in the 1980s, emerged from research on how leadership communication and language influence employee motivation, engagement, and performance. It offers leaders a guiding framework for effective leadership.[26] "Work is communication and communication is work," notes Jacqueline Mayfield. "You can't get anything done in an organization without communication."[27] The Mayfields' deep dive into what makes a leader's message truly impactful led them to consult with experts in sports psychology and military history, seeking to understand what drives passion and sparks action. As the Mayfields remind us, "Communication shapes culture, and culture shapes communication."[28]

Through their years of research, the Mayfields discovered that the most powerful motivational speeches, regardless of the setting, generally contain three essential elements: *direction giving, expressions of empathy*, and *meaning making*. They found that when leaders understand and incorporate these elements into their communication, they can ignite passion, cultivate a sense of purpose, and inspire action. Leaders who master these tools are able to push their teams beyond basic performance, fostering a deeper commitment to the mission and its overarching goals.

- The first key element—direction giving—focuses on providing clarity and guidance. A strong motivational message needs to help listeners understand exactly what needs to be done, how to do it, and why it matters. For example, a human resources (HR) manager might detail how learning a new software platform is going to help them do their work more efficiently, while a sales manager might provide a clear road map to hit a sales target. The purpose here is to reduce uncertainty and create focus, giving someone a clear vision of the path ahead. It's about offering practical guidance, ensuring everyone knows what role they play in the larger picture.

- The second element—expressions of empathy—connects the leader with their team on an emotional level. Motivational messages should never just be about what and how; they need to show that the leader understands the challenges their teams face. This can be done through praise, acknowledgment, or gratitude. The HR manager might say, "I appreciate that it will take some time and effort to learn this new platform," while the sales manager might tell their team, "I know this target looks daunting, but I believe in you." This is where leaders can humanize the task at hand, reminding their team members that their efforts are noticed and valued.

- Finally, the most powerful speeches are those that help listeners connect their efforts to a larger purpose—this is the meaning-making element. Research by the Mayfields reveals that only half of managers leverage this approach when motivating their teams—an opportunity that is clearly being overlooked.[29] Leaders benefit when they connect their team's actions to a purpose larger than the immediate goal and demonstrate how achieving the task aligns with the organization's broader mission or an individual's personal values. For the HR manager, it might look like this: "If you can learn this new software, it will free up countless hours of work for you in the future." The sales manager might remind their team, "Hitting this goal means not just meeting a target but also showing senior leadership that you are talented, driven, and can accomplish great things." This is where the leader instills a sense of purpose—helping the team see how their success will resonate beyond just the task at hand.

I recently spoke with the Mayfields about their ongoing research—as well as that of others—into motivating language. Their latest findings, based on studies across various organizations worldwide, uncovered an intriguing insight: motivating language isn't just effective when a boss communicates with their team; it's equally impactful in peer-to-peer interactions, especially when the message being delivered is rooted in inspiration or motivation. Additionally, they stressed that motivating language should be seen as a dialogue, not a monologue.[30]

By understanding and applying three key elements—direction giving, expressions of empathy, and meaning making—leaders can ignite passion, cultivate commitment, and empower their teams to achieve their full potential. According to the Mayfields, leaders who use motivating language can boost trust and elevate their perceived competence by as much as 70 percent.[31] Whether in the home, office, or classroom, motivating language can do more than boost performance—it can reshape how others perceive their purpose and help them unlock their full potential.

Mental Contrasting

Gabriele Oettingen, a German academic and professor of psychology at New York University, first introduced the concept of *mental contrasting* in the early 1990s, where she explored the effects of positive fantasies and the role of contrasting those fantasies with the present reality.[32]

Mental contrasting is a motivational tool that can help leaders inspire their teams to achieve goals by combining positive visualization with a realistic assessment of the effort and sacrifices required. It encourages team members to envision a desired outcome while also acknowledging the obstacles they may encounter. This approach not only helps them set realistic, attainable goals but also strengthens their motivation to overcome challenges and commit to the actions necessary for success. As the Stoic philosopher Marcus Aurelius famously said, "The impediment to action advances action. What stands in the way becomes the way."[33]

A pair of studies by Andreas Kappes and his team at University College London highlighted mental contrasting as a game changer in goal pursuit. Consistent with previous research, their findings showed that when individuals used mental contrasting and believed in their potential for success, they began to view challenges not as roadblocks, but as obstacles to be overcome. This shift in mindset significantly enhanced their ability to stay focused and motivated toward achieving their goals.[34]

How Leaders Drive Passion and Purpose

Building on Oettingen's research, the mental contrasting process I employ follows a simple three-step formula designed to help teams move from where they are to where they want to be:

1. It starts by *describing the present state*, where the current situation is clearly defined, and the goal or problem that needs to be addressed is outlined. This step also includes an understanding of the impact the situation has in the present moment.

2. The next step encourages *imagining a positive future* by painting a vivid picture of success. This is where the team envisions the positive outcomes and transformative effects of achieving the goal, helping to create an inspiring vision for the future.

3. The third step is *identifying obstacles*, acknowledging the challenges and barriers that could arise, while stressing the importance of overcoming these difficulties together. Here, the process calls for a commitment to action, urging the team to dedicate themselves to the effort required, take specific actions, and remain determined despite any challenges or setbacks.

To demonstrate how this works, let's imagine a boss using the mental contrasting formula to motivate their team for an upcoming project.

First, the leader describes the present state: "Team, we're in the early stages of this project, still navigating planning and resource challenges." Next, the leader shifts to imagining the positive future: "But imagine, by the end of this quarter, we've launched the product, received great feedback, and smashed our sales targets." Then, the leader identifies potential obstacles: "We'll likely face tight deadlines and unexpected setbacks along the way." Finally, they ask for commitment: "I'm asking each of you to stay focused, tackle obstacles head-on, and push forward together. Are you with me?"

As you reflect on past projects or challenges your team has encountered, think about how you could have framed your message using motivating language theory or mental contrasting. Both approaches are powerful tools for igniting passion and purpose, helping your team see their efforts as part of a larger, more meaningful goal.

In Part IV, we'll delve into how storytelling serves as a powerful tool for leaders—not only in communicating their purpose with clarity and authenticity but also in fostering deeper emotional connections and motivating their teams to take action.

Part IV

Storytelling

Chapter 10

The Undeniable Power of Narrative

In the end, we'll all become stories.

—Margaret Atwood

The Appeal of Storytelling

In today's fast-paced business world, storytelling has become a powerful tool for communication—one that anyone can harness to their advantage. Great leaders are often exceptional storytellers, and the most influential communicators recognize the profound impact of narrative. While direct selling and persuasion are push strategies, storytelling takes a pull approach, gradually unfolding to subtly draw the listener in. A well-crafted story not only makes your message more memorable but it also fosters a deeper connection with your audience, making your ideas more relatable and your message more impactful.

By weaving in emotion, context, and authenticity, storytelling can transform complex concepts into something clear and compelling, ensuring that your message resonates long after the conversation ends. Values are just words unless you act on them and incorporate them into the fabric of your organization's culture. Stories can help you do that quickly and efficiently.

In an experiment conducted with students at Stanford University to compare the memorability of facts versus stories, researchers had participants give one-minute speeches on crime, using statistics provided to them. On average, each student included 2.5 statistics in their speech, while only 1 in 10 chose to tell a story. After the speeches, the researchers tested the students' recall of the information they had heard. The results were striking: only 5 percent of students could remember specific statistics, while 63 percent were able to recall the stories. The takeaway is clear: stories are far more memorable than statistics, likely due to the emotional engagement they evoke.[1]

Scott Galloway, the popular podcaster and professor of marketing at New York University's Stern School of Business, is frequently asked about the most important skill children need to master in order to succeed in adulthood. His response: "Hands down, if I could inculcate my sons in any domain expertise, in any skill, it would be storytelling." He explains why: "Storytelling—it's how you raise money, it's how you find a mate, it's how you get a job, it's how you convince people to work with you. Our superpower as a species is cooperation. That's the reason why we went from being in caves to having arms treaties and espresso and Netflix. We are the apex predator. And the reason why is we paint pictures or draw pictures on cave walls such that the next generation learns faster than instinct."[2]

As Galloway reminds us, storytelling is a practice we've engaged in since the dawn of humanity and is hardwired into human nature. The earliest examples of storytelling can be traced to the cave paintings created by our ancestors more than 50,000 years ago. Rather than being mere art, these types of images served as vital lessons and guides for survival, depicting crucial information, such as how to hunt, gather, and navigate the challenges of daily life.[3]

The discovery of fire further revolutionized storytelling, as early humans would gather around the warmth of the campfire at night, cooking and staying safe while sharing stories. This nightly ritual offered a vital space for education, the exchange of knowledge, and the discussion of life beyond the shelter of the cave. It was through these shared experiences and stories that early humans could learn, connect, and prepare for the world around them.[4]

Although we've thankfully moved beyond the confines of those early caves, our attraction to and reliance on storytelling remains as strong as ever. Whether it's over Zoom, during a commute, or at a bar after the workday has ended, we're still captivated by stories—and by the people who know how to tell them well. Humans have been telling stories long before they had written language. Some of the earliest written documents evolved from oral traditions, preserving stories, laws, religious teachings, and historical events that had been passed down through generations. Notable examples include *The Iliad* and *The Odyssey*, as well as the Bible.

While modern technology and the increasing amount of time we spend in digital spaces have reshaped how and where we direct our attention, the human craving for narrative remains unchanged. Alexis Ohanian, cofounder of the social media platform Reddit, spotlights humanity's enduring desire for stories. "Thousands of years ago . . . we were sitting around a campfire and that great storyteller was doing the voices and the impressions. That's ingrained in our species." Ohanian believes that live theater will experience a resurgence in the next decade. "We'll look at all these screens with all these AI-polished images, and we'll actually want to sit in a room with other humans to be captivated for a couple hours in a dark room to feel the goosebumps of seeing live human performances."[5] A recent survey by Workday supports this view, revealing that 83 percent of respondents believe the growing use of AI will make human skills—such as empathy, communication, and relationship building—even more essential.[6]

If you pause to reflect on the prevalence of story in our lives, you'll realize just how much of your day involves relaying information to others through narrative. Unsurprisingly, we also enjoy talking about ourselves. Researchers at UC Santa Barbara explored why human

145

The Undeniable Power of Narrative

beings spend so much time talking about their thoughts and feelings. The study revealed that talking about ourselves, whether in person or on social media, increased activity in the same brain regions associated with the sense of reward gained from food, money, and sex.[7]

In his paper "Gossip in Evolutionary Perspective," evolutionary psychologist Robin Dunbar found that social topics—especially gossip—make up a staggering 65 percent of all human conversations in public spaces.[8] As humans, we are naturally drawn to gossip, finding excitement in the exchange of such information, even when the topics at hand are relatively mundane. This fascination stems from the social value that gossip provides—it helps us learn about the people in our personal or professional circles. Those who hold and selectively share this information often accrue social capital, gaining influence and strengthening their connections. Through this dynamic, gossip and stories become more than just idle chatter; they become a tool for building relationships and asserting social status.[9]

Though today we may spend less time gathering around a literal campfire, there are many metaphorical campfires in the modern world where people come together to share information. Podcasts, a term first coined in 2004, have become a powerful medium for information in the digital age, with a staggering 546 million listeners worldwide. One study found that 47 percent of the US population over the age of 12 listens to a podcast at least once a week. Advertising spending on podcasts was expected to surpass $4 billion in 2024.[10]

TED Talks provide another popular platform for communal learning and the sharing of stories and ideas. Over the years, TED—short for "Technology, Entertainment, and Design"—has featured many influential speakers, including Adam Driver, Al Gore, and Sheryl Sandberg. These TED sessions, as well as TEDx Talks, consistently attract millions of viewers across social media platforms. Previous TED Talks have showcased remarkable speakers and ideas, such as Daryl Davis, a Black man who attended Ku Klux Klan rallies to challenge hate and encourage dialogue; Tan Le, a scientist who introduced a groundbreaking headset capable of reading brainwaves; and a parrot named Einstein, who demonstrated the astonishing cognitive abilities of birds.[11] Interestingly, research into the 500 most popular TED Talks found that those that went viral followed a clear structure: 65 percent personal stories, 25 percent facts and figures, and 10 percent content to establish the speaker's credibility on the topic.[12]

Anyone who has shed a tear at the end of a book or felt their heart race during a suspenseful action scene in a film knows the profound emotional impact stories can have to move us. In a business setting, a well-crafted story can evoke powerful emotions and serve as a valuable tool for overcoming objections, simplifying complex ideas, building rapport, and demonstrating value. As the old saying goes: *facts tell, stories sell.*

The connection between storytelling and science received a significant boost in 2010, when Uri Hasson, a researcher at Princeton University, used magnetic resonance imaging to study the brain's response to storytelling. Hasson discovered that when a person tells an emotional story, "extensive neural coupling" occurs, aligning the brain activity of both the speaker and the listener—almost like a "mind-meld."[13] This contributes to the neural entrainment phenomenon we spoke about previously.

When human beings hear a story, our brains respond as though we're experiencing the events ourselves, a phenomenon known as *transportation*. The auditory cortex processes the sounds of the story, while the sensory cortex activates, helping us imagine details like sights, sounds, smells, and even tastes. However, Hasson's research revealed an important caveat: if the speaker is an ineffective storyteller, the neural coupling diminishes, and the connection between speaker and listener is significantly weakened.[14]

As a story unfolds, the motor cortex becomes activated, preparing us to take action or respond. In his research at Princeton, Hasson

147

The Undeniable Power of Narrative

and his team discovered that when participants heard action-oriented messages, their motor cortices lit up as though they were physically performing the actions described. This mind-body connection is a powerful tool that leaders can harness, using storytelling to inspire and motivate their teams to take meaningful action.[15]

Dr. Paul J. Zak, a leading expert on storytelling, explains how emotional narratives trigger the release of oxytocin in the brain—a neurotransmitter often called the *love hormone*. This has important implications for leaders managing teams, as oxytocin fosters trust, compassion, and empathy—crucial ingredients for effective collaboration. Zak's research has been pivotal in demonstrating how the use of storytelling can influence our brains, bring strangers together, and encourage greater compassion and generosity.

The immersive experience of hearing an emotional story not only captivates us but also has the power to boost motivation. Says Zak, "Character-driven stories with emotional content result in a better understanding of the key points a speaker wishes to make and . . . blows the standard PowerPoint presentation to bits."[16] Tension builds when conflict arises in the story, particularly when something significant is at stake for the main character. As risks are taken and challenges faced, a series of events unfold, steadily building momentum toward the story's climax. This sense of urgency and uncertainty keeps the audience engaged, eager to see how the character will navigate the mounting stakes.

Applying the Hero's Journey to Modern Leadership

Andrew Stanton has been a major creative force at Pixar Animation Studios since 1990, writing and directing classic films such as *Toy Story*, *WALL-E*, *Monsters, Inc.*, and *A Bug's Life*.[17] From an early age, Stanton was drawn to storytelling and the power of narrative. "We all love stories," he explains. "Stories affirm who we are. We all want affirmations that our lives have meaning. And nothing does a greater affirmation than when we connect through stories."[18]

In 1998, Andrew Stanton had just completed writing Pixar's hit films *Toy Story* and *A Bug's Life* and was fully immersed in the art of screenwriting. Despite the critical acclaim and box office success of his films, Stanton was far from satisfied and was determined to continue honing his craft. "I wanted to become much better at it," said Stanton. "So I researched everything I possibly could, and I finally came across this fantastic quote by a British playwright, William Archer: 'Drama is anticipation mingled with uncertainty.' It's an incredibly insightful definition. When you're telling a story, have you constructed anticipation? In the short term, have you made me want to know what will happen next? But more importantly, have you made me want to know how it will all conclude in the long term? Have you constructed honest conflicts with truth that creates doubt in what the outcome might be?"

Stanton later went on to write and direct *Finding Nemo*, a captivating animated tale about a spirited clownfish named Nemo who is separated from his family and embarks on an unforgettable journey to reunite with them. Along the way, Nemo faces perilous challenges and encounters dangerous predators in the vast, unpredictable ocean. The film earned Stanton an Academy Award for Best Animated Feature and became one of Pixar's most successful and beloved releases, grossing nearly $1 billion worldwide.

Finding Nemo follows one of the most enduring narrative structures in storytelling: the "hero's journey." This framework, first identified by scholar Joseph Campbell in his book *The Hero with a Thousand Faces*, outlines a universal pattern found across myths, legends, and stories from various cultures. Campbell called this pattern the *monomyth*—a series of stages that a hero typically experiences during their adventure, transformation, and eventual return.[19]

149

The Undeniable Power of Narrative

This structure, which follows a protagonist's journey through various challenges and triumphs, is a familiar framework for anyone who enjoys movies or books. Whether it's Macaulay Culkin's clever survival in *Home Alone*, Jodie Foster's intense pursuit of justice in *The Silence of the Lambs*, or Sacha Baron Cohen's outrageous adventures in the *Borat* movies, the hero's journey serves as the backbone of countless iconic stories. Each of these characters embarks on a unique adventure, facing obstacles that ultimately lead to personal growth and a deeper understanding of the world around them. In a story, obstacles are essential to generate conflict, and as screenwriting expert Robert McKee aptly reminds us, "Nothing moves forward in a story except through conflict."[20]

In business and sales, a leader can leverage the hero's journey to inspire initiative and drive action. The key points of the hero's journey relevant to the sales and marketing process are this: your hero (the customer) has a problem. Your hero (the customer) takes a journey toward solving that problem. Your hero (the customer) meets a mentor (your company) that helps them with their journey. Your hero (the customer) eventually achieves success as a result of the association with their mentor (your company). This narrative approach helps to create a sense of partnership and empowers the customer to take decisive action.

The hero's journey can also be used for leaders managing a team. For example, faced with the difficult decision to reduce their head count due to budget constraints, a manager can frame the remaining team members as the heroes of the story, navigating tough circumstances and rising to new challenges: longer hours, heavier workloads, and greater responsibilities. Through the frame of the hero's journey, that manager can position themselves as a supportive guide, whose role is to provide the resources, guidance, and encouragement needed to help this resilient and talented team succeed in achieving their goals.

When sharing a story in a corporate setting, be mindful of positioning yourself as the hero—unless you're in a job interview or performance review, where highlighting your skills and accomplishments is the goal. Portraying yourself as the central figure can come across as boastful or self-serving, which may alienate your audience or colleagues. Instead, focus on making others the hero of the story—for example, your audience or employees. This approach demonstrates appreciation for their contributions and reinforces the value of teamwork.

The ability to use storytelling to inspire and motivate others is an essential skill for any leader. While data and facts appeal to the intellect, stories pack an emotional punch, forging a deeper connection. By mastering the classic hero's journey and applying it to your storytelling, you can deliver your business messages with passion and impact, fostering greater engagement and driving meaningful results.

Elements of a Compelling Story: Understanding Dramatic Structure

The question of whether good storytellers are born or made is one that's been debated for a long time, and the answer is probably a mix of both nature and nurture. Some people seem to have a natural gift for storytelling and the ability to captivate an audience. As a result, they might be more inclined to develop an interest in storytelling from an early age, absorbing techniques unconsciously through their experiences or environment. However, storytelling is a skill that can be cultivated and refined over time.

When I work with leaders who don't consider themselves natural storytellers, I always emphasize that storytelling is a skill, not an innate talent. Even if you don't feel you were born with an instinct for narrative, you can still learn and master the key elements of effective storytelling. My own journey began at 15, when I started studying storytelling with professionals from the Playwrights' Center and the Guthrie Theater in Minneapolis. That experience was a turning point, and I've spent decades experimenting with storytelling and structure ever since. With each new project, I'm reminded of one key truth: storytelling is a skill that can be learned and honed. As John August, the award-winning screenwriter notes, "When something is well-structured, you feel beginnings and endings, you feel closure of moments, you feel there's a rhythm to it, and you've recognized what the audience needs."[21] The foundation of this process lies in a strong understanding of dramatic structure and the core elements that make a story truly compelling.

Aristotle, the renowned philosopher of the 4th century BCE, was the first to propose that stories should adhere to a specific structure. In his seminal work *Poetics*, Aristotle laid the foundation for dramatic theory and the art of storytelling, arguing that a well-crafted narrative should consist of three essential parts: a beginning (exposition), a middle (complication), and an end (resolution).[22] About 2,100 years later, the German novelist and playwright Gustav Freytag built on Aristotle's work and introduced a more formalized model of dramatic plot, now known as *Freytag's pyramid*. This simple narrative structure divides a story into five distinct sections: *exposition, rising action, climax, falling action*, and *resolution*. Freytag's pyramid continues to be widely used by writers across genres today.[23] Modern storytelling experts, however, have adapted Freytag's model to include a sixth crucial element: the *inciting incident*.

The framework for dramatic structure I recommend for storytelling is centered on six key elements (see Figure 10.1).

To show how these elements work together, let's break them down using *The Wizard of Oz* as an example:

Exposition. The first element in dramatic structure, *exposition*, provides essential background information that helps the

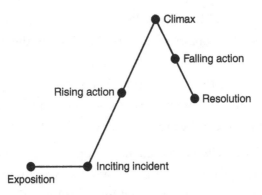

Figure 10.1 Dramatic structure

audience understand the context of the story and establish the who, what, where, and when. It introduces the characters, setting, and time period, while subtly hinting at the conflict that will propel the plot forward. In *The Wizard of Oz*, the exposition introduces Dorothy, a young girl living on a farm in rural Kansas with her family and her dog, Toto, in the early 20th century.

Inciting incident. The second element is the *inciting incident*, which is the event that triggers the main plot and sets everything in motion. It introduces the central conflict—presenting either an opportunity or a threat—and forces the protagonist to take action. In *The Wizard of Oz*, the inciting incident occurs when a tornado sweeps Dorothy and her house away to a strange, magical land, setting her journey in motion.

Rising action. The *rising action* is the third element, where the majority of the narrative unfolds. Here, obstacles and complications are introduced, and the protagonist must face these challenges to achieve their goal. As the conflict intensifies, the stakes grow, pulling the audience deeper into the story. In *The Wizard of Oz*, the rising action begins when

Dorothy accidentally kills the Wicked Witch of the East, setting off a chain of events that incites the Wicked Witch of the West to pursue her. Here, Dorothy also meets key characters—the Scarecrow, Tin Man, Cowardly Lion, and eventually the Wizard of Oz—who will assist her in her quest to return home.

Climax. The *climax* comes next, representing the moment of highest tension in the story, where everything turns for the protagonist. It's the pivotal point where the main conflict reaches its peak. In *The Wizard of Oz*, the climax occurs when Dorothy, in a desperate act of defiance, throws a bucket of water on the Wicked Witch of the West, causing her to melt. This moment resolves the central conflict as the Wicked Witch is defeated and her pursuit of Dorothy ends.

Falling action. Following the climax, the *falling action* occurs, where the pace slows and the narrative begins to wind down. The tension eases, and the story starts to draw toward its conclusion. In *The Wizard of Oz*, after the Wicked Witch of the West is vanquished, the falling action reveals that Dorothy has the power to return home using the magic of her ruby slippers. She bids farewell to her newfound friends and clicks her heels three times, wishing to return to Kansas.

Resolution. Finally, the *resolution* provides the conclusion of the story, tying up loose ends and reinforcing the central message or theme. It offers closure and emotional release for the audience. In *The Wizard of Oz*, the resolution occurs when Dorothy returns home to Kansas and is reunited with her family. Her iconic line, "There's no place like home," encapsulates her journey. Through her adventure, Dorothy has learned that the true value of her life lies in the love, security, and stability found in her family and home.

Harnessing *In Medias Res* for Impact

Once you're comfortable with the dramatic structure of Freytag's pyramid, you can experiment with another classic narrative technique: *in medias res*. This Latin phrase, meaning "in the midst of things," refers to starting a story in the middle of the action and gradually revealing key details—such as the who, what, when, and where—through dialogue, flashbacks, or other narrative devices.[24] Many iconic works of literature and film use this technique to create immediate engagement. For instance, Homer's *The Iliad* opens in the heat of the Trojan War, plunging readers directly into the conflict. Similarly, Christopher Nolan's *The Dark Knight* kicks off with a high-stakes bank heist orchestrated by the Joker. In both examples, the story unfolds around the initial action, keeping the audience intrigued as they piece together the backstory. I even used *in medias res* to tell the opening story of this book.

One of the most powerful examples of *in medias res* occurs in the opening scene of the television series *Breaking Bad*. The pilot episode begins with a frantic, nearly naked man in a gas mask, driving a battered RV while being chased by an unknown threat. Right from the start, viewers are thrown into the action: the man speeds down a desolate New Mexico road, clearly terrified for his life. We have no idea who he is, what he's done to provoke such a pursuit, or whether he's the hero or villain of the story.

Creator Vince Gilligan deliberately disorients the audience, plunging us straight into the heart of the drama with no exposition or context. Before the opening credits even roll, the man—who we later learn is Walter White, the show's protagonist—grabs a gun from a lifeless body on the RV's floor, steps outside, and points it at the approaching police cars, their sirens growing louder. This high-stakes, adrenaline-pumping introduction immediately sets the tone for the entire series and sparks curiosity: *who is this man and what events led up to this life-or-death standoff?* By withholding information and starting in the middle of the action, *Breaking Bad* grabs our attention and keeps us craving answers.

A leader can harness the power of *in medias res* to immediately capture an audience's attention, and it is particularly effective for emphasizing a critical challenge, pivotal change, or transformation within a business. Imagine a CEO is speaking to their team about a major crisis the company previously overcame, like a near-collapse due to a financial crisis. Instead of starting with a long buildup or background context, the CEO jumps straight into a pivotal moment: "I still remember the feeling of panic that hit when the market crashed. We were in a meeting, stunned, trying to process the news, when the phone rang. It was the head of marketing, telling us that our largest client had just called, requesting we cancel their $50 million contract."

To incorporate *in medias res* into your story, begin at a climactic or pivotal moment of your narrative—something that's both dramatic and crucial to the plot. By diving straight into the heart of the action, you'll draw the audience in from the very beginning, sparking curiosity about the events that led to this moment and what will happen next.

In business, storytelling that evokes emotion humanizes a company's or team's journey, creating a deeper connection with the audience by showcasing both challenges and triumphs. This emotional resonance not only makes the audience feel personally invested in the outcome but also inspires them to take action or embrace the changes ahead.

Next, in Chapter 11, we'll explore how leaders can leverage stories and anecdotes to navigate change, foster alignment, and support their teams during periods of uncertainty and challenge.

Chapter 11

Managing Change Through Storytelling

*We cannot change the cards we are dealt, just how we play
the hand.*

—Randy Pausch

Turning Uncertainty into Opportunity

The past few years of pandemic and post-pandemic work have taught
us a crucial lesson: change is inevitable. What feels like the norm
today can be completely upended tomorrow. While we all crave stability and predictability, the modern workplace is in a constant state
of flux. As I mentioned in the Introduction to this book, Gallup's
latest research reveals a staggering reality: overall job satisfaction
among global employees has sunk to a historic low. This alarming
trend has been labeled the *Great Detachment.*

Several factors have contributed to this sharp decline in engagement, with the relentless pace of change in the workplace being
the most significant. Employees are grappling with challenges like
constant organizational restructuring, the growing pains of hybrid
and remote work, and shifting expectations from both leadership
and customers. On top of that, the lingering effects of the pandemic,
coupled with a sluggish job market and persistent inflation, have left
many workers feeling stuck, disconnected, and demotivated.[1]

Leaders who want to maintain engagement and productivity during times of transition or upheaval should begin by harnessing the

power of storytelling to inspire and motivate their teams. As Steve Denning, head of talent management for the World Bank, noted, "When it comes to inspiring people to embrace a vision or a change in behavior, storytelling isn't just better than the other tools; it's the only thing that works."[2]

Research has shown that up to 88 percent of business transformations fail to achieve their original ambitions[3] and only 10 percent of leaders have the skills necessary to guide teams through challenging times.[4] As we've mentioned before, people tend to resist change, often preferring what's familiar and comfortable. Therefore, when advocating for change, it's crucial that team members understand the why—how it connects to their individual roles and supports the organization's broader mission.

Change can be daunting, especially when not managed effectively. When leaders fail to guide their teams through it thoughtfully, it can undermine employee morale, fueling anxiety, fear, or even resentment. A 2023 study underscored the growing severity of the issue, revealing that 44 percent of workers worldwide—and a staggering 52 percent in the United States—reported feeling stressed on the job, marking an all-time high.[5] In this challenging environment, storytelling emerges as a powerful tool for leaders. When used strategically, storytelling can shift the focus of change from something disruptive to an opportunity for growth, alignment, and shared purpose. As Jon Kabat-Zinn, an author and scientist, wisely puts it, "You can't stop the waves, but you can learn to surf."[6] Storytelling enables leaders to help employees navigate the waves of change with resilience and clarity.

Effective change initiatives are always driven by forward momentum and action, and a carefully chosen story or anecdote—employed strategically—can be a powerful tool for leaders to engage their teams. Whether it's reassuring the anxious, persuading the resistant, or challenging the complacent, storytelling can create a shared sense of purpose and direction. As Jacqueline Novogratz eloquently writes

158

Synergy and Sparks

in *Manifesto for a Moral Revolution*, "The job of a moral leader—which is the job of all of us—is to learn to tell stories that matter, stories that unite and inspire, reinforcing our individual and collective potential, and paint a picture of the future that we can build and inhabit together." This ability to share meaningful stories is key to guiding teams through change and helping them envision the future they can create together.[7]

Abraham Lincoln, widely regarded as one of the most important figures in US history and the president who brought an end to slavery in the United States, was deeply influenced by one particular story that helped shape his views on abolition. In 1852, Harriet Beecher Stowe published *Uncle Tom's Cabin*, an antislavery novel that became the second best-selling book of the 19th century, surpassed only by the Bible. The novel, which chronicled the tragic journey of the morally steadfast slave, Uncle Tom, as he suffers under the cruelty of various masters, had a profound impact on Lincoln when he read it, solidifying his stance on slavery and galvanizing the abolitionist movement. Legend has it that when Beecher Stowe met Lincoln in Washington, DC, he greeted her with the famous words, "So you're the little woman who wrote the book that started this great war."[8]

When choosing the right story to tell, it's essential to consider both the context and the audience. Start by identifying the challenges your audience is facing and the type of change they are experiencing—or that needs to happen. From there, tailor your story to resonate with them by understanding their values, concerns, and interests. This makes your message more relatable and impactful. Craft your story to connect emotionally, using vivid imagery and specific language to forge a deeper connection with your listeners. Seek out stories of transformation that highlight an individual, team, or company navigating and overcoming challenges. These narratives tend to be naturally compelling and relatable. Finally, whenever possible, conclude your story with a clear call to action, inspiring your audience to take the next step.

Crafting a Vision That Resonates

Stories involving change are ubiquitous, and many of them carry powerful, easily digestible lessons. One compelling example involves the story of Blockbuster CEO John Antioco during the early days of the digital revolution. In 2000, Reed Hastings, the CEO of Netflix, approached Antioco with an offer to sell Blockbuster his fledgling DVD rental service for just $50 million. Antioco, skeptical of Netflix's potential and convinced that the future of video rentals lay in Blockbuster's traditional brick-and-mortar model, turned down the offer.

Fast-forward to today, and Netflix is worth nearly $250 billion, revolutionizing entertainment through streaming and original content production, while Blockbuster has all but disappeared, relegated to a corporate punchline and a cautionary tale. Antioco's resistance to change, particularly in an industry on the brink of digital disruption, not only cost him the chance to profit from a transformative new business model but also enabled Netflix to become the dominant player in an industry that Blockbuster once ruled.[9]

Conversely, if you wanted to share a story of a CEO faced with difficult circumstances who effectively embraced change, you could recount the story of Domino's Pizza CEO Patrick Doyle, who took the reins in 2010 during a very challenging period in the company's history. "We were the 30-minute guys," said Doyle, "We were the delivery guys who were going to get a pizza to you that's going to be OK, but we're going to get it to you quickly."[10] With the pizza chain's reputation in shambles and its stock price anemic, Doyle decided to ask customers directly what they thought of Domino's product. Their feedback was not good, with people saying it tasted like "cardboard," describing it as "bland" and the "worst pizza I ever had."[11]

But instead of quietly reshaping the Domino's brand in private, Doyle decided to take a different approach. He created a new marketing campaign—dubbed "Domino's Pizza Turnaround"—where he didn't hide from the negative feedback; he actually included the comments in Domino's television and print ads. Doyle even appeared himself, accepting the withering criticism, and promising to "work days, nights, and weekends" to make improvements.[12] By doing so, he acknowledged his company had fallen short and the time had come for them to reimagine their product. "Our problems were self-inflicted," said Doyle, "because the pizza wasn't as good as it could be."[13] The product revamp worked, creating a vastly improved recipe and brand. In the first year alone, Domino's sales grew by 10 percent and their stock increased by 130 percent.[14] Doyle's "Pizza Turnaround" initiative was a success and remains one of Doyle's proudest accomplishments as Domino's CEO.

Doyle's strategy showed a commitment to radical transparency as a leader. His bold approach not only demonstrated honesty and humility but also resonated with consumers, showing that the company was willing to acknowledge its shortcomings and take action. This approach highlights the power of being transparent about challenges and change, which can build credibility and trust with both customers and employees.

Stories Versus Anecdotes

In Chapter 10, we explored two classic narrative structures that can be used to craft compelling business stories: Freytag's pyramid and *in medias res*. But what if you don't have time to tell a full story during your speech or presentation? In that case, you can turn to an anecdote. While a story typically unfolds with a beginning, middle, and end—complete with sensory details and emotional depth—an anecdote is a more concise and straightforward retelling of a specific event or experience. In a business context, both stories and anecdotes are powerful

161

Managing Change Through Storytelling

tools for communicating ideas, building connections, and imparting lessons. However, they serve different purposes, vary in scope, and follow distinct structures. A business story is typically more expansive, used to convey a broader message, highlight a pivotal moment, or embody core values. These stories tend to be more detailed, focusing on significant events or transformational journeys, and are often employed to inspire, persuade, or motivate an audience. For instance, a leader might share a story about how their company overcame a major challenge, leading to growth or innovation, in an effort to demonstrate resilience and strategic thinking. By weaving in these larger narratives, stories engage audiences on a deeper level and provide context for the lessons being shared.

By contrast, an anecdote is shorter and more focused, usually centered on a specific moment or event. Anecdotes tend to be more casual and concise, often used to highlight a key point or offer insight into a particular situation. They are commonly shared in conversations or informal settings, serving as quick, relatable examples, sometimes with a touch of humor, to build rapport. For example, a business leader might share an anecdote about a memorable interaction with a satisfied customer to underscore the importance of personalized service.

Frameworks for Anecdotes

When sharing an anecdote, you can use one of these three frameworks to ensure it's clear, concise, and impactful:

- Past/present/future
- Cause/effect/remedy
- Before/event/result

Each of these three anecdote formulas serves a unique storytelling purpose and can be employed strategically depending on your intent. *Past/present/future* works well when guiding the audience through a personal or professional journey, offering insight into growth or transformation. Use *cause/effect/remedy* when addressing a problem, especially in persuasive writing or speeches, as it logically breaks down an issue and presents a solution. *Before/event/result* is ideal for spotlighting a pivotal moment—often used to emphasize turning points, key decisions, or impactful experiences—making it perfect for interviews, testimonials, or case studies.

Imagine you're having a conversation with your teenager about technology, emphasizing the importance of being mindful of the devices they use and the personal information they share. A great way to approach the conversation is by using the *past/present/future* framework, like this:

> When I was growing up, we didn't have smartphones, so my parents had no way of knowing where I was or what I was doing most of the time [past]. Today, with the devices you use, I can track your location and contact you almost anytime [present]. In the future, though, as technology advances, this ability for others to track us could start to feel like an invasion of privacy [future].

The *cause/effect/remedy* framework is another simple and effective way to structure your anecdote. For example, imagine you're explaining to your team why customer complaints about shipping delays have been increasing and what you're doing to fix it:

> Recently, we've noticed a rise in customer complaints about shipping times being too long. The is a result of our outdated

warehouse management system, which is prone to errors and causes delays [cause]. As a result, customers are receiving their orders later than expected, which negatively affects their satisfaction with our service [effect]. To address this, we're implementing a new warehouse management system that will improve efficiency and reduce errors [remedy].

For the third example, if your boss questions the cost of a new software platform, you can employ the *before/event/result* framework like this:

I completely understand your concerns about investing in a platform like this—I had the same reservations, initially [before]. However, after running a pilot with the new software, the results were impressive [event]. Within just six months, every salesperson who used it experienced a 20 percent increase in their close rate [result].

A recent survey found that 76 percent of CEOs believe the ability to adapt to change will be a critical source of competitive advantage in the future.[15] Leaders will need to become skilled at navigating change, and storytelling can be a powerful tool to manage expectations, gain commitment, and align teams around a shared vision. It's important to remember that effective storytelling isn't just about sharing information; it's about creating an emotional connection that inspires people to embrace the change you're advocating.

The Enduring Impact of Stories in Leadership

Prime Minister Narendra Modi of India has won three consecutive elections, and currently boasts an impressive 70 percent approval rating with the Indian people.[16] He has garnered considerable influence over time, boasting more than 107 million followers on X (formerly Twitter).[17] A recent article in the *New York Times* explored Modi's widespread popularity and the factors behind his strong connection with the Indian public.[18] Not surprisingly, much of his success stems from his ability to craft compelling narratives and present himself as an authentic, relatable leader. One of the most notable ways Modi does this is through his weekly radio show, a modern-day equivalent to the radio addresses once delivered by President Franklin Delano Roosevelt in the United States during the 1930s.

Modi launched his radio show *Mann Ki Baat* in 2014, just months after becoming prime minister of India. Aired on the last Sunday of each month, the show quickly became a cornerstone of Modi's communication strategy, enabling him to connect directly with the Indian people, bypassing traditional media channels. Through a personal and conversational tone, Modi effectively conveyed his government's key initiatives—from providing free rations to improving infrastructure. During the COVID pandemic, *Mann Ki Baat* played a crucial role in shaping public discourse, with Modi using one episode to encourage vaccination as he guided citizens through the crisis. His skillful blend of populist storytelling and direct engagement helped him strengthen his rapport with the nation. World leaders like Modi understand the importance of creating a narrative to move and inspire people. As John Blake wrote for *CNN*, "A country needs a unifying story like a human being needs oxygen."[19]

Business leaders can draw valuable lessons from Modi's approach and adapt it to their own organizations. By hosting town halls, question and answer sessions, or recording messages for distribution across multiple platforms, leaders can foster direct, transparent communication with employees, building stronger connections and a more engaged workforce.[20]

In the United States, current and past presidents have leveraged storytelling for years to help the public manage uncertainty and change. "Stories are essential to holding a nation together," says Kermit Roosevelt III, a historian and author.[21] Two of America's most gifted communicators—Ronald Reagan and Barack Obama—knew how to use narrative to inspire a nation and promote the ideals of liberal democracy. In his farewell speech at the end of his second term as president, Reagan spoke passionately about how immigrants were the source of America's greatness: "While other countries cling to the stale past, here in America we breathe life into dreams. Thanks to each wave of new arrivals to this land of opportunity, we're a nation forever young, forever bursting with energy and new ideas."[22]

Former president Obama frequently used stories from his personal experiences growing up as the son of a white mother from Kansas and Black father from Kenya as proof that the American dream was possible for anyone. "I stand here knowing that my story is part of the larger American story," said Obama, during his speech at the 2004 Democratic National Convention in Boston, "that I owe a debt to all of those who came before me, and that, in no other country on Earth is my story even possible."[23]

Even Donald Trump, a dominant political figure in recent years who, after being defeated by Joe Biden in 2020, would return to win a second presidential term in 2024, used narrative and imagery to shape public perception. However, Trump's tone differed sharply from that of Reagan or Obama. In all three of his presidential campaigns, Trump portrayed America in stark, dire terms, declaring, "We are a nation in decline, we are a failing nation."[24] In his 2017 inaugural address, Trump famously coined the phrase "American carnage" to describe the nation's condition. He painted a grim, pessimistic picture of America, describing "mothers and children trapped in poverty in our inner cities, rusted-out factories, scattered like tombstones across the landscape of our nation . . . and the crime, and the gangs, and the drugs that have stolen too many lives and robbed our country of so much."[25]

166

Synergy and Sparks

Metaphors and Echoes

Storytelling techniques used by screenwriters and playwrights to captivate audiences in film and theater can be equally effective in leadership and communication. Two particularly powerful tools are *metaphor* and *thematic echo*. These techniques are not only key for crafting compelling narratives in movies and plays but are also invaluable for leaders who recognize the impact of storytelling in shaping public perception and driving change. Leaders like Ronald Reagan, Barack Obama, and Donald Trump all skillfully used these elements to connect with audiences and reinforce their messages.

According to anthropologist Mary Catherine Bateson, "Our species thinks in metaphors and learns through stories."[26] In ancient Greece, where oratory was prized over written communication, metaphors were particularly valued by those in power for their ability to persuade and inspire. Aristotle loved metaphors, saying, "To be a master of metaphor is the greatest thing by far."[27] A well-crafted metaphor used in a business context, such as "the finish line is finally in sight" or "this is going to be a tough hill to climb," can take abstract ideas and connect them to something familiar, making the intangible more accessible. By transforming complex situations into concrete images, metaphors help audiences grasp and emotionally engage with new concepts, turning uncertainty into something comprehensible and actionable. One important tip: when using a metaphor, make sure it's simpler than the concept you're explaining and also easy for your audience to relate to.

Reagan used metaphor effectively on the eve of his election in 1980 when he famously referred to America as "a shining city on a hill." That image became a touchstone for his entire presidency.

Barack Obama, similarly, preferred metaphors of roads and landscapes in his description of the nation's "rugged path towards prosperity and freedom." Obama's use of the journey metaphor became so prevalent that his official campaign logo even reflected it: a naturalist scene with a rising sun and stripes of the flag running over a hillside.[28]

Donald Trump's use of visceral metaphors such as "drain the swamp" and "build the wall" were repeated so often during his first campaign, they became a mantra of sorts for his followers. Trump effectively used them as simple-to-understand rallying cries for millions of disaffected voters who felt like their political leaders had abandoned them.[29]

In a screenplay, a *thematic echo* is a technique used to reinforce a story's central message by strategically including echoes throughout the narrative to deepen the audience's understanding of the movie's theme and conflict.[30] This is generally done through the use or repetition of imagery and symbols. For example, in *The Godfather*, the theme of family loyalty is echoed throughout the film through the repeated imagery of the family home. The film opens and closes with scenes of the Corleone family gathered at their home, a symbol of unity and power. In the *Star Wars* saga, the theme of balance between good and evil is echoed through both visual and narrative elements. Luke Skywalker's journey mirrors that of his father, Anakin Skywalker, highlighting how the choices between the light and dark sides of the Force are constantly in tension. You might even have noticed how I've used the word *spark* as a recurring motif throughout this book.

Thematic echo can also be applied in a business setting to reinforce core values or strategic goals, ensuring consistency and clarity in messaging. Ronald Reagan used thematic echoes in his farewell address as president in 1989 when he returned to his earlier metaphor of America as a "shining city on a hill" from his speech nine years earlier. "We made the city stronger," said Reagan, "We made the city freer. And we left her in good hands."[31]

Obama, leaning in to his optimism for a prosperous and inclusive future, used thematic echoing when he employed the phrase, "Yes, We Can" as a rallying cry for the nation, saying, "When we have faced down impossible odds, when we've been told we're not ready or that we shouldn't try or that we can't, generations of Americans have responded with a simple creed that sums up the spirit of a people: Yes, we can. Yes, we can. Yes, we can."[32]

Throughout his presidential campaigns, Donald Trump leveraged the phrase "Make America Great Again," not merely as a slogan but as a thematic anchor that unified his policy proposals, speeches, and actions. By repeatedly using the phrase, he created a resonant echo that reinforced his core message, weaving a cohesive narrative of national renewal. Though the phrase had previously been used by other politicians such as Ronald Reagan, George H. W. Bush, and Bill Clinton going back as far as 1980, Trump claimed it as his own in 2015, boasting, "Make America Great Again, the phrase, that was mine, I came up with it about a year ago."[33] Trump's strategic repetition, combined with the slogan's widespread presence on branded merchandise, helped solidify its place in the public consciousness. For Trump's supporters, it became more than just a catchphrase—it evolved into a symbol of an alternative future, steeped in the nostalgia of a perceived golden past.

For business leaders looking to use thematic echoes in storytelling, start by defining the central message or theme you want to convey—think of it like a newspaper headline that encapsulates the essence of the story. This step is crucial, says John Medina of the University of Washington School of Medicine, because it not only helps grab your audience's attention but also helps them focus on a single, clear idea. "When a listener doesn't grasp the overarching idea being presented," Medina warns, "they have a hard time digesting the information." A well-defined theme provides a throughline that guides the entire narrative, ensuring that each piece of the story reinforces and supports the central message. By consistently echoing that theme in different contexts, you help your audience understand and internalize the message more effectively.[34]

169

Managing Change Through Storytelling

Once you've decided on a central message, brainstorm and create imagery that embodies this theme, either literally or metaphorically. Introduce visual echoes at key moments of conflict or character development, using repetition to emphasize their significance. For example, a leader might repeatedly reference a symbol of unity—like a handshake or a bridge—throughout speeches, reinforcing the theme of collaboration during times of division.

As the story unfolds, let the imagery evolve to mirror the character's growth and any shifts in the theme. For instance, a leader might begin with a focus on overcoming obstacles, using images of breaking chains or opening doors, and as progress is made, shift to imagery of building or constructing—such as laying foundations or raising structures—to represent growth and achievement. These repeated, evolving images help solidify the leader's core message while visually guiding their audience through the narrative.[35]

Metaphor and thematic resonance enhance both the emotional and intellectual impact of a story. When used by leaders, these tools can inspire action, build trust, and guide team members through change. Like skilled screenwriters, a boss or manager can use metaphors to simplify complex transitions, making them more accessible. By weaving these elements into their business stories, leaders can connect with their audiences on a deeper level, creating alignment and motivation.

In Chapter 12, we'll explore the five essential business stories every leader should possess, offering practical guidance on how and when to deploy them for maximum impact. These stories not only inspire and influence but also serve as powerful tools for building trust and driving action.

Chapter 12

Choosing a Business Story to Tell

How could you live and have no story to tell?

—Fyodor Dostoevsky

Storytelling as a Retention Booster

Every leader carries with them a wealth of stories and lessons drawn from both personal and professional experiences. These stories—whether recounting triumphs or challenges—serve as invaluable assets, helping to shape and enhance collaboration and communication with others. Oprah Winfrey, the legendary talk show host, actor, and entrepreneur, has long harnessed the power of storytelling to build and propel her brand. "I'm in the storytelling business," she has said. "I believe that the humanity that all of us share is the stories of our lives, and everybody has a story. Your story is as important as the next person's story."[1] This perspective is also echoed by Richard Branson, the charismatic and innovative founder of Virgin Airlines. "Today, if you want to succeed as an entrepreneur or leader," Branson advises, "you also have to be a storyteller."[2]

An article in *MIT Sloan Management Review* highlighted research showing that storytelling, when integrated into executive development programs, outperformed many other initiatives in enhancing leadership skills.[3] When we tell stories, our teams and clients are far more likely to remember the message. Studies reveal that within the first hour of learning new information, more than half of it is forgotten. By the end of the first day, another 10 percent slips away, and after a month, an additional 14 percent is lost.[4] A well-crafted story not only makes a message more memorable but it can also help clarify meaning and illustrate complex concepts or ideas. Because stories often carry an emotional charge, they can be more effective in defining an organization's culture or promoting its values than a company vision statement or motto. As author Alan Weiss wisely observes, "Logic makes people think; emotion makes them act."[5]

Research by Thomas Graeber, an assistant professor of business administration at Harvard Business School, reveals that if you want your message to truly resonate and be remembered, packaging your information in a story can be a powerful strategy. Through a series of controlled experiments, Graeber and his team examined how different types of information lose their impact over time. While the effect of a story faded by approximately 30 percent within a single day, the decay of a statistic was much more pronounced, dropping by 73 percent.[6] Graeber's research revealed that stories are more easily recalled by listeners because they incorporate details, context, and emotions, all of which enhance retention and memory. According to Graeber, "In the moment people receive information, they usually understand that statistics tend to be more informative than stories. But after a day, stories are simply more memorable."[7]

When managers use storytelling to resolve conflicts and address issues within their teams, they significantly enhance their ability to achieve positive outcomes.[8] Storytelling serves as a powerful tool in these situations by creating a relatable framework that makes complex ideas easier to digest. In high-stakes or intricate scenarios, stories can distill large amounts of information into clear, concise messages, enabling team members to grasp key concepts quickly and effectively. A well-crafted anecdote or narrative doesn't just convey information—it engages emotions, fosters empathy, and can break

172

Synergy and Sparks

down barriers of misunderstanding. Through storytelling, abstract concepts are made tangible, helping individuals relate to a situation more personally and understand diverse perspectives. What might take hours of explanation or an avalanche of technical jargon can be communicated in a few minutes with the right story, making it a vital skill for managers looking to foster cooperation, alignment, and understanding within their teams.

Mining Your Past: The Five Essential Stories

Each of us carries a rich, intricate tapestry of stories—woven from our experiences, challenges, and triumphs—that define who we are and how we lead. In my travels around the world delivering keynote speeches and facilitating executive coaching sessions, I've seen time and again how storytelling is far more than a communication skill. It's a catalyst for connection, a driver of transformation, and a powerful force for inspiring action. At its core, storytelling builds trust and cultivates empathy—but in some contexts, it becomes even more profound. It can be a lifeline. A quiet act of defiance. A way to preserve our humanity when the world tries to silence it.

Recently, I had the profound honor of leading a storytelling session with a group of young women and girls living in Kabul, Afghanistan—a place where, since 2021, the Taliban has imposed harsh restrictions that forbid women from receiving an education or working. Despite the immense risks they face, these brave young voices gathered to share and to listen. After the session, one of the girls reached out with words that have stayed with me: "Storytelling is our quiet form of resistance," she explained. "It's how we survive. How we remain human when everything around us tries to reduce us to silence." Her message was a powerful reminder that even in the darkest of circumstances, storytelling offers a lifeline—a way to reclaim identity, dignity, and hope.[9]

Through my work with leaders at all levels, I've identified five essential types of stories that every leader should have in their communication toolkit. These stories are not just impactful—they are the cornerstone of effective leadership communication. They serve to engage audiences, engender trust, and build lasting relationships that transcend transactional interactions. Whether delivering a speech, leading a team meeting, or navigating a challenging conversation, these stories can elevate a leader's influence, humanize their message, and ensure their vision resonates. The five types of stories every leader should master are detailed in the following sections, with specific examples demonstrating each.

The Origin Story: Airbnb

An origin story is crucial for both leaders and organizations, as it humanizes them and creates a deeper emotional connection. By sharing their roots, leaders and companies invite others to relate on a personal level, fostering trust and empathy. It reveals the motivations, values, and principles that have shaped them, providing clarity not only about what they do, but why they do it. Whether it's the story of how you met your partner, how you ended up in your current city, or why you chose your profession, these personal narratives help build stronger relationships with customers, employees, investors, and other stakeholders, making you more relatable and authentic.

Additionally, an origin story for an organization specifically clarifies the company's purpose, reinforcing its identity and ensuring that everyone—internally and externally—understands its mission and priorities. It also helps differentiate the brand in a competitive marketplace by showcasing the company's unique journey and the passion behind its products or services. For leaders, an origin story demonstrates authenticity, showing where they come from and how they've grown, making them more approachable and trustworthy.

An origin story is not just a recounting of the past; it's a strategic tool that shapes perception, fosters loyalty, and builds lasting connections with audiences.

In a recent episode of the *Pod Save America* podcast, host Tommy Vietor offered his thoughts on leaders—especially politicians—sharing their origin stories: "You can't just say, 'This is my platform. These are my plans.' You have to say, 'This is who I am, this is who raised me. This is where I came from, and this is how that origin story informed my values and what I care about.'"[10] This perspective is equally applicable for leaders outside the political realm. Whether in business, nonprofit work, or any other field, sharing your origin story is a powerful way to build rapport, cultivate trust, and establish credibility with others.

A compelling example of an origin story is the founding of Airbnb, the US company that revolutionized the way people travel by connecting hosts with travelers seeking short- and long-term accommodations. It all started in 2007 when Brian Chesky and Joe Gebbia, two friends who met at the Rhode Island School of Design, were living in San Francisco and struggling to pay their rent.[11] When a major design conference came to the Bay Area, they noticed all the hotels were fully booked. Seeing an opportunity, the enterprising duo came up with a creative solution: they would rent out air mattresses in their living room to conference attendees who had nowhere else to stay. They launched a simple website called Airbed & Breakfast, offering guests a place to sleep and a homemade breakfast in the morning.

The idea was a hit. As demand and interest grew, they decided to take things further. They brought in Nathan Blecharczyk, Chesky's former roommate, as their third cofounder and chief technology officer. Together, they rebranded the concept into what we now know as Airbnb, a platform that allowed anyone with extra space to rent it out to travelers.

As Airbnb gained popularity, it evolved from offering just air mattresses to featuring a wide range of accommodations, from spare rooms and apartments to unique stays like treehouses, castles, and even igloos. Today, Airbnb stands as a global leader in the travel industry, with listings in over 200 countries and a market capitalization of approximately $80 billion. The company has revolutionized travel by offering affordable, authentic, and unique experiences that continue to reshape the tourism landscape.[12]

The origin story of Airbnb is a powerful example of how creativity and entrepreneurship can transform a simple idea into a global business, embodying the essence of the adage, "Think big but focus small." This mindset encourages individuals to set bold, ambitious goals (thinking big) while remaining grounded in the details and actions that bring those goals to life (focusing small). By identifying an unmet need and leveraging their resourcefulness, Airbnb's cofounders demonstrated that innovation often starts with a willingness to think outside the box, take calculated risks, and adapt to new opportunities. Their journey proves that transformative ideas can emerge from modest beginnings and a commitment to challenging the status quo.

As you reflect on this, consider your own origin story as a leader. How did you begin your leadership journey, and what pivotal experiences shaped the leader you are today? These stories are more than just chapters of your past; they are powerful lessons that reveal the foundation of your leadership style, offering insight and inspiration that can guide and motivate your team.

The Value Story: Nike

A value story can take two powerful paths for a leader. First, it can serve as a window into the values that guide the leader or the organization, revealing what is truly important to them and what they stand for. By sharing these values, a leader can offer clarity and transparency, helping others understand the principles that shape decisions, actions, and long-term goals. Second, a value story can spark excitement and build trust by clearly demonstrating the tangible impact the organization has had in the past. Whether highlighting specific outcomes or detailing how the work benefits clients, customers, the community—or even society at large—a well-crafted value story creates a compelling narrative that shows the real-world value the company delivers and why it matters. In both cases, the value story connects people to a shared sense of purpose and reinforces the organization's commitment to making a positive difference.

One of the most iconic brands in history owes much of its success to its ability to convey its value (and values) to consumers and the public through the stories it tells. Most people are familiar with the origin story of Nike, the iconic athletic footwear and apparel brand, and how its founders, Bill Bowerman and Phil Knight, launched the company in 1971. According to the tale, Bowerman, eager to create a shoe that was lighter and faster, famously used a waffle iron in his kitchen to design the now-iconic "waffle sole," a feature that became a hallmark of Nike running shoes.[13] But today, what truly sets Nike apart from its competitors is its emphasis on the company's core values in its television and print advertising—beginning with its iconic slogan, "Just Do It."

The appeal of the "Just Do It" message lies in its universal versatility—it casts the consumer as the hero of their own story. Whether you're a high school athlete, an Olympic champion, or an energetic senior taking a jazzercise class, the slogan offers a motivating, inclusive call to action that adapts to each individual's unique journey. Nike has consistently embraced this spirit of empowerment, while also taking bold stances on social issues. In 2018, when NFL player and Nike-sponsored athlete Colin Kaepernick protested police brutality and racial injustice, Nike chose to support him. The company aligned itself with Kaepernick's message of standing up for what you believe in—even at personal cost. One iconic Nike ad

177

Choosing a Business Story to Tell

famously featured Kaepernick with the powerful tagline: "Believe in something. Even if it means sacrificing everything." The spot went on to win an Emmy Award for Outstanding Commercial at the 2019 Creative Arts Emmy Awards.[14]

In 2019, Nike championed women's rights with its powerful ad campaign "Dream Crazier," narrated by Serena Williams and featuring an all-star lineup of female athletes, including gymnast Simone Biles, fencer Ibtihaj Muhammad (the first Muslim woman to wear a hijab while competing for the US Olympic team), snowboarder Chloe Kim, and members of the US Women's National Soccer Team. This bold, high-energy campaign celebrated the physical strength and mental determination of sportswomen. By investing in this message, Nike not only demonstrated its brand values but also made a strong statement: female athletes possess the same toughness, ambition, and drive as their male counterparts.[15]

Reflect on moments when your leadership choices clearly reflected your core values, whether through making tough decisions or supporting the growth of others. Consider times when your actions created meaningful value for those around you. Stories such as these not only highlight your leadership approach but also serve as inspiration for your team to act with purpose and integrity.

The Crucible Story: Bumble

The crucible story is a powerful narrative that illustrates a significant challenge or demanding situation faced by you or your company, and the actions taken to adapt, survive, and ultimately overcome it. This could involve a variety of obstacles, such as the emergence of a new competitor, an unexpected economic downturn, or a personal health battle. These stories not only showcase your ability to overcome adversity but also highlight your flexibility, resilience, and tenacity—key qualities that resonate with customers and team members alike.

Sharing these experiences enables you to connect on a deeper level with your audience, showing that you have the capability to persevere in the face of uncertainty and emerge stronger as a result.

Whitney Wolfe Herd, the founder of the popular dating app Bumble, made history at 31 when she became the youngest woman ever to take a company public. Just two hours after Bumble's stock soared, making her a billionaire, Wolfe Herd sat on a pink velvet couch in her office, holding back tears. Her remarkable success had not come easily. As a woman in the male-dominated tech industry, she faced relentless challenges, constantly battling the misogyny that pervaded the sector—and all the obstacles that came with it.

Wolfe Herd had previously been one of the cofounders of the dating app Tinder, where she was allegedly harassed by an executive (who was also her boyfriend at the time), got dumped, and was subsequently ousted from the company. She went on to sue for sexual harassment before leaving to start Bumble.[16] After the toxicity of the work environment at Tinder, Wolfe Herd used that experience to define her leadership approach and shape her new business venture. Wolfe Herd created a feature on the Bumble app that allows only women to initiate the first message when users match. In a digital dating environment where women, especially women of color, often face bullying and harassment, Wolfe Herd aimed to create a platform that offers a safer space for online romance. Said Wolfe Herd, "Honestly, my ambition comes from abusive relationships. I've never had this healthy male relationship until I created it. I engineered an ecosystem of healthy male relationships in my life."[17]

By the time Bumble went public, the company had already facilitated 8.6 billion connections across 237 countries, generating $582 million in revenue—boasting an impressive 26 percent profit margin.[18] When asked why, as one of the few female tech founders to reach billionaire status, she believes platform behavior is her responsibility, Wolfe Herd replied simply, "I don't think it's a coincidence."[19]

179

Choosing a Business Story to Tell

Wolfe Herd's powerful crucible story demonstrates how she used those difficult experiences—often painful and isolating—as a source of strength, fueling her commitment to creating a company that prioritizes kindness, respect, and safety. By embracing her vulnerabilities and confronting adversity head-on, Wolfe Herd inspired countless female entrepreneurs to rise above the challenges they face, proving that resilience, empathy, and a deep sense of responsibility can be powerful drivers of success.

What are some of the key challenges or obstacles you've faced in your life or career that helped shape the leader you are today? Reflect on the experiences that pushed you to grow, the lessons you learned from each, and how those insights can guide your team. How can you use your past to help others navigate their own challenges and avoid similar pitfalls?

The Solution Story: Zoom

A solution story demonstrates how you or your organization identified a specific problem or customer need and successfully addressed it through your products, services, or expertise. In this type of story, you highlight an actual challenge faced by a previous customer and show how your solution made a meaningful impact. It serves as a powerful tool not only for persuading potential customers to move forward with a deal or proposal but also for motivating your team by showcasing a concrete example of the value you or your organization has delivered. By illustrating your ability to solve problems and achieve positive outcomes, a well-crafted solution story builds trust and confidence, making it easier to cultivate new business relationships and strengthen internal alignment.

An excellent story of a company providing a solution for millions of desperate consumers involved the open collaboration network known as Zoom. When the COVID pandemic forced the world into lockdown in 2020, Eric Yuan, Zoom's founder and CEO, recognized that millions of leaders and organizations would suddenly be relying on his platform to keep their businesses running. Under Eric Yuan's leadership, Zoom became the go-to platform for remote meetings, education, and collaboration.

Recognizing the critical need for businesses and schools to stay connected during the pandemic, Yuan and his team quickly adapted, scaling the platform's infrastructure to handle the surge in demand. They even offered free access to schools and nonprofits to help them remain operational. By March 2020, Zoom's downloads had skyrocketed by 700 percent, and its value more than quadrupled, underscoring its pivotal role in the global shift toward hybrid work and learning.[20] As Yuan puts it, "Work is no longer a place; it's a space where Zoom empowers your teams to connect and bring their best ideas to life."[21] It's clear that Zoom played a defining role in the remote work revolution that began in 2020, and the platform's value is likely to remain indispensable in the years to come, as companies continue to embrace more flexible, distributed, and collaborative ways of working.

Reflect on your life and career, and think of the moments when you identified a problem or when someone came to you for help. What was it that enabled you to see beyond the surface of the issue? How did your foresight and creativity enable you to offer a solution that not only resolved the problem but also left a lasting positive impact on the person or situation? Consider how those moments of insight shaped the way you approach challenges, and how your ability to think critically and act with intention made a real difference.

The Pie-in-the-Face Story: Kodak

The pie-in-the-face narrative is a powerful tool for leaders to demonstrate humility and vulnerability. By sharing a story where you or your

181

Choosing a Business Story to Tell

organization made a mistake, faced a setback, or fell short in some way, you invite others to connect with you on a deeper, more human level. This type of narrative can be as simple as a personal anecdote laced with self-deprecating humor or a larger misstep that took place at the organizational level. What makes these stories so compelling is their authenticity—when leaders openly acknowledge their flaws or failures, they become more relatable and approachable, which fosters trust and creates a genuine connection with their audience.

The real strength of a pie-in-the-face story lies not just in the failure itself but also in the lessons it reveals. By sharing how you or your team took a setback and turned it into an opportunity for growth, you showcase resilience, self-awareness, and a commitment to continuous learning. These stories remind us that even the most successful leaders and organizations are not immune to mistakes—what truly defines us is how we respond to and learn from those moments. In fact, a study from the Kellogg School of Management found that teams who shared embarrassing or failure-related stories—so-called "pie-in-the-face" moments—generated 26 percent more ideas, along with a broader and more diverse range of ideas during collaboration or brainstorming.[22]

A striking example of a powerful brand making a costly miscalculation is Kodak, the iconic US company once synonymous with film photography. In the 1970s, Kodak dominated the industry, controlling nearly 90 percent of the market and selling hundreds of millions of rolls of film each year. At the peak of its success, Kodak's brand was inseparable from photography, with its products found in nearly every household. Yet, the company made a critical misstep that ultimately contributed to its decline.[23]

In 1975, Steven Sasson, an electrical engineer at Kodak, marched into his boss's office, proudly presenting a bulky, unconventional metal device. With excitement in his voice, Sasson revealed that he had just invented the world's first digital camera—no film required.

This groundbreaking innovation should have been the dawn of a new era for Kodak, positioning the company at the forefront of the digital photography revolution. Instead, as history shows, Kodak failed to seize the opportunity, letting this game-changing invention slip through its fingers.

The reason? A profound lack of vision and foresight among Kodak's senior leadership. Instead of recognizing the digital camera as an opportunity to lead their consumers into a new technological frontier, they saw it as a threat to their core business—film. Deeply entrenched in the success of traditional film, the company's leaders were reluctant to embrace a digital future that could jeopardize their highly profitable film sales. So when Sasson presented his invention—a camera that didn't need film—the reception from his bosses was anything but warm.

In an interview many years later, Sasson recounted, "[I]t was filmless photography, so management's reaction was, 'that's cute—but don't tell anyone about it.'"[24] This reaction, combined with Kodak's leadership's failure to envision the future of photography beyond film, proved to be a costly mistake.[25] By the time Kodak's executives finally recognized the potential of digital technology, it was too late. Competitors had already surged ahead, capitalizing on the digital revolution while Kodak struggled to adapt. The company's inability to pivot in time set the stage for decades of decline, ultimately leading to its Chapter 11 bankruptcy filing in 2012.[26] Kodak's story is a classic example of how complacency and an unwillingness to embrace change can lead to a company's downfall.

Consider the moments in your life where you miscalculated, fell short or made a mistake. How did those experiences of failure or disappointment make you feel at the time? What lessons did you learn from each setback, and how did those lessons shape your growth? Think about how these blunders or missteps, though difficult, made you smarter, stronger, and more resilient as a leader.

We all carry untold stories within us, waiting to be shared—not just you, but everyone you meet: your boss, your accountant, your mail carrier. Every person has a rich tapestry of experiences that can inspire, teach, or open new perspectives. As you hone your story-telling skills, make it a priority to uncover not just your own stories but also those of the people around you—especially mentors, colleagues, and leaders in your organization. These stories, if shared, can ripple outward, motivating and uniting others. Become a collector of stories, and embrace the art of sharing meaningful moments from your own life. By doing so, you'll build deeper connections and inspire others to open up about their own experiences.

As you begin to collect and share stories, it's essential to create an environment where trust and mutual respect can thrive. In Section V, we'll explore tools and techniques for fostering these essential elements in your collaborations, ensuring that your team is not only motivated but also united in a shared vision.

Part V

Collaboration

Chapter 13

Establishing Trust and Mutual Respect

What is an ocean, but a multitude of drops?

—David Mitchell

A Crossroad of Cultures: The NUMMI Experiment and Its Legacy

The story of NUMMI (New United Motor Manufacturing, Inc.) is a fascinating chapter in automotive history, offering valuable lessons on the power of collaboration.[1] Established in 1984, NUMMI was a joint venture between Toyota and General Motors (GM)—two fierce competitors—and was aimed at revitalizing GM's struggling factory in Fremont, California. At the time, the plant was plagued by poor performance, low morale, and labor unrest.

Toyota, the renowned Japanese automaker celebrated for its efficient production methods and high-quality vehicles, was aiming to strengthen its foothold in the US market. GM viewed the partnership as a chance to learn from Toyota's highly regarded Toyota Production System (TPS), while Toyota saw it as an opportunity to better understand US manufacturing practices and consumer preferences.

At the time, GM's factories, particularly the Fremont plant, were plagued by inefficiency and poor product quality. Management had lost control of the facility, and workers often engaged in disruptive behavior: drinking, using drugs, and even having sex on the factory floor—when they showed up to work at all. Absenteeism was consistently above 20 percent.[2] Workers were constantly going on strike and the quality of the products was not good. Bruce Lee, who oversaw the western region for the United Auto Workers Union, had a stark assessment of the teams in Fremont. "It was considered the worst workforce in the automobile industry," said Lee, a reputation he acknowledged was "well-earned."[3] Not surprisingly, morale had plummeted, and the factory suffered from a rigid, top-down management style, where workers had little involvement in decision-making. This lack of collaboration eroded trust and further exacerbated the plant's problems.

By contrast, Toyota was known for its focus on *kaizen*, a Japanese concept meaning "continuous improvement," which emphasized waste reduction and worker empowerment. TPS relied on a highly efficient production model where workers in the factories were given the authority to stop the production line if they identified a problem. This was done using a nylon cord: if something went wrong, workers could pull the cord, halt the line, and correct the issue immediately. This policy stood in stark contrast to GM's approach, which was to *never stop the line under any circumstances*—even if it meant producing defective products or sacrificing quality. By empowering workers to address problems as they arose, Toyota ensured that quality was built into every stage of production. The NUMMI project sought to bring these Japanese systems and methods into GM's operation, leading to some surprising discoveries for both parties.

At first, many GM workers were resistant to Toyota's practices, as they were used to a more rigid, hierarchical structure. But over time, Toyota's focus on worker empowerment began to take hold. NUMMI workers were encouraged to think beyond their specific tasks and to stop the line if they noticed a problem, which, as mentioned, was a stark departure from GM's previous practices. This empowered GM employees to take more responsibility and contribute to continuous improvement. The shift in workplace culture also included a focus

188

Synergy and Sparks

on cleanliness, organization, and teamwork. NUMMI's factory floor at the Fremont plant was transformed into a model of meticulous organization, with workers trained to maintain clean and efficient workstations. Again, another striking contrast to the chaotic environment that had previously existed.

For GM, NUMMI became a valuable testing ground for implementing Toyota's principles across its own factories. The most important lesson GM learned was the critical role of worker engagement and respect. The culture at NUMMI was far more collaborative than at GM's other plants, where the relationship between management and labor was often adversarial. At NUMMI, workers were seen as problem-solvers rather than mere cogs in the machine.

The results at NUMMI were striking. Productivity and product quality improved dramatically. Despite initial skepticism about Toyota's methods, NUMMI workers at the Fremont plant began to embrace the changes and take pride in their work. The factory became a model for how teamwork, respect for workers, and a focus on continuous improvement could yield better outcomes. Productivity per worker at NUMMI even surpassed that of GM's other US plants.

Despite NUMMI's success, the joint venture ended in 2009 when GM declared bankruptcy and was forced to close the Fremont factory soon after as part of its restructuring. However, through NUMMI, both GM and Toyota learned how creating a culture of mutual respect, worker empowerment, and continuous learning could transform not only a factory's output but also employees' attitudes and morale—leading to remarkable results.

The NUMMI experiment provides valuable insights into the power of effective collaboration in shaping a productive and engaged workforce. It highlights how fostering an environment where workers are encouraged to take ownership of their work and solve problems as they arise can lead to tangible improvements in both performance and morale. As you reflect on this story, how do these lessons make

189

Establishing Trust and Mutual Respect

you look at your own company's culture? Are there any tangible changes you could implement right now to foster greater collaboration, empower your team members, and build a more engaged and high-performing workforce?

Collaborative Communication

In any workplace, trust and mutual respect form the foundation of healthy and productive relationships. These elements are crucial not just for fostering collaboration but also for ensuring that individuals feel valued and understood in their roles. Sociologist Erving Goffman, extending his famous analogy of people as actors on a stage, observed that "in their capacity as performers, individuals will be concerned with maintaining the impression that they are living up to the many standards by which they and their products are judged."[4] This concept suggests that, just like actors in a play, individuals are constantly performing in their professional environments, managing how they are perceived by others to align with both personal and organizational expectations.

Studies show that employees who feel valued and respected by their managers are significantly more likely to stay in their jobs, with 79 percent of workers citing lack of appreciation as the main reason for leaving.[5] This highlights the critical role mutual respect plays in building trust and loyalty within teams. Leaders can't just declare an "open-door" policy; they must actively foster a culture of belonging where employees feel genuinely heard, supported, and safe sharing their ideas. After all, an open-door policy isn't truly effective if no one feels comfortable enough to walk through it.

Trust is also built through meaningful communication, which is often lacking in workplace environments. Gallup's research shows that 50 percent of employees leave their jobs because of poor relationships with their managers.[6] Additionally, studies on communication highlight that one of the biggest costs of ineffective interactions in the workplace is wasted time.[7] When managers fail to recognize the emotional and practical impact of their decisions and leadership style, it leads to disengagement and resentment—not necessarily out of malice but due to a lack of awareness and connection.

True collaboration, especially in times of difficulty, requires the ability to work alongside people with diverse perspectives and varying viewpoints. It's in these challenging moments that the real value of collaboration is tested. As Frank Evers notes, "Collaboration is interesting when there are conflicting values or limited time and resources. How do you work together as a team when the pressure is on? Real collaboration should be exciting and allow you to step out of your own level of experience and even work productively with people you don't like or who have very different values than you." This highlights the importance of embracing the discomfort that often comes with working in diverse teams. The ability to navigate differences in values, work styles, and opinions can lead to creative solutions and stronger team cohesion. When done well, collaboration doesn't just solve problems—it fosters growth, broadens perspectives, and strengthens relationships, even among people who may initially seem difficult to work with.[8]

Creating a workplace where employees feel trusted and respected is key to long-term commitment. Studies show that employees who find meaning in their roles are three times more likely to stay with an organization, highlighting that respect for personal values and contributions strengthens trust and generates deeper loyalty.[9] In healthy work environments, where creative conflict is viewed as a necessary and productive force rather than something to avoid, teams can merge diverse ideas, reduce risks, and drive innovation. However, this type of culture doesn't emerge on its own; it requires leadership that consistently seeks to understand and value the experiences of others.

Whether you're working with colleagues to solve a complex problem, negotiating with a challenging client, or figuring out who's taking the family dog to the vet, we're constantly engaging with others—both at work and in our personal lives. From team projects to daily interactions, collaboration and communication are central to everything we do. In today's business world, mastering these skills is essential for success. In fact, in 2021, employers ranked a candidate's "ability to work in teams" as the most important skill for recent college graduates.[10]

During collaboration, leaders play a crucial role in shaping the behavior of their teams by modeling the actions and attitudes they wish to see in others. When leaders consistently demonstrate qualities like accountability, integrity, empathy, and dedication, they set a clear example for their team members to follow. This modeling creates a powerful form of *social contagion*, where the behaviors and values of the leader begin to resonate with the team, encouraging them to adopt similar practices.[11]

How we feel at the end of the workday—whether it's a good day or a bad one—often depends on the success or challenges of our interactions with others throughout the day. The quality of these interactions can have a significant impact on our mood, productivity, and overall job satisfaction. A recent study reveals that the average employee spends about 85 percent of their workweek engaged in activities involving communication and collaboration.[12] This is a substantial portion of our time, underscoring just how critical effective teamwork is to our daily work experiences. Whether it's solving problems, making decisions, or simply staying connected, the way we engage with others shapes not only our outcomes but also our sense of accomplishment and well-being.

There's an apocryphal story about a janitor's encounter with President John F. Kennedy during NASA's early days that has made the rounds for decades. The story goes like this: while visiting Cape Canaveral, the president is said to have asked the man, who was holding a broom, "What do you do?" To which the janitor proudly replied, "Well, Mr. President, I'm helping to put a man on the moon."[13] This anecdote highlights an important point: in any organization, every team member—regardless of their role or status—should feel valued and appreciated. When individuals understand how their contributions align with the broader mission, collaboration flourishes, and success becomes a collective achievement.

Coming of age as an artist in Chicago's vibrant theater scene of the late 1980s and early 1990s, I was immersed in the dynamic world of Chicago-style theater—known for its bold, scrappy, ensemble-driven ethos. Performances often featured live rock bands, nudity, and staged violence, unfolding in intimate spaces such as lofts, parks, church basements, and storefronts. In these raw environments, creativity flourished despite limited resources. It was here that I discovered the true power of collaboration, realizing how each member of the ensemble plays a vital role in shaping the overall performance.

The success of a play relies on the collective efforts of everyone involved—actors, directors, designers, and technicians—each playing an essential role in creating a cohesive and impactful production. This mirrors the dynamics of most corporate teams and organizations, where collaboration is equally critical to success. However, much like in theater, effective teamwork doesn't always happen instinctively. The ability to work together seamlessly, communicate clearly, and contribute meaningfully to a shared goal is a skill that requires continuous cultivation and refinement.

A defining aspect of human societies over time has been our ability to work together toward a common goal. Collaborative communication is more than just talking and listening; it's an intricate dance of contributing ideas, providing feedback and hearing other perspectives in a way that fosters mutual respect and achieves results. It involves empathy, open-mindedness, and a genuine interest in the contributions of others. Collaborative communication goes beyond just letting the other person be heard; it's about genuinely understanding them while also making sure they fully understand you. Unfortunately, we're often not as skilled at it as we think.

Take, for example, the common belief among many young people that they excel at collaboration. Research paints a different picture. A survey by the Association of American Colleges and Universities found a notable gap between students' self-perception and employers' assessments of their teamwork skills. While 64 percent of students felt they worked well with others, only 37 percent of employers agreed.[14]

In today's fast-paced and constantly evolving workplace, effective collaboration is the glue that brings diverse individuals together, helping them work productively toward common goals. While studies show that 75 percent of employees recognize the importance of collaboration,[15] we don't always view our colleagues as effective collaborators. In fact, a striking 86 percent of people identified poor collaboration and communication as the main reasons for workplace failure,[16] and 39 percent believed that people in their own organization didn't collaborate enough.[17]

As I often highlight in my coaching and training sessions, trust is the foundation of all successful business relationships. Without it, collaboration becomes little more than an empty buzzword. To build trust, transparency is key. Teams and leaders must embrace an open-book mentality, where information flows freely, creative conflict is welcomed, and decisions are made with input from all relevant stakeholders. This kind of open communication creates a supportive environment that boosts morale, motivation, and productivity—sometimes by as much as 25 percent.[18] Such transparency not only aligns the team but also empowers individuals, making them feel truly invested in the team's success.

Leadership, of course, plays a crucial role in fostering collaborative communication. Bosses and managers need to be role models, demonstrating effective collaboration and setting the tone for the rest of the team. As author and entrepreneur Seth Godin reminds us, "Leaders create the conditions where people choose new actions . . . . You can't make people change. But you can create an environment where they choose to."[19] In any collaborative work environment, especially within a corporate setting, challenges are inevitable—problems arise, setbacks occur, and crises demand attention. However, being part of a cohesive team provides significant advantages when navigating these difficult situations.

Teams bring diverse perspectives, shared resources, and collective support, all of which make it easier to adapt and find solutions when faced with challenges. By tackling obstacles together, the responsibility is spread across the group, which not only alleviates stress but also enhances motivation. Moreover, achieving success as a team can be far more rewarding and morale boosting than individual accomplishments, as the shared sense of victory fosters a deeper connection and a stronger sense of collective purpose.

Amplification for Voice and Vision

A team is a melting pot of diverse backgrounds, experiences, and perspectives, and harnessing this diversity, if done effectively, can turn it into a powerful asset. Encouraging team members to share their unique viewpoints can help foster a culture of innovation and creativity. It can break down silos and encourage teamwork, leading to solutions that are well-rounded and comprehensive. And there's more good news: when you truly listen to your employees, they are nearly five times more likely to feel empowered to do their best at work.[20]

Many of us have felt the frustration of having our ideas dismissed in a meeting or seeing someone else take credit for an idea we originally shared. A recent study shed light on this common issue by observing 78 team meetings to analyze what happens when people present ideas and opinions. The results revealed troubling patterns: ideas were often dismissed, overlooked, and at times reintroduced without crediting the original contributor. These issues were particularly pronounced when the person presenting the idea was someone considered lower power or was a woman, a person of color, or a member of another underrepresented group—individuals who are disproportionately ignored in collaborative environments.[21] Fortunately, there is a simple technique to address these situations and challenges: it's called *amplification*.

Amplification is a straightforward yet powerful strategy that involves colleagues actively repeating and reinforcing each other's points, while ensuring that the original speaker is credited for their contribution. By doing so, the strategy creates a supportive environment where the person who initially shared the idea is acknowledged, and their input is given the attention it deserves, fostering a more inclusive and equitable discussion.

Dr. Kristin Bain, assistant professor of management at Rochester Institute of Technology, conducted a study titled "Amplifying Voice in Organizations." In this research, Bain and her team sought to explore the benefits of amplification in organizational settings. They set out to answer three main questions:

- Does amplifying someone make their contribution seem better?
- Does amplifying someone else make the amplifier (the person doing the amplifying) look good, too?
- Can groups use amplification to help underrepresented voices be heard?

In three studies in the United States, Bain and her team found that the answer to all three questions was a resounding yes.[22]

Bain's findings revealed that when participants observed someone amplifying another team member's idea in a meeting, they not only considered the amplified idea to be better, but also perceived the original speaker as more influential and higher status within the group. Furthermore, the person doing the amplification was seen as more high status, even when compared to instances where they had proposed their own original idea.[23] Additionally, Bain and her team concluded that amplification is a powerful tool for helping underrepresented or lower-status employees have their voices heard. As Bain summarized in her findings, "Amplification can help make sure more people are heard at work, that teams are considering all suggestions, and people get proper credit for the ideas they have."[24]

To effectively use amplification as a leader, begin by listening intentionally during meetings. Pay close attention to the contributions of others, especially those from underrepresented groups. If you notice that a colleague's feedback or ideas are being overlooked, dismissed, or miscredited, seize the opportunity to reinforce their point by repeating it, giving credit where it's due, and elaborating on its value. This not only helps ensure that important ideas or opinions are acknowledged but also fosters a culture of respect and inclusion.

Unlocking Creativity Through Collaborative Teamwork

Given the diversity within most teams, leaders must be intentional about creating an environment where all perspectives and voices are heard. By actively encouraging input from every team member, regardless of their age, background, or role, leaders can ensure that diverse viewpoints contribute to decision-making and problem-solving. Ultimately, the best outcomes arise when all voices are given the space to be heard and respected.

Research by Myers-Briggs shows that 56.8 percent of people worldwide tend to lean toward introversion in how they communicate and collaborate.[25] This preference underscores the need for bosses and managers to adapt their leadership styles to better meet the needs and preferences of their team members. Unfortunately, studies also reveal a clear leadership bias against introverts, with 65 percent of senior executives viewing introversion as a "barrier to leadership,"[26] despite numerous studies showing that introverted and extroverted leaders are equally effective in driving team and company performance.[27] As leaders, it's crucial to challenge and overcome these biases.

In general, extroverts gain energy from social interactions while introverts lose energy from interactions. By recognizing and respecting the introverted tendencies of one's various team members, leaders can develop stronger group dynamics and greater overall engagement.[28] Leaders should make a conscious effort to actively seek input from introverted or lower-status members of their team, as these voices can often be overshadowed or crowded out by more dominant or higher-ranking executives in the room.

Collaborative teamwork is a powerful approach to brainstorming and problem-solving, where individuals come together to identify, analyze, and address challenges by openly sharing their perspectives, ideas, and information. Essentially, it's about solving problems or generating ideas as a group effort. This method emphasizes inclusive participation, ensuring that every team member has a voice in the decision-making process, rather than allowing one person to dominate or impose a solution.[29] While individual problem-solving is certainly possible, collaborative teamwork encourages a richer exchange of ideas, helping the group find the most effective solutions. It also builds trust, fosters creative thinking, and creates a supportive environment where even introverted or lower-status members feel empowered to contribute.[30]

Here's how to employ collaborative teamwork in your next team meeting:

1. Start by bringing your team together and ensuring everyone has a shared understanding of the issue. Clearly define the problem,

highlighting key details and potential root causes. For example, you might frame the issue with specific questions like, "How can we improve customer service?" or "Which current processes can be simplified or streamlined for better efficiency?" Crafting a clear and precise problem statement is crucial to ensure everyone is aligned and focused on the same goal.

2. Once the team is aligned on the problem, break them into smaller groups of three to four people for breakout sessions. These smaller work groups will help create an environment where team members who may be more introverted or from lower-status roles feel more comfortable contributing their ideas and suggestions. Provide clear instructions on the objectives of the session, the time limit, and the process each group should follow. Allow enough time for thoughtful brainstorming but ensure the session is concise enough to maintain a sense of urgency without making participants feel rushed.

3. During the breakout sessions, ask each group to work privately, ideally away from other groups to prevent distractions and external influence. Assign each group a specific objective, such as "Come up with two actionable ideas to improve our customer service" or "Identify one current company process that could be streamlined for better efficiency." Encourage open brainstorming, ensuring that all ideas are captured, whether on paper or a whiteboard, and that every group member has a chance to contribute. This inclusive approach ensures that a wide range of perspectives are considered and that the process isn't dominated by just a few voices.

4. As the breakout sessions wrap up, ask each group to select a spokesperson who will present their ideas to the larger group. Once everyone reconvenes, have the spokesperson from each group share their team's insights and recommendations.

199

Establishing Trust and Mutual Respect

Capture these ideas on a whiteboard or shared screen so that everyone can see them. Facilitate a discussion where team members can ask questions, provide feedback, or seek clarification on the ideas presented.

5. By the end of the session, you should have a clear understanding of which ideas resonated most with the group. Highlight any suggestions or proposals that warrant further exploration, and outline the next steps for implementation. This structured approach will not only generate a range of potential solutions but also foster a sense of shared ownership and commitment to the outcomes.

Effective teamwork goes beyond simple collaboration—it requires intentional effort to build trust and navigate conflict in a healthy, productive way. Conflict, when approached constructively, does not imply disrespect; rather, it can be a catalyst for growth and innovation. This approach not only drives the achievement of shared goals but also boosts morale and contributes to long-term organizational success.

In Chapter 14, we'll discuss how a leader can thoughtfully approach and effectively deliver feedback to team members, with the goal of fostering growth, enhancing performance, and driving overall team productivity.

Chapter 14

Enhancing Performance Through Feedback

To avoid criticism, do nothing, say nothing, and be nothing.

—Aristotle

Shaping PepsiCo's Future: A Cultural Transformation

The story of Indra Nooyi's leadership is a powerful testament to the transformative role of feedback in shaping both personal growth and corporate success. Born in Chennai, India, Nooyi became the CEO of PepsiCo in 2006, after joining the company in 1994. From the start, her impact was profound, guiding PepsiCo through pivotal strategic shifts, playing a crucial role in spinning off PepsiCo's restaurant division—including Pizza Hut, KFC, and Taco Bell—for $4.5 billion, and leading the acquisitions of Tropicana and Quaker Oats, which significantly strengthened PepsiCo's portfolio.[1]

Widely regarded as one of the world's most influential women, Nooyi was not only the first woman of color and immigrant to lead a Fortune 50 company but also an inspiring example of how feedback—both given and received—can drive innovation and leadership.[2] Her journey reflects how embracing constructive criticism and using it to refine strategies can help companies navigate change, build resilience, and ultimately thrive. Nooyi's story offers invaluable lessons on the power of feedback in leadership, innovation, and corporate success.

When Nooyi became PepsiCo's CEO in 2006, she quickly realized that the company needed to evolve in response to shifting consumer preferences, especially as health-consciousness grew among customers. PepsiCo was known for its sugary sodas and snacks, and Nooyi understood that the company had to diversify its product portfolio to include healthier options. This was a bold challenge, but Nooyi viewed it as an opportunity for innovation—something that could only succeed with strong engagement from all levels of the organization.

Fortunately, Nooyi was not only a champion of giving feedback but also receiving it. She frequently sought input from her colleagues, employees, and even external stakeholders to ensure she had a clear sense of how the company was performing and where improvements could be made. At PepsiCo, Nooyi asked employees to assess their managers annually. This helped her identify weak points not just within management but also within the company as a whole, as weak managers generally end up leading weak teams.[3]

Nooyi's leadership created a collaborative culture where feedback could flow freely in both directions. Employees felt safe to express their ideas and concerns, which led to more innovation and a stronger sense of ownership over the company's success. Nooyi's openness to feedback, her commitment to giving constructive input, and her ability to create an environment of trust became foundational to PepsiCo's success during her tenure. "As a leader, I am tough on myself and I raise the standard for everybody," said Nooyi. "However, I am very caring because I want people to excel at what they are doing so that they can aspire to be me in the future."[4]

When Indra Nooyi's 12-year tenure as CEO of PepsiCo came to a close, the company had seen its revenue grow by more than 80 percent, and the company's portfolio of more-healthful options grew from about 38 percent of revenue in 2006 to roughly 50 percent by 2017.[5] Nooyi's journey demonstrates that feedback is not just a tool for evaluation; it is essential for both personal and organizational growth. Whether giving or receiving, feedback should be embraced as an opportunity to learn, innovate, and improve.

Feedback as a Catalyst for Growth

Much of our communication during a given workweek involves providing feedback or opinions to others—be it on a phone call, in a performance review, or during a meeting with a client. Feedback—both positive and constructive—is essential for growth, as it provides individuals with the opportunity to learn and improve. Positive feedback reinforces good habits and outcomes, while constructive feedback offers valuable guidance for further development. However, recent reporting reveals that managers are falling short when it comes to feedback, with less than half of workers indicating that they know what is expected of them at work[6] and 35 percent saying they would like to see more action taken on the feedback they provide.[7]

Constructive feedback should focus on behaviors and outcomes rather than personal attributes. It should be specific, actionable, and delivered with empathy. When team members feel that feedback is aimed at their growth and development, they are more likely to embrace it and use it to improve their performance. Unfortunately, many leaders struggle with providing feedback, as studies show that 9 out of 10 managers avoid giving it due to concerns about how employees will react.[8] And while 96 percent of employees see feedback as "a good thing," 41 percent have reported leaving a previous job due to feeling unheard or receiving little to no feedback.[9]

Younger workers today expect more than just feedback from their managers—they crave authentic feedback. Research shows that employees who receive genuine recognition are more than five times more likely to see a clear path for growth within their organization.[10]

203

Enhancing Performance Through Feedback

This desire for constant, meaningful feedback among younger workers can be traced to their upbringing in the digital age, where instant responses and validation on social media have become the norm. As KeyAnna Schmiedl, chief human experience officer at Workhuman, notes, younger workers are increasingly focused on how their company will support and help them grow. They are particularly motivated by regular microdoses of feedback and recognition, which play a crucial role in keeping them engaged and invested in their work. For managers seeking to inspire and engage a younger team, offering honest, constructive feedback is essential to cultivating a supportive and motivating workplace culture.[11]

Mindsets That Matter: From Fixed to Growth

Before diving into the mechanics of delivering effective feedback, it's important to first understand the role mindset plays in shaping how individuals receive and respond to it. Specifically, let's explore the distinction between a *fixed* mindset and a *growth* mindset—concepts pioneered by Stanford professor Carol Dweck.[12] For anyone working as part of a team, understanding this distinction is crucial, as it influences not only how we receive and process feedback but also how we approach challenges and opportunities for growth.

So, what's the difference between the two? A fixed mindset is rooted in the belief that our abilities, intelligence, and character traits are inherent and unchangeable. People with this mindset tend to see talent and skills as fixed qualities that can't be developed over time. As a result, they often prioritize avoiding failure to maintain the illusion of being "smart" or "competent." This can create a fear of taking risks or stepping outside their comfort zone, leading to complacency. Individuals with a fixed mindset may resist feedback—particularly if it challenges their self-image—and are likely to avoid roles or tasks that might expose their weaknesses.

By contrast, a growth mindset embraces the idea that abilities and intelligence can be developed through effort, learning, and perseverance. People with a growth mindset view failure not as something to be avoided but as a crucial stepping stone in the learning process. For example, a person with a growth mindset who receives feedback about a presentation won't feel discouraged by critiques but instead sees them as opportunities to refine their skills for the next time. They see challenges, whether in the form of complex projects or new roles, as opportunities to stretch their capabilities and grow, rather than obstacles to be feared. This mindset encourages resilience, adaptability, and a passion for continuous development.

Leaders and individuals with a growth mindset actively seek feedback, especially when it's constructive, because they recognize it as a valuable tool for personal growth. For example, a manager with a growth mindset might ask their team for suggestions on how to improve after a project, seeing each piece of feedback as an opportunity to enhance their leadership skills and achieve better results in the future.

To cultivate a growth mindset as a leader, start with humility. Research published in the *Journal of Management* highlights the power of humble leadership, showing that bosses or managers who embrace humility are more likely to delegate effectively and foster innovation. This approach leads to higher employee satisfaction and stronger company performance.[13] For leaders, this means owning your mistakes, offering sincere apologies when necessary, and being open to seeking help. It also means embracing the idea of being the second smartest person in the room, especially if you've done well in hiring talented people—because chances are, they'll have valuable insights.

The mindset we adopt—whether fixed or growth—shapes our behavior, influencing how we handle success, setbacks, and the way we approach personal and professional challenges. These mindsets

205

Enhancing Performance Through Feedback

are formed early in life but can evolve over time with self-awareness and intentional effort. Ultimately, they affect our ability to stay motivated, learn from our experiences, and achieve long-term success. As the saying goes, "Old keys don't unlock new doors." To unlock new opportunities for growth, we need to adopt a mindset that is open to learning, experimentation, and improvement.

Three Types of Feedback: Evaluative, Exploratory, and Directive

As a leader, you have three main types of feedback at your disposal to guide and motivate your team. Each type serves a distinct purpose and can be tailored to the specific situation and individual you're addressing.

Evaluative Feedback The most common type of feedback leaders provide is evaluative feedback, typically tied to performance reviews. This feedback involves assessing a team member's performance over a specific period—usually annually—and discussing their accomplishments, challenges, and areas for improvement. When delivering evaluative feedback, it's essential to be both thorough and balanced—recognizing strengths while also addressing areas for growth. A well-rounded approach ensures the feedback is constructive and fosters continuous development.

Exploratory Feedback The second type of feedback is exploratory feedback, which encourages self-reflection and empowers individuals to evaluate their own performance. Instead of merely pointing out areas for improvement, you ask open-ended questions that prompt the team member to reflect on their work and identify opportunities for growth. For example, after reviewing past areas of focus, you might ask, "How do you feel you

206

Synergy and Sparks

performed in these areas?" or "What might you have done differently?" This type of feedback fosters self-awareness and ownership of personal development. By guiding employees through the process of self-evaluation, you help them build confidence, accountability, and a proactive mindset toward continuous improvement.

Directive Feedback The third type of feedback is directive feedback. With this type of feedback leaders provide clear, actionable guidance for improvement. It is used when specific behaviors or actions need to be addressed immediately. It is direct and future-focused, outlining exactly what changes are expected. For example, "Over the past month, I noticed you've struggled with meeting deadlines. Moving forward, I need you to prioritize your time better and ensure that tasks are completed on schedule." Directive feedback helps individuals understand what is expected of them and provides concrete steps to help them improve.

When preparing to give feedback, think about which type—evaluative, exploratory, or directive—best fits the situation and the individual. Depending on the context, you may use a combination of all three to motivate, guide, and support your team members in their development. Effective feedback isn't just about pointing out what's wrong—it's about helping others improve, and each feedback type plays a crucial role in that process.

Providing Feedback to Improve Performance

Feedback is a powerful tool for both the person receiving it and the person delivering it, contributing to both personal development and a deeper sense of trust. Offering a sincere compliment or helpful suggestion to a team member to help them do their job better doesn't cost anything, but it holds the potential to boost morale and strengthen relationships. It also creates a positive cycle, making both the giver and the recipient feel better.

When providing constructive feedback, it's crucial to be clear and direct. Feedback should be concise, firm, and specific, ensuring the recipient fully understands both the message and its significance. Research shows that, especially when delivering criticism or negative feedback, most people prefer directness and candor, with minimal small talk or buffering.[14] So, get to it. This straightforward approach eliminates ambiguity, making the message more impactful.

Studies have shown that nearly half of employees don't feel comfortable raising issues or providing feedback to their boss or manager.[15] This represents a missed opportunity for both employees and organizations, as evidenced by Indra Nooyi's experiences leading PepsiCo. When providing feedback to a boss or manager, it's essential to approach the conversation thoughtfully. One key step is to ask for permission before sharing any thoughts or opinions. This shows respect for the other person's time and perspective and helps create an environment where feedback can be exchanged constructively. By creating clear channels for upward feedback, organizations can foster greater innovation, enhance employee engagement, and cultivate more effective leadership.

When given the opportunity to share feedback with your boss, approach the conversation with a solution-oriented mindset. Focus on the work itself and balance constructive criticism with positive feedback. Always deliver feedback privately, maintaining a professional and considerate tone. During the discussion, show genuine curiosity about the decision-making process by asking thoughtful questions to better understand the reasoning or motivations behind leadership's actions. Use specific, recent examples to illustrate your points, and direct your comments toward solutions, offering practical ideas for improvement rather than simply highlighting problems.

Synergy and Sparks

This approach will result in a more productive, collaborative dialogue that can lead to meaningful change.

A notable incident involving Emmy Award–winning actress Sarah Paulson serves as a cautionary tale about the risks of offering unsolicited or unwelcome feedback.

In 2013, Paulson was starring in a revival of the play *Talley's Folly* Off-Broadway. Both her performance and the production received glowing reviews, including praise in the *New York Times*. However, things took an unexpected turn when Trish Hawkins—who had originated the same role during the play's first 1980 Broadway run and was now in her late 70s—attended a performance.

On the *SmartLess* podcast, Paulson recounted the awkward encounter that followed. After the show, Hawkins came backstage to meet her, but rather than offering congratulations or positive feedback, Hawkins began to criticize the production. Paulson recalls, "She came to the play, proceeded to say . . . 'Your dress is yellow. Mine was pink.' And I thought, 'What?' Cut to two days later." Two days later, Paulson received an email from Hawkins—six pages long—detailing extensive notes on how Paulson could improve her performance. Hawkins also included a breakdown of how she had portrayed the role 33 years earlier. The unsolicited feedback enraged Paulson, who found the criticism not only unwelcome but overstepping. More than a decade later, Paulson still seethed when recalling the incident, describing Hawkins's actions as "outrageous" and making her feelings unmistakably clear: "Trish Hawkins, I haven't forgotten," declared Paulson. "And I hope I never see you again."[16]

Organizational psychologist Adam Grant suggests that when providing feedback—especially critical feedback—it's helpful to spotlight your intention to reduce defensiveness. In one study, researchers found that feedback effectiveness increased by 40 percent when the critical comments were prefaced with a positive phrase like, "I'm sharing this with you because I have high expectations and I'm confident

209

Enhancing Performance Through Feedback

you can meet them."[17] This approach helps frame the feedback as a tool for growth, rather than criticism.

Interestingly, in situations involving both good and bad news, research suggests that frontloading the bad news helps ensure the entire message resonates effectively. A study conducted by the University of California, Riverside, found that recipients of messages containing both bad news and good news overwhelmingly prefer to hear the negative information first, while those delivering the news tend to favor starting with the good news.[18] The reasoning behind these preferences is simple: for the news-giver, sharing good news is easy; but for the listener, when they know bad news is coming, it dominates their attention, making it difficult to absorb the good news. By delivering the bad news up front, news-givers enable the recipient to process it without distraction, ensuring that the good news is then received with greater clarity and impact.

Timing also plays a crucial role in how feedback is received and acted on. Providing feedback too early can disrupt an employee's workflow, create unnecessary anxiety, or even be perceived as micromanagement. Conversely, offering feedback too late may lead to missed opportunities to address issues, diminish its effectiveness, or give the impression of indifference.

Research indicates that 75 percent of workers feel they don't receive feedback often enough to improve their performance.[19] By contrast, companies that manage the timing of feedback reap numerous benefits, such as a more motivated workforce and lower turnover rates.[20]

A leader should deliver feedback in a way that gives the recipient ample time to absorb the information and make any necessary adjustments. One study shows a massive disconnect between employers and employees when it comes to the timeliness and frequency of feedback, with more than 90 percent of employees saying they want their manager to address performance mistakes or development opportunities in

210

Synergy and Sparks

real time, versus weeks or months later during a performance review.[21] Research by Todd Thornock, a scholar at the University of Nebraska–Lincoln, also underscores the importance of feedback timing, showing that delayed feedback from a manager can hinder an employee's growth and learning, whereas immediate feedback "most effectively promotes learning and [improves] future performance."[22]

When delivering critical feedback, leaders should not only anticipate questions but also actively encourage open dialogue. This involves being ready to clarify any points that might be unclear and creating an environment where the recipient feels comfortable expressing their thoughts and concerns. When responding to questions, it's crucial to listen fully before offering solutions or making assumptions. Giving the individual space to speak without interruption promotes a more meaningful exchange. Such conversations—where questions are welcomed and thoughtfully addressed—enhance clarity, deepen understanding, and ensure the feedback is both heard and actionable. Additionally, if the recipient doesn't ask questions right away, the leader should take the initiative to invite them to do so, creating a culture of ongoing communication and growth.

Think about how many questions you asked as a child, when everything around you was new and fascinating. As children, we embraced our curiosity, asking questions freely without fear of looking silly. However, as we grow older, factors such as ego, reputational concerns, or personal insecurities often hold us back from asking questions. According to the *Harvard Business Review*, parents estimate that around 70–80 percent of their children's conversations consist of questions. By contrast, among adults, that figure drops to just 15–25 percent. This shift highlights how, over time, we tend to lose our natural curiosity and our willingness to inquire.[23] Since adults often ask fewer questions, it's essential for leaders to foster a culture where team members feel safe and encouraged to seek clarity—particularly when receiving feedback. This not only ensures that feedback is fully understood but also helps cultivate a culture of continuous learning and improvement.

When delivering critical feedback, leaders should not only highlight areas for improvement but also provide a clear, actionable plan for moving forward. Feedback should drive growth, so it's essential to help the individual translate it into concrete steps. This includes offering guidance on how to address the issues, setting specific milestones to track progress, and checking in regularly to ensure they stay on track. Leaders should stay engaged in the development process, offering encouragement, resources, and support as needed. Taking a partnership approach to the follow-through—helping the team member implement changes and providing ongoing feedback—reinforces a commitment to their success. This collaborative approach fosters improvement while strengthening trust and accountability within the team.

The effectiveness of feedback hinges on a key concept: mutuality. In this context, *mutuality* refers to a shared understanding and commitment between the giver and receiver of feedback to work toward improvement or a common goal. It emphasizes that feedback is not a one-sided exchange, but a collaborative process where both parties are equally invested in each other's growth and success. In essence, mutuality means that both the leader and the team member have each other's best interests at heart, fostering a positive, open environment where constructive conversations can thrive and lead to meaningful progress.

In practice, mutuality means that both parties view feedback as a two-way process. The receiver may share their perspective or ask questions for clarification, and the giver is open to listening and providing support. It also ensures that the feedback session is not just about pointing out shortcomings but about collaborating to find solutions and set clear goals for improvement. As a leader providing feedback, it's important to remind yourself that leadership is not about titles or authority—it's about impact, influence, and inspiration.

Embracing the Gift of Feedback

Receiving feedback can be challenging, but it is a vital skill for personal and professional growth. Just as giving honest, constructive feedback is important, so is the ability to receive it with openness and humility. Effective leaders recognize that true growth requires them to be open to feedback. One way to invite this feedback is by asking team members or direct reports questions like, "What am I doing well?" "What am I doing that I should I stop doing?" and "How can I better support you?" By inviting and soliciting feedback, leaders show receptivity and humility, setting an example that encourages others to do the same.

When receiving feedback, it's important to follow a few key guidelines:

- First and foremost, keep an open mind. Remember that feedback is a gift—its purpose is to help you grow and improve, not to criticize or attack. The insights you're about to receive are meant to support your development, not to highlight your shortcomings. No one is perfect, and everyone has areas where they can refine their skills or expand their knowledge. Instead of viewing feedback as a challenge, embrace it as an invaluable opportunity for growth, and see it as a stepping stone toward becoming a better version of yourself.

- When receiving feedback, focus on listening to understand rather than responding immediately. Resist the urge to jump to conclusions or filter the feedback through preconceived biases. Pay attention to your mental, physiological, and emotional reactions as the feedback is shared, and create space between your emotions and your response. This pause enables you to process the information more thoughtfully. As feedback is being delivered, take notes on key points to help absorb the message and retain important details for later reflection.

213

Enhancing Performance Through Feedback

- One of the toughest challenges in a feedback session is keeping your ego in check. While it's natural to want to be accepted and appreciated, it's crucial to focus on how the feedback can help you become smarter, more effective, or more productive. Resist the urge to dismiss feedback outright as unfair or unjustified. Letting pride or emotions cloud your judgment can prevent growth and hinder progress. The feedback or criticism you're receiving is about your performance, not your character, so try not to take it personally. Accept it with grace, even if you don't agree with every point. Thank the person for sharing their perspective and recognize it as an opportunity to improve. If anything is unclear, ask clarifying questions to ensure you fully understand the feedback and can make meaningful adjustments to enhance your performance.

Finally, after receiving feedback, take time to reflect before taking action. It can be helpful to give yourself some space to process the information fully. Consider sharing the feedback with someone you trust—a spouse, friend, or mentor—to gain their perspective and insights. Allow yourself a day or two to absorb the feedback and process your emotions before tackling next steps. This reflection period helps you to approach the feedback with a clearer, more balanced mindset, enabling you to develop a thoughtful, effective plan for improvement. By taking this time to reflect, you also prepare yourself for the inevitable challenging conversations that may arise as you work to implement changes.

In Chapter 15, we'll dive into how to approach these difficult discussions with confidence and grace, exploring practical strategies to communicate clearly, stay composed under pressure, and foster understanding—especially when the stakes are high.

Chapter 15

Mastering Challenging Conversations

It's not what you say, it's what they hear.

—Red Auerbach

Leadership, Layoffs, and Lessons: The Better Fiasco

In business, leaders frequently face the challenge of delivering difficult news to stakeholders or addressing hostile, distracted, or apprehensive audiences. Whether it's presenting disappointing financial results, explaining tough decisions, or navigating a crisis, leaders must remain calm, composed, and in control under pressure. Their ability to communicate effectively in these high-stakes situations is crucial—not only to ensure their message is understood but also to maintain credibility and preserve trust with their audience. For example, when delivering bad news about company performance, leaders who approach the situation with transparency, empathy, and a clear plan for moving forward can mitigate anxiety and help stakeholders focus on solutions rather than getting caught up in negative emotions.

Vishal Garg, the ambitious and entrepreneurial CEO of Better.com, was born in India and moved to Queens, New York, with his family at a young age. Growing up in a bustling urban environment, Garg quickly developed a drive for success. He attended several prestigious schools and went on to graduate from New York University,

215

where he honed his academic and professional aspirations. After completing his studies, Garg built a diverse career, gaining valuable experience in both the finance and technology sectors. Drawing on these experiences, he founded Better in 2014, with the goal of revolutionizing the way people bought mortgages through innovative, technology-driven solutions.[1]

Garg's goal with Better was to disrupt the mortgage industry by using technology to make home buying faster, more transparent, and affordable, with lower fees than traditional lenders. By the end of 2020, the company was valued at $4 billion.[2]

Better quickly gained momentum, attracting hundreds of millions in investment, and Garg became a celebrated figure in fintech. In 2021, after a $750 million infusion, he decided to take the company public, with a valuation of $7.7 billion.[3] Everything seemed on track for the young CEO—until the day after the funding announcement, when things took a dark turn.

On December 1, 2021, Garg called a mandatory meeting with 900 Better employees, many of whom joined a one-way Zoom call, uncertain of what was about to unfold. When Garg finally kicked off the meeting, looking visibly uncomfortable, slouched in his chair, he stated, "This is the second time in my career I'm doing this, and I do not want to do this. The last time I did it, I cried. This time, I hope to be stronger." Then, in the same flat, emotionless tone, he informed all 900 meeting attendees that they were "part of the unlucky group that is being laid off," adding, brusquely, "your employment here is terminated, effective immediately."[4]

Garg's tone-deaf pity party at the start of the call, combined with his impersonal delivery of such devastating news, angered his laid-off workers, who understandably felt blindsided. The video of the meeting was leaked and quickly went viral, instantly villainizing Garg as a heartless CEO, and becoming a symbol of how not to manage mass layoffs in the digital age.

216

Synergy and Sparks

As the press examined Garg's leadership, troubling details emerged, revealing a pattern of toxic management and fear-based leadership.[5] Reports also exposed multiple lawsuits from previous business associates accusing him of fraud and misappropriating millions—funds allegedly used to launch Better. In one disturbing deposition, Garg reportedly threatened to burn a former partner alive.[6]

Subsequent leaks of old emails from Garg to his employees at Better painted an even more troubling portrait of his autocratic leadership style. In one email, he berated his team with the message, "You are TOO DAMN SLOW. You are a bunch of DUMB DOLPHINS and . . . DUMB DOLPHINS get caught in nets and eaten by sharks. SO STOP IT. STOP IT. STOP IT RIGHT NOW. YOU ARE EMBARRASSING ME." Garg's aggressive language and disregard for basic professionalism created a toxic workplace culture where respect was clearly in short supply.[7]

The fallout from Garg's public relations disaster was swift, with three top executives at Better resigning in protest.[8] In the aftermath of the controversy, Garg was placed on leave as he sought to rehabilitate his image. However, just one month later, he returned to the CEO position, where he remains to this day.[9] The incident has become a widely cited example of how not to handle layoffs in the corporate world, serving as a reminder about the importance of leadership, empathy, and compassion in the workplace.

Cultivating Trust Through Psychological Safety

The Vishal Garg saga—and its aftermath—serves as a stark reminder that when a difficult conversation occurs, team members are unlikely to fully absorb or engage with the message if they don't feel their leader genuinely cares about their well-being or has their best interests at heart. In high-stakes moments like these, trust and emotional support are crucial to delivering tough news in a way that can be constructive and productive. Without these foundational elements—empathy, understanding, and mutual respect—even well-intentioned messages can feel dismissive or demotivating. Leaders must prioritize building a strong rapport and trust with their teams if they hope to navigate tough conversations effectively and inspire lasting change.

The term *psychological safety*, popularized by Harvard Business School professor Amy Edmondson, is defined as "a belief that one will not be punished or humiliated for speaking up with ideas, questions, concerns, or mistakes."[10] This concept refers to creating an environment in which individuals feel secure enough to share their thoughts openly and take interpersonal risks without fear of negative consequences. Psychological safety in the workplace encourages trust, collaboration, and innovation, enabling teams to engage in candid discussions that drive progress and growth.[11]

Studies of teamwork at Google showed that psychological safety, more than anything else, is critical to making a team work effectively.[12] Without psychological safety and mutuality being established early on in a collaborative relationship, you run the risk of team members clamming up, withholding information, or just stewing in resentment. Says Edmonson, "People in positions of power or supervision can and do create more psychological safety when they ask more questions, listen to the answers, and when they acknowledge their own shortcomings."[13] A 2015 report coauthored by Edmondson suggests that psychological safety can serve as an "antidote" to the challenges that arise from a workforce's diversity of backgrounds, thoughts, and experiences. By fostering an environment where individuals feel safe to speak up, it enables everyone to contribute their unique perspectives more effectively.[14]

To foster psychological safety, a leader must lead by example. When addressing difficult conversations or sensitive topics, a leader should approach them in a constructive, nonjudgmental way, modeling the behavior they expect from their team. Bosses or managers should

218

Synergy and Sparks

create an environment of receptivity, where team members feel comfortable raising concerns or sharing their opinions at every stage of the process. "Leaders must prioritize a culture of learning and innovation for team members to be comfortable speaking up, taking risks, and sharing information," says Edmondson. She reminded us, "This does not happen by default. It emerges with effort and curiosity and care."[15]

Encouraging risk-taking and actively applauding team members for stepping outside their comfort zones significantly strengthens psychological safety within the team as well, creating an environment where individuals feel supported in taking initiative and experimenting without fear of judgment. Conversely, studies show that when people withhold their ideas, questions, and doubts, their team's risk of making mistakes and experiencing failure increases.[16]

Equally important is publicly acknowledging and celebrating the unique skills and contributions of each team member. With nearly 84 percent of workers reporting that recognition affects their motivation, this practice not only highlights individual value but also reinforces a culture of respect.[17] By fostering a sense of belonging, it inspires everyone to perform at their best and contribute more meaningfully to the team's success.

A fundamental way for leaders to establish psychological safety within their teams is by framing mistakes as valuable learning opportunities. As Steve Jobs famously said, "You can't connect the dots looking forward; you can only connect them looking backwards."[18] This perspective encourages a mindset shift where mistakes are not seen as failures, but as stepping stones to deeper understanding and growth. When mistakes occur, effective leaders should not only acknowledge them but also assess their impact and focus on the lessons learned to prevent similar issues in the future. By establishing an environment where mistakes are viewed as part of the learning process, leaders help build a culture where team members feel safe to take risks, innovate, and experiment without fear of blame or retribution.

Mastering Challenging Conversations

Strategies for Reflection: Pre-mortem and Post-mortem Analysis

To foster a collaborative and supportive environment, leaders should incorporate debriefing sessions into every project, giving teams the chance to reflect and improve. Two powerful tools for this are *pre-mortems* and *post-mortems*. Used at the start and end of a project, these tools help identify risks, learn from successes and challenges, and improve future performance. Let's start by focusing on the more familiar one: the post-mortem.

- In medicine, a post-mortem, or autopsy, is the detailed examination of a body to determine the cause of death and gain insights into the circumstances surrounding it. In a business context, a post-mortem serves a similar function—analyzing a project or initiative after its completion, especially when it has failed or underperformed. This process helps teams understand the underlying reasons for the lack of success, uncovering any missteps, inefficiencies, or unmet expectations. A business post-mortem also provides an opportunity to identify gaps in strategy, communication, or execution, enabling organizations to address these weaknesses and improve their approach for future projects.

- A pre-mortem, however, is a proactive exercise conducted before a project begins, but after the team has been briefed on the initiative's goals and objectives. Unlike post-mortems, which assess what went wrong *after* the fact, a pre-mortem focuses on identifying potential risks and challenges in advance, enabling the team to anticipate obstacles and develop strategies to mitigate them from the outset.

Here's the approach: the leader starts by acknowledging that, despite everyone's best efforts, the project has failed or underperformed.

220

Synergy and Sparks

Each team member then shares their perspective on what went wrong, answering the question: *what factors contributed to the failure—and why?* The team then discusses each factor or concern, exploring ways to mitigate risks or adjust the plan to avoid issues before the project begins. Research by the Wharton School, Cornell University, and the University of Colorado has shown that employing this type of "prospective hindsight"—imagining that the project has already failed—can boost a team's ability to identify potential risks by 30 percent, ultimately improving their chances of success.[19]

The questions a leader uses in both a pre-mortem and post-mortem should align closely, ensuring consistency. By asking the same key questions at the start and end of a project, leaders can set clear expectations up front and then reassess them afterward. Questions should focus on key areas such as planning failures, communication failures, execution failures, and results failures.[20] Planning failures stem from poor preparation or unrealistic expectations before a project begins. Communication failures involve breakdowns in messaging that hinder collaboration or clarity. Execution failures occur during implementation, such as delays, resource challenges, or quality issues. Results failures focus on how the project met—or failed to meet—its goals and performance metrics, and the factors that contributed to those outcomes.

Communicating Through Conflict

When challenges arise during collaboration, it's essential for leaders to communicate more, not less. In difficult moments, silence or withholding information can create confusion, frustration, and mistrust. Transparency and openness should be the norm, not the exception, as clear communication helps keep the team aligned and focused on the shared goal. As Howard Schultz, former CEO of Starbucks, wisely states, "It's very easy to lead when things are going great, and you've got the wind at your back. It gets really hard when you've got headwinds, disappointments, and people are telling you you're going the wrong way."[21] This captures the true test of leadership—steering the team through adversity.

Creative conflict in a team should be welcomed, not avoided, as it helps the team work through difficulties, synthesize different perspectives, and ultimately arrive at the best solutions to complex problems. In these moments, a leader's ability to encourage open dialogue and manage differing viewpoints can transform challenges into opportunities for innovation and growth.

For leaders who tend to avoid conflict, Peter Bromberg offers a powerful reminder: "When we avoid difficult conversations, we trade short-term discomfort for long-term dysfunction."[22] While facilitating a tough conversation can be intimidating, approaching such interactions with honesty and candor is essential to make sure the message is understood. As Howard Schultz reminds us, "Most people generally have difficulty with conflict, and many are conflict-avoidant. It's not conflict you're trying to expose yourself to; it's honesty. If you're not being honest with those around you, you become part of the problem."[23] Embracing openness and candor by focusing on the *impact* caused by the issue or situation being addressed not only improves leadership effectiveness but also builds a transparent and trustworthy culture.

As a leader, your ability to stay calm under pressure is key to your effectiveness. It's crucial to manage your emotions in a way that supports your goals. A single word or comment, once spoken, can't be taken back—what's said is said. In leadership, your words and reactions carry significant weight. "When something happens," says Kris Lee, a behavioral science expert from Northeastern University, "our brain's automatic response is to be reactive. When our amygdala, the small part of our brain that regulates fight-or-flight is set off, we have to avoid taking the bait of our raw emotional reactions that make us want to overreact."[24]

222

Synergy and Sparks

Anger and stress are among the most common emotions experienced in the workplace, particularly when managing conflict. These emotions often arise in high-pressure situations or when there are interpersonal tensions. Author Susan David explains that when you're feeling emotional, "the attention you give your thoughts and feelings crowds your mind; there's no room to examine them."[25] This highlights how, in moments of strong emotion, we can become so focused on our immediate reactions that we lose the ability to step back and reflect on what's really driving those feelings. For leaders, cultivating *emotional agility*—the ability to navigate your own emotions and engage more effectively with others—is crucial. By enhancing this skill, leaders can better manage their emotions and create stronger, more collaborative relationships within their teams.

Groucho Marx once said, "Speak when you're angry and you'll make the best speech you'll ever regret."[26] Anger is one of the most difficult emotions for leaders to manage. As tensions rise, clear thinking fades, and instincts often push us into fight mode. In these moments, pausing to silently acknowledge what you're feeling—a technique known as *labeling*—can be incredibly helpful. By naming the emotion, such as, "I'm feeling angry because I think my coworker is being disrespectful," you create mental distance, allowing for greater control.[27] Jeanne Brett, a dispute resolution expert at the Kellogg School of Management, suggests visualizing hurtful or provocative words as though they are simply passing over your shoulder, rather than striking you directly.[28]

Research shows that failing to acknowledge and address emotions can increase stress and harm both mental and physical health.[29] By contrast, labeling emotions offers significant benefits, helping you regain composure and stay focused. By identifying and naming your feelings, you create the space to respond more thoughtfully. David Rock, a leader in human performance coaching, notes that emotional labeling can reduce stress by up to 50 percent. He writes, "Without

223

Mastering Challenging Conversations

this ability to stand outside your experience, without self-awareness, you would have little ability to moderate and direct your behavior moment to moment."[30]

For managers, mastering emotional agility is a game changer—almost like a superpower. In high-stakes conversations, where emotions run deep and tensions are high, reacting impulsively can quickly derail productive dialogue. Instead, pausing—both physically and emotionally—is often more effective. Organizational psychologist Adam Grant puts it this way, "A mark of intelligence is not internalizing everything you feel. Thoughts and emotions are possibilities to ponder, not facts to accept."[31] Taking a moment to breathe, step back, or take a short break allows you to return with greater composure, clarity, and focus, leading to more constructive outcomes. "When we buy time," says Kris Lee, "We then have access to the frontal lobes of our brains, where we have access to reasoning, better problem-solving and perspective. We never have to take the bait of primitive emotions."[32]

Leaders must also carefully consider the mode of delivery they use when handling conflict or emotionally charged conversations. As Vishal Garg showed, choosing the wrong platform can lead to significant issues. We've all encountered the pitfalls of trying to resolve a heated discussion via text or email—it's rarely effective. Research supports this, with studies showing that written communication is often misinterpreted, leading to misunderstandings. A study detailed in *Forbes* found that 80 percent of people attributed workplace misunderstandings to text messages, and 87 percent to emails. Such miscommunications often trigger resentment, frustration, or anger.[33] Texting and email can complicate conflict resolution because they lack the nuance and tone of voice that help convey meaning in face-to-face conversations.

Our growing preference for texting over email and phone calls—particularly among the younger generations—has led to an increase in the number of interactions, but a decrease in the quality of those interactions, ultimately harming relationships.[34] According to psychologist Maggie Mulqueen, the primary issue with texting is that it "reduces conversation to words or photos on a screen" and "converts the rich exchange of human connection into brief, stilted fragments." This shift diminishes the depth and warmth of communication, making it harder to build meaningful connections and resolve issues effectively.[35]

Texting during emotionally charged exchanges is particularly risky, as it often triggers impulsive reactions. Without the visual cues of facial expressions or gestures, and tone of voice, it's easy to respond with anger or sarcasm. Texting can also encourage passive-aggressive behavior, leading to what Mulqueen calls "hit-and-run" communication—brief, harsh messages that would likely never be said face-to-face. This can escalate tensions and undermine the potential for constructive dialogue.[36]

Texting also makes lying easier, as the written word on a screen doesn't reveal the intent behind a message the way tone of voice or body language can in a virtual call or face-to-face conversation. Without those cues, it's easier to mask true intentions. Additionally, texting can encourage laziness—it's much quicker to send a cake emoji for someone's birthday than to actually bake one. As Mulqueen warns, "Our skills for conversing are getting rusty and will only get worse as more people use virtual assistants, online shopping, and other apps that help us avoid actually talking to another human being. Texting breeds not just grammar and spelling illiteracy but, more importantly, emotional illiteracy as well."[37]

A Formula for Difficult Conversations

If you manage or lead people, you're likely familiar with workplace conflict. Whether it's personality clashes, shifting deadlines, heightened competition, or market pressures, these challenges are part of everyday organizational dynamics that often drain productivity and morale. A report by *CPP Inc.*, the publishers of the Myers-Briggs Assessment, reveals that employees spend an average of 2.8 hours per week managing conflicts, leading to a staggering $359 billion in lost productivity each year. Unresolved conflicts not only disrupt workflows but also impose a heavy financial burden on businesses globally.[38]

Conflicts are inevitable in any workplace, and learning to navigate difficult conversations is a crucial skill for leaders. Common triggers include a lack of trust, cited by 73 percent of respondents, and personality clashes, mentioned by 72 percent.[39] How you handle these conflicts can significantly affect your career. Research from Columbia University shows that your response to conflict can either advance or hinder your progress and growth. Overly aggressive behavior can harm your performance by alienating peers, while being too passive can prevent you from achieving your goals. Striking the right balance between assertiveness and diplomacy is crucial for resolving conflicts effectively and building an empowered workforce.[40]

In 2014, Satya Nadella, the CEO of Microsoft, had the difficult task of announcing the layoff of 18,000 employees due to restructuring. However, unlike Vishal Garg at Better, Nadella delivered this difficult news with honesty and empathy, acknowledging the financial challenges Microsoft faced and the need to adapt to a rapidly changing industry.

"The first step to building the right organization for our ambitions is to realign our workforce. With this in mind, we will begin to reduce the size of our overall workforce by up to 18,000 jobs in the next year," Nadella stated. His message: long-term progress will require short-term pain. He then went on to express empathy by reassuring employees that the company would support those affected. "While we are eliminating roles in some areas, we are adding roles in certain other strategic areas. My promise to you is that we will go through this process in the most thoughtful and transparent way possible . . . and everyone can expect to be treated with the respect they deserve for their contributions to Microsoft."[41]

Nadella's approach prioritized empathy and transparent communication, which not only helped sustain trust within the organization but also demonstrated a culture of openness and collaboration. By being both direct and compassionate, he positioned himself as a leader who balanced the pursuit of business goals with a genuine commitment to the well-being of his employees. This combination of clarity and care reinforced Nadella's reputation as a leader who viewed people as integral to Microsoft's success, not just as resources.

When delivering difficult news or handling emotionally charged situations, a structured approach is essential for ensuring clarity, empathy, and a constructive outcome. Having a clear framework helps you remain calm and focused, reducing the risk of misunderstandings or emotional escalation. It also steers the conversation toward resolution, ensuring that core issues are addressed rather than getting lost in reactive responses. Without a road map, it's easy for conversations to become unproductive or even counterproductive. Here's a simple, three-step framework that can be highly effective in managing such conversations:

Step 1: Set the context. First, like Nadella did at Microsoft, set the stage by clearly explaining the situation to your team member and outlining its impact on others. Provide relevant context and acknowledge any emotions that may be involved. This step helps establish a constructive tone, prepares the listener for the conversation, and emphasizes the importance of addressing the issue. By framing the discussion this way, you make it easier for the other person to absorb the information and create a shared understanding of its urgency and significance.

Step 2: Gain perspective. Next, focus on gaining the other person's perspective. After outlining the issue and its impact,

227

Mastering Challenging Conversations

invite their response and actively listen to their thoughts, feelings, and reactions without interrupting or becoming defensive. It's tempting to dive into solutions immediately, but holding back from doing so allows you to understand the full scope of their concerns. Giving the other person space to share their perspective makes them feel heard, which can defuse tension and build mutual respect.

Step 3: Agree on action. Finally, guide the conversation toward finding a way forward and agree on a clear course of action. Work together to explore potential solutions, ensuring the other person feels both supported and empowered as they move ahead. Focusing on a positive, forward-looking vision helps everyone feel more engaged and confident in resolving the issue. Conclude by clearly defining the next steps, ensuring both parties understand what needs to happen. This promotes accountability and reinforces the other person's role in driving the solution. By aligning on specific actions, you create a shared sense of responsibility and provide the conversation with a clear direction, helping both parties feel confident and motivated to move forward.

As you guide the conversation toward a positive resolution, it's essential to approach the process with empathy and compassion. In Chapter 16, we'll explore how embracing these qualities in leadership not only strengthens your ability to support others but also fosters trust and deeper connections.

Synergy and Sparks

Part VI

Connection

Chapter 16

The Case for Empathy in Leadership

Compassion is not a virtue—it is a commitment.

—Brené Brown

Hidden Kindness: The CEO and the Civil Rights Icon

Compassion is a fundamental trait for effective leadership, as it nurtures trust, promotes collaboration, and deepens the connection between leaders and their teams. Compassionate leaders don't just listen to their team members' concerns—they respond with empathy and a sincere commitment to helping. This approach cultivates a supportive work environment where individuals feel valued and respected, enhancing both morale and engagement. Unfortunately, a recent study revealed that 77 percent of CEOs fear they will lose respect if they show empathy, highlighting a significant barrier to embracing a more compassionate leadership style.[1]

One powerful example of leadership, generosity, and compassion comes from Michael Ilitch, the founder and owner of the international fast food franchise Little Caesars Pizza. Ilitch was born in Detroit, Michigan, and at the age of 30, he and his wife, Marian, invested their family savings to open the first Little Caesars store in Garden City, Michigan. They grew the brand into the third-largest pizza chain in the world, with locations in more than 27 countries and territories, including all 50 US states. In addition to building a global pizza empire, the couple went on to acquire the Detroit Red Wings hockey team in 1982 and the Detroit Tigers baseball team in 1992.[2]

Throughout his life, Mike Ilitch remained deeply committed to his hometown, tirelessly working to help Detroit thrive and restore pride to the city. In 1988, he and Marian purchased the neglected Fox Theatre and meticulously restored it to its original 1928 splendor. A firm believer in giving back, Ilitch created programs to support veterans and families in need. Since 2000, grants and donations from the Ilitches' companies and their charitable affiliates have totaled more than $220 million.[3] Mike Ilitch passed away in 2017 at the age of 88, but three years before his death, an article in *Sports Business Journal* highlighted an act of kindness that perfectly captured his leadership approach and the impact of his generosity.

In 1994, Rosa Parks, the iconic civil rights activist who famously refused to give up her seat on a segregated bus in 1955, was living in Detroit. That August, at the age of 81, Parks was robbed and assaulted in her home. In response, Judge Damon Keith reached out to a real estate developer to help find a safer place for Parks to live. When news of the attack and Parks's search for new housing became public, Mike Ilitch was deeply moved. He contacted Judge Keith and offered to cover Parks's rent in her new apartment, pledging to support her financially for as long as needed. With no fanfare or public announcement, Ilitch quietly funded Parks's housing for over a decade, continuing until her death in 2005.[4]

Ilitch's kind assistance, provided without seeking recognition, is a powerful example of empathetic leadership. It shows how a compassionate leader cannot only help those in need but also inspire others in positions of power to make a meaningful difference themselves. Said Judge Keith, "It's important that people know what Mr. Mike Ilitch did for Ms. Rosa Parks because it's symbolic of what he has always done for the people of our city."[5]

Why Leaders Should Care

We live in a time of increasing division, where people often talk *at* each other rather than *with* each other. One of the key reasons for this divide is the way we consume and use information, which tends to reinforce existing beliefs and can fuel misunderstanding, creating an "us versus them" mentality that makes it harder to connect with others. Many of us can recall moments—whether at work, over drinks, or during family gatherings—when a comment or opinion sparked an emotional exchange that damaged or altered a relationship.

A landmark study in 2010 found that Americans were less empathetic than their counterparts were 30 years earlier.[6] Empathy levels dropped significantly during the COVID pandemic, with a United Way NCA survey revealing a 14 percent decline in respondents' empathy ratings from 2019 to 2022.[7] This decline was driven by a combination of factors, including technology, social media algorithms, and rising political tribalism.[8]

In a letter to the American people in 2025, US Surgeon General Vivek Murthy expressed concern over the growing division and polarization in American society, warning that these forces are eroding our sense of optimism and taking a toll on both our mental and physical health. "Relationships keep us grounded and bonded to each other," noted Murthy, "Service, from formal volunteering to informal small acts of kindness, is about helping each other. And purpose gives our life a sense of direction and meaning."[9]

One interesting initiative designed to help foster empathy originated in Denmark in 2000: the Human Library Organization. This nonprofit—whose motto is "Unjudge Someone"—is committed to fostering dialogue, building meaningful connections, and challenging stereotypes. The concept behind the Human Library is simple yet powerful: people can "borrow" human "books"—individuals with unique life experiences—who then share their stories in open, nonjudgmental conversations. These exchanges promote empathy, challenge prejudices, and encourage cross-cultural understanding. The initiative has since expanded globally, with Human Libraries now operating in more than 85 countries, offering an innovative way to bridge divides and foster greater social cohesion.[10]

Actors rely on empathy to portray characters authentically, even when playing villainous or unsympathetic roles. By connecting to the emotions, desires, and fears driving their characters, they create multidimensional portrayals that feel true to life. This requires suspending judgment and seeing the world through the character's eyes. Through empathy, actors bring humanity to any role, allowing audiences to explore complex aspects of human nature, even in morally ambiguous or flawed characters. As Bill English, artistic director of the San Francisco Playhouse, aptly puts it, "Theater is like a gym for empathy. It's where we go to build our compassion muscles, to practice listening, understanding, and engaging with people who are not just like ourselves. We practice sitting down, paying attention, and learning from others' actions. We practice caring."[11]

Sadly, with the rise of cable news and social media—and the intentionally combative and divisive leadership style of Donald Trump—many of us increasingly retreat into our own "tribes," seeking out only information that reinforces our existing beliefs—what's known as *confirmation bias*. This happens because engaging with opposing viewpoints feels uncomfortable—it challenges our sense of truth and forces us to confront uncertainty or contradictions. This discomfort often leads us to avoid listening, deepening divisions and hindering meaningful dialogue. Neuroscientists at the Brain and Creativity Institute at the University of Southern California studied individuals with strong political views using functional magnetic resonance imaging scanners to observe brain activity when their beliefs were challenged. Some areas of their brains lit up as if they were facing a life-threatening danger—similar to the response triggered by the sight of a bear chasing them.[12]

UCLA political scientist Lynn Vavreck argues that the current US electorate is not just polarized but calcified, with the country almost evenly split into two rigid factions that remain firmly fixed in their political loyalties, making it increasingly difficult for either side to bridge the divide. This deeply entrenched division is precisely what Donald Trump was referencing when he famously boasted, "I could stand in the middle of Fifth Avenue and shoot somebody, and I wouldn't lose any voters."[13]

The rise of partisan news outlets and media platforms, fueled by algorithms designed to reinforce existing beliefs, has led many to engage primarily with like-minded individuals while actively avoiding opposing viewpoints. This is unhealthy for collaboration, especially in the workplace. Allstate CEO Tom Wilson has warned that society is suffering from an "addiction to divisiveness and negativity."[14] Gaining a genuine understanding of others—whether in the workplace or socially—demands actively listening to and truly considering the concerns and perspectives of those we engage with. A recent Georgetown University study highlights a rise in workplace incivility, with serious consequences, including decreased performance, worsened customer experiences, and higher turnover rates.[15]

Empathy—the ability to truly understand and share the feelings of others—is an essential quality for anyone leading a team or managing an organization. It goes beyond sympathy; it requires actively considering the challenges, concerns, and emotions of those you work with and integrating these perspectives into your decision-making. For leaders, recognizing the distinction between sympathy and empathy is an important first step toward fostering a supportive and effective work environment. While sympathy involves feeling pity or sorrow for someone, empathy requires understanding and sharing in their experience from their perspective.

Demonstrating empathy through both verbal and nonverbal communication is a powerful tool for any leader. It shows team members that they are heard and understood, which can help align the group, engage employees, and make people feel valued. To effectively show empathy, a leader must be authentic, genuine, and nonjudgmental, especially when considering differing or opposing viewpoints. Empathy requires a leader to momentarily step into another person's shoes, understanding their emotions and perspective in that moment—much like an actor embracing a new role.

The time-tested techniques that professional actors use to empathize with others offer valuable lessons for leaders in the business world. Actors excel at imagining the struggles and emotions of people from diverse backgrounds. As Meryl Streep once said, "An actor's only job is to enter the lives of people who are different from us and let you feel what that feels like." This skill is equally vital for effective leadership, as it strengthens connections, improves decision-making, and allows leaders to genuinely appreciate others' perspectives.[16]

In their book *Emotional Intelligence 2.0*, authors Travis Bradberry and Jean Greaves argue that "walking in the shoes of another is social awareness at its best—and it's not just for actors. It's for all of us who want to gain perspective, deepen our understanding of others, [and] improve our communication."[17] Unfortunately, a report in *Harvard Business Review* revealed that empathy is most lacking among senior executives and middle managers.[18] This is particularly concerning because leaders' decisions have the greatest influence on their teams, and a lack of empathy at the top can significantly affect workplace culture and employee engagement.

When you think about your peers and the team members within your organization, how well do you listen to them and show empathy? Do you feel like you have a clear understanding of the challenges they face each day? Are you aware of any impending deadlines or specific budget concerns that may be weighing on their mind? Do you know if they're dealing with personal challenges at the moment? If you can't identify the specific challenges your employees are facing, it's likely a sign you need to engage with them more deeply.

Colin Powell, the highly accomplished and respected four-star general who made history as the first African American Secretary of State, shared the following insight when asked what defines an effective leader: "Leadership ultimately comes down to creating conditions of trust within an organization," said Powell, "The essence of leadership is . . . taking that extra step and giving it that spark. And that spark comes from getting people to trust you, so that they will follow you. If only out of curiosity."[19] For leaders, empathy and trust go hand in hand.

A study conducted by researchers at the University College London Division of Psychological and Language Sciences found that audience members' hearts actually synchronize while watching live theater. Interestingly, not only did their emotional responses align as they experienced the play, but their heart rates also synchronized, with their pulses speeding up and slowing down in harmony.[20] In simple terms, when we truly listen and connect with others—whether in a theater or a boardroom—we can genuinely feel what they feel and experience what they experience.

In studies done by the Management Research Group, empathy was identified as the most important competence for effective leadership, and one of the top three predictors of leadership success.[21] When a leader lacks compassion or treats others with disrespect, it undermines the entire organizational culture. Meryl Streep, in a speech in 2017, highlighted the dangers of such leadership, remarking, "This instinct to humiliate, when it's modeled by someone in a public platform, by someone powerful, it filters down into everybody's life, because it gives permission for other people to do the same thing. Disrespect invites disrespect."[22]

237

The Case for Empathy in Leadership

Leadership Strategies to Boost Empathy

Communication often falters because we quickly leap to the worst possible conclusions about others, neglecting to consider their circumstances or perspective. We've already discussed two key factors that contribute to this tendency: overconfidence and confirmation bias. However, the most significant—and potentially most damaging—misstep is a cognitive bias known as the *fundamental attribution error*.

As defined in an article by Harvard Business School Online, fundamental attribution error refers to "an individual's tendency to attribute another's actions to their character or personality, while attributing one's own behavior to external situational factors outside of their control." In other words, you tend to cut yourself a break while holding others 100 percent accountable for their actions.[23]

Imagine you're driving down the road when another car suddenly cuts you off and speeds away. Your immediate reaction might be, "What a rude, inconsiderate driver," assuming they're just being reckless and have no regard for others. But what you don't know is that the driver just received an urgent call from their child's school, informing them that their daughter was having an allergic reaction and needed medication right away. In this case, your assumption—that the driver was being thoughtless—illustrates the fundamental attribution error. We tend to overlook situational factors and instead blame people's actions on their character.

To avoid making fundamental attribution errors when managing a team, leaders should focus on extending grace and giving team members the benefit of the doubt, when warranted. Instead of making sweeping generalizations like, "Jordan is always late for meetings" or "Chris has terrible people skills," take time to assess the situation more thoughtfully. Look for patterns of behavior that support such judgments and test any hypotheses before drawing conclusions. Additionally, before focusing solely on a team member's shortcomings, pause to reflect on their positive contributions to the team and organization. This helps maintain a balanced perspective and ensures a fairer approach to addressing the issue.

As you engage with your coworkers, family members, or social media contacts, make a conscious effort to truly listen to what they say, without being dismissive or judgmental. Approach conversations with an open mind, asking questions to gain context and a deeper understanding of their circumstances and emotions. Try to separate your personal feelings about them from your assessment of their actions. Assume there may be a reasonable explanation for their behavior—whether it's an action or an omission. This approach will help cultivate a more empathetic and collaborative environment, where misunderstandings are less likely to derail progress or damage relationships.

To enhance your empathy and understanding of others, try this simple exercise: start by identifying someone with whom you have significant political, cultural, religious, or philosophical differences. Think of a specific statement or viewpoint they've expressed that you disagree with or find difficult to understand. Then, take a moment to reflect on their perspective by imagining at least two possible reasons why they might hold that opinion. Writing these reasons down can help you step into their shoes and see things from their point of view. Next, seek an opportunity to ask them about their perspective, but do so with curiosity and respect. Instead of challenging their viewpoint, inquire about the experiences or beliefs that led them to form that opinion. When they respond, listen attentively without judgment. Resist the urge to interrupt, argue, or offer counterpoints. Your goal is simply to understand their experience and reasoning. Allow them to express themselves fully. After they've shared their thoughts, thank them for their openness, and take some time to reflect on what you've learned. Consider how their personal experiences and

239

The Case for Empathy in Leadership

perspectives may have shaped their views, and think about any new understanding or empathy you've developed from the exchange.

Gratitude, Recognition, and Servant Leadership

As a leader, every decision you make communicates a message to those around you, as does every decision you choose not to make. Prioritizing the needs and well-being of your team over your own is a cornerstone of empathetic leadership. By demonstrating care and consideration for others, leaders foster a culture of mutual respect and shared purpose. True leadership lies in recognizing that the success of a team is built on trust, collaboration, and a commitment to the collective well-being.

In 1970, Robert K. Greenleaf, an AT&T executive and director of management development, published his groundbreaking essay "The Servant as Leader," which introduced the concept of *servant leadership*. In it, Greenleaf explored the idea that effective leadership is rooted in a leader's commitment to serving others. Unlike traditional leadership, which often focuses on the accumulation and exercise of power by those at the top of an organization, Greenleaf's model flips this dynamic. A servant leader shares power, prioritizes the needs of others, and fosters growth by consistently empowering and supporting their team. "The servant leader is servant first," wrote Greenleaf, "It begins with the natural feeling that one wants to serve . . . . Then conscious choice brings one to aspire to lead. That person is sharply different from one who is leader first, perhaps because of the need to assuage an unusual power drive or to acquire material possessions . . . . The difference manifests itself in the care taken by the servant first to make sure that other people's . . . needs are being served."[24]

Recognition and gratitude are fundamental principles of servant leadership, offering bosses and managers the opportunity to acknowledge and appreciate their team members' contributions.

This fosters a positive, supportive environment where individuals feel valued, empowered, and motivated to perform at their best. Naturally, employees want to feel that their work matters and that their efforts are appreciated. A recent study found that nearly 84 percent of people believe recognition plays a key role in motivating them to succeed at work, with 80 percent saying they'd be more productive if leadership recognized their efforts more often.[25] This highlights the importance of consistently seizing opportunities to recognize team members for their efforts and accomplishments. Unfortunately, despite organizations' efforts to improve employee engagement, Gallup reports that progress has been slow. In 2024, only 21 percent of employees strongly agreed that their organization cared about their overall well-being, marking a record low.[26]

In the fast-paced world of corporate leadership, one of the most powerful yet often overlooked practices is expressing genuine gratitude. Acknowledging the efforts of a team or individual stakeholder can significantly boost morale, strengthen relationships, increase engagement, and inspire loyalty. Leaders can express gratitude in various ways—publicly, during team meetings or company-wide town halls, or privately, through personal emails or one-on-one conversations. Teams motivated by recognition and guided by servant leadership principles are more likely to go above and beyond, ultimately driving higher productivity and revenue.[27]

Arthur C. Brooks, a Harvard Business School professor and author, highlights the benefits of practicing gratitude, particularly its ability to rewire the brain and counteract our natural negativity bias—the survival mechanism discussed previously that prioritizes threats over rewards. He explains that we are wired with more brain space dedicated to negative emotions than positive ones because, as he puts it, "Positive emotions are nice to have. Negative emotions will keep you alive."[28] By expressing gratitude, we can shift our focus from potential problems to positive aspects and accomplishments.

When showing gratitude to team members, a leader should be consistent, equitable, and inclusive. Consistency ensures that employees know their efforts will be regularly recognized, fostering engagement and accountability. Equity guarantees fairness, making all team members feel valued, while inclusivity ensures diverse contributions are acknowledged, promoting a collaborative and innovative culture. Fair and inclusive recognition boosts morale, strengthens team cohesion, and improves retention, leading to better performance and long-term success.

As William James, the founder of US psychology, noted, "The deepest principle in human nature is the craving to be appreciated."[29] This fundamental need for recognition is central to our sense of self-worth and motivation. In the corporate world, appreciation directly affects morale and performance. For leaders, understanding this need is essential—not just for acknowledging accomplishments but also for fostering an environment of empathy and compassion. Think about your team and your leadership approach: how often, and in what ways, do you show gratitude? Consider whether your recognition is consistent, specific, and genuine, and reflect on how you can make gratitude a more intentional part of your leadership style.

Empathetic leaders recognize the emotions and struggles of their teams, and actively support and elevate their people. When bosses and managers display servant leadership, they build trust, loyalty, and a positive culture where individuals feel engaged and motivated. Ultimately, leading with empathy isn't just about recognition; it's about creating an environment where everyone feels seen, respected, and valued.

More Than Winning: A Story of Integrity, Empathy, and Leadership

One remarkable story of selflessness and empathy took place in 2012 at a cross-country race in the Navarre region of northern Spain, where Abel Kiprop Mutai, a Kenyan runner, and Iván Fernández Anaya, a runner from Spain, were racing each other. With only a few meters to go in the race, Mutai, who had led from the start, began to show signs of fatigue. In a moment of confusion, he misjudged the location of the finish line and started to slow down, thinking the race was over and he had won.

As the Kenyan eased into a victory jog, Anaya, trailing just behind, quickly realized what was happening. He shouted at Mutai to keep running, but since Mutai didn't speak Spanish, he couldn't understand the instructions. In that critical moment, Ayana made a split-second decision to do something extraordinary: he chose to help. Rather than taking advantage of Mutai's confusion to steal the victory for himself, Ayana ran up to his opponent, tapped him on the shoulder, and gently guided him toward the finish line, ensuring that Mutai crossed the line first. His selfless act enabled Mutai to keep his lead and win the race, despite the moment of misunderstanding.

When the race ended, Mutai expressed his deep gratitude to Anaya, acknowledging that he would surely have lost the race had it not been for the Spaniard's intervention. When asked by the press why he let Mutai win the race instead of passing him, Anaya responded, "I didn't deserve to win it," adding, "He was the rightful winner."[30]

Anaya's act of sportsmanship quickly spread across social media, demonstrating that true victory isn't just about crossing the line first but also about the character and integrity displayed while competing. "I have earned more of a name having done what I did than if I had won," said Anaya. He added, "And that is very important, because today, with the way things are . . . in society, in politics, where it seems anything goes, a gesture of honesty goes down well."[31]

The moment between these two fierce competitors offered a powerful lesson for leaders. Just as Anaya chose to uplift his competitor instead of seizing an easy victory, leaders can inspire loyalty and respect by putting the well-being of their teams first, even when faced with opportunities for personal gain. This act of compassion is a reminder that true leadership isn't defined by individual success, but by the ability to foster a culture of humanity, collaboration, and integrity within a team.

In Chapter 17, we'll explore the importance of active listening and the deep human need to connect with others, both socially and professionally, to build stronger relationships and create more productive teams.

Chapter 17

Cultivating Authentic Dialogue

Eventually, everything connects—people, ideas, objects.

—Charles Eames

No More Tears: A Journey from Prison to Purpose

Lonnie Morris's life is a compelling testament to the transformative power of human connection, showing how it can illuminate even the darkest of paths. Growing up in a family of migrant workers and alcoholics, Lonnie faced a troubled childhood. After his mother's death from cirrhosis when he was 12, his family fell into chaos. Lonnie's brothers turned to crime to survive, pulling him into a violent world. By 26, his criminal record was long and filled with time in jail and prison.[1]

Everything changed on August 4, 1977. Out on parole, Lonnie and an accomplice robbed a jewelry store in San Pablo, California. During the robbery, Lonnie shot a police officer, who later died. That tragic act sealed his fate: sentenced to seven years to life behind bars, he was sent to the notorious San Quentin State Prison.[2]

For the next two decades Lonnie settled into a life of incarceration. He went before the parole board time after time, only to have his parole request repeatedly denied. But something changed in the early 2000s. San Quentin's overcrowding saw an influx of young men from the Bay Area, and Lonnie, now older and more reflective, saw an opportunity. He began talking to these young men, learning about their experiences and the violence they faced on the streets.

As he listened, Lonnie realized that many of these young men were heading down the same path he had taken. Though he would likely never leave prison, these young men would eventually return to the streets. Lonnie saw this as a chance to make a real impact. "If I could cultivate in them a relationship, maybe I could influence them to do something different with their lives," he said.[3]

This sparked the idea for No More Tears, a program focused on building genuine connections with young men—especially those resistant to the system's rehabilitation efforts. Lonnie aimed to reach men who spent their time in the yard smoking, gambling, and fighting, as well as the influential "shot-callers" at San Quentin. He knew that if he could get them to participate, others would follow. Convincing these groups wasn't easy. Many were skeptical, assuming Lonnie had ulterior motives. "You just want us to come to the group to get some money," they'd say.[4] Lonnie understood that trust was key. "Nobody cares how much you know, until they know how much you care," he recalled a friend telling him. So, he set out to build relationships—spending time with these men, playing games, talking, and listening. Slowly but surely, they began to listen to him, too.[5]

With patience and persistence, Lonnie assembled his first cohort and launched the program, guiding the men through explorations of trauma, its consequences, and personal responsibility. Over the next 25 years, No More Tears would evolve into one of California's most impactful prison rehabilitation programs, helping more than 3,000 men confront the trauma and choices that had led them to incarceration. The results were striking: 85 percent of graduates who were released remained free, nearly double the national average.[6]

As the decades passed, Lonnie continued to develop himself and others. He earned a BA degree, honed his talents as a songwriter and filmmaker, and dedicated himself to helping other incarcerated

246

Synergy and Sparks

individuals escape the cycle of violence. In 2021, after 44 years of incarceration and 22 parole denials, Lonnie's tireless work and transformation culminated in a breakthrough: after filing a petition for habeas corpus, the courts ordered Lonnie's release. At the age of 70, Lonnie walked out of San Quentin Prison as a free man, but his mission was far from complete.

Today, Lonnie continues to lead No More Tears from the outside, regularly returning to San Quentin to mentor men while traveling globally to share his powerful story. I first met Lonnie in 2022 through my daughter, who was volunteering with the program at San Quentin. When I asked Lonnie about the lasting impact of his work, he simply said, "I don't really think about it. I do what I do and it does what it does. I set out to do some things and help some people, and if I did that, great."[7]

Lonnie Morris's story is a powerful reminder that it's never too late to change and rise again, no matter where we come from or how far we've fallen. Through connection and resilience, he's created a lasting legacy of hope, proving that human relationships can break even the toughest cycles.

Leadership, Loneliness, and Our Need to Connect

In any environment—whether a corporate setting, theater company, or even a prison—success depends not only on skill and strategy but also on building meaningful relationships. Leaders must earn trust from their teams, peers, and clients, especially where trust is scarce. Like Lonnie, leaders who invest in empathy and understanding can break down barriers, foster loyalty, and inspire growth. Just as Lonnie gained the respect of skeptical inmates, corporate leaders can drive collaboration and innovation by understanding the unique experiences of their colleagues and clients. Effective leadership is rooted in connection. As author Andy Stanley says, "Leaders who don't listen will eventually be surrounded by people who have nothing to say."[8] Reflect on the worst bosses you've had. What made them ineffective? How did their communication or collaboration style contribute to their shortcomings?

Connection is essential for both actors and leaders. For actors, building a deep connection with scene partners, as well as their character, is key to delivering authentic performances. Collaborating effectively with the cast and crew of a play or film is important for turning a shared vision into a powerful narrative. Similarly, leaders must cultivate strong bonds within their teams. When team members feel valued, heard, and understood, they are more likely to engage, contribute their best work, and collaborate toward common goals. Without connection, a team risks fragmentation and may never reach its full potential.

Every leader you've encountered—whether a boss, manager, or mentor—has taught you something valuable about connection and leadership. Some led by example, showing how to empower and motivate a team, while others made mistakes that taught you what to avoid. But true growth requires more than observation—it calls for curiosity, self-reflection, and a willingness to learn through authentic dialogue.

The world today is facing a crisis of connection, deeply affecting both personal and professional relationships. German researchers found that half of people who regularly wear headphones do so to avoid talking to others.[9] Psychologists and sociologists have warned of a growing loneliness epidemic in the United States, which has been declared a public health crisis. The effects are profound: isolation is now linked to an increased risk of premature death, as much as obesity and alcoholism.[10] Recently, US Surgeon General Dr. Vivek Murthy highlighted this issue, revealing that nearly half of US adults report significant loneliness. In the United Kingdom, the government appointed a "Minister for Loneliness" in 2018 to address the struggles of the nine million citizens who feel isolated.[11] In Japan, companies

248

Synergy and Sparks

have even started offering actors to play the roles of friends, family members, and romantic partners for those seeking companionship.[12]

The decline of friendships and social interactions began before the pandemic but was significantly worsened by it.[13] We've already discussed how the growing amount of time spent in front of screens often comes at the expense of real, face-to-face conversations. The rise of remote work has further limited in-person interactions, with fully remote employees reporting much higher levels of loneliness (25 percent) compared to their fully on-site counterparts (16 percent).[14] Ironically, despite our constant use of social media, we seem to be growing more disconnected. As former US transportation secretary Pete Buttigieg pointed out in *Rolling Stone*, "We've never had more connections, and we've never been more disconnected."[15]

According to a recent Gallup survey, more than one in five adults worldwide reported experiencing loneliness for much of the previous day.[16] And in a separate study, 58 percent of people said they trust strangers more than their own boss.[17] While this may not be the most encouraging news for those leading teams, it underscores a crucial truth: as leaders, we still have a lot of work to do in building a culture of trust and support within our organizations.

A lack of connection can have profound consequences on both our physical and mental health. Harvard professor and Gallup senior scientist Lisa Berkman and her colleagues conducted a study in which they examined the relationship between social ties and mortality rates over a nine-year period. The findings were striking: individuals with limited social connections had a mortality risk twice as high as those with strong community and social ties.[18] This underscores the importance of social bonds—not just in our personal lives but also in the workplace.

Feeling connected at work is a key driver of productivity. Research published in the *Journal of Knowledge Management* found that team members are more willing to share information with colleagues when they feel a sense of trust and connection. When employees view their coworkers as friends rather than competitors, they are less territorial and more open to collaboration.[19] For example, teams that prioritize building relationships often experience smoother communication, faster problem-solving, and a stronger sense of camaraderie, all of which contribute to better outcomes.

Gallup's research on emotions further highlights the impact of connection, revealing that women who have a best friend at work are more than twice as likely to be engaged in their jobs compared to those without one.[20] This sense of friendship and support not only boosts morale but also drives engagement—employees with close work relationships are more committed, productive, and loyal to the organization. In practice, when employees feel supported and connected, they're more likely to go the extra mile, take on new challenges, and contribute to a positive work culture.

As leaders, bosses, and managers, we can help foster connection by consistently engaging with our team members, checking in on their progress, and offering both guidance and support. Simple yet impactful questions—such as "How's everything going?" and "Is there anything you need?" can make a significant difference. In fact, a Google study found that leaders who demonstrate genuine concern for their team members' success and well-being consistently outperform others in both the quality and quantity of work produced.[21] These small gestures of care and engagement can help create a more connected, motivated, and high-performing team.

Active Listening: Engaging Every Moment

As we navigate the rhythms of hybrid work, shifting between home offices and in-person meetings, it's a good time to reawaken our social skills. Reengaging with colleagues across both virtual and physical spaces takes intention—and a little flexibility. Whether we're catching up over coffee or collaborating on a video call, finding our footing in this blended environment can lead to stronger connections and more dynamic teamwork. Everyone has a network of connections and contacts, and being able to have productive and meaningful conversations can serve you well as you grow and advance in your career. Even chance encounters or small talk can lead to important connections that may pay off down the road.

As mentioned previously in this chapter, a key element of meaningful conversations is demonstrating genuine curiosity about others. The best way to truly get to know someone is by asking thoughtful questions and listening intently to their answers. In Chapter 10, we discussed our natural tendency to focus on ourselves in conversation, driven by the dopamine rush we get from talking about our own experiences. In fact, one study found that people spend about 60 percent of their conversations talking about themselves. This can be a barrier to building real connections.[22] As the saying goes, "When you're talking, you're not learning anything new."

When meeting someone for the first time, it's important to assume they have passions, interests, and hobbies—many of which you may share. The key is to discover these commonalities through open-ended questions. For instance, instead of asking, "Do you like sports?" try something more open like, "What do you like to do in your free time?" This invites a broader response and gives people space to share what truly excites them. You can then offer your own experiences to build a natural rapport, sharing a similar interest or asking follow-up questions.

Above all, as psychologist Jacqueline Mayfield advises, treat the other person as "a person of consequence."[23] This means valuing their thoughts, feelings, and experiences, rather than simply waiting for your turn to speak. When people feel truly heard, they're more likely to open up, creating a stronger bond. For example, when a colleague shares a challenge they're facing at work, instead of jumping

251

Cultivating Authentic Dialogue

straight into offering advice or shifting the focus to your own experiences, take a moment to empathize, ask questions, and really understand their perspective.

Research has shown that when two strangers communicate with each other "disclosure begets disclosure."[24] If I share something about myself, your impulse is to do the same in return. One benefit of being able to ask questions during a conversation is that the mere act of doing it actually increases your level of likability in the eyes of others. According to one Harvard study, asking a question and then asking at least two follow-up questions will dramatically increase how likable you are.[25]

Active listening, a concept first introduced by psychologists Carl Rogers and Richard Farson in 1957, involves fully focusing on, understanding, responding to, and remembering what someone is saying.[26] As Rogers explained, when practicing active listening, one should "hear the words, the thoughts, the feeling tones, the personal meaning, even the meaning that is below the conscious intent of the speaker."[27] This distinction highlights the crucial difference between simply hearing and truly listening. As the saying goes, "Hearing is the sound hitting your ears; listening is the sound reaching your brain."

Active listening techniques are crucial for staying present and engaged in any conversation. Whether you're in a brainstorming session, a performance review, or simply chatting over drinks, think of each interaction as a spotlight shifting back and forth between people. In a conversation, we take turns allowing each other to step into the spotlight, sharing and receiving attention. Effective listening requires temporarily setting aside your own ego and self-interest, making space for the other person to truly shine. Leaders who excel at this demonstrate what psychologists call *conversational sensitivity*—the ability to not only focus on the words being spoken but also to pick up on underlying messages as well.[28]

An excellent anecdote about conversational sensitivity involves NBA superstar Michael Jordan and his agent, David Falk. In an interview with *Cigar Aficionado*, Jordan recounted how he and Falk were having dinner at a restaurant one evening. As the night wore on, Falk, known in the industry for his aggressive personality and brash communication style, continued to interrupt Jordan throughout dinner, often changing subjects mid-discussion. "I couldn't get a word in," recalled Jordan. Finally, growing increasingly frustrated, the basketball legend had enough. He flagged down the waiter and proceeded to order a bottle of the most expensive wine on the menu.

Falk, who was paying for the dinner, immediately took notice and fell silent. Seeing that he finally had Falk's attention, Jordan leaned in and, with a slight grin, said, "Every time you interrupt what we're talking about, I'm going to order another bottle." From that moment on, Falk stopped interrupting, became more attentive, and allowed the conversation to flow naturally for the rest of the evening.[29]

Despite the numerous benefits of effective listening, most people still fall short of fully mastering this crucial skill. Among the most common bad listening behaviors: interrupting, responding vaguely or illogically to what was just said, checking a phone or watch, and not maintaining eye contact with the speaker.[30] Think about how often you've been in the middle of a conversation only to have the other person check their phone or start texting someone who's not even part of the discussion. It's frustrating, and it can make you feel dismissed or disrespected. Additionally, approximately 15 percent of Americans—around 51 million people—experience some degree of hearing loss.[31] This creates additional challenges, as many individuals have difficulty hearing and their brains must work harder to compensate. These factors highlight the importance of being patient and intentional when communicating with others.

As we've discussed, a good conversation is like a spotlight that shifts back and forth between participants, an intentional ebb and

253

Cultivating Authentic Dialogue

flow. However, some people struggle with this balance. Those who dominate conversations or only enjoy hearing the sound of their own voice are often referred to as *conversational narcissists*. A healthy conversation between people should be a free flow of ideas, with both parties contributing, engaging, and feeling heard. As Bill Nye the Science Guy wisely reminds us, "Everyone you will ever meet knows something you don't."[32] In this context, let's discuss some active listening initiatives that can help you become a more mindful and effective listener.

Mastering Support and Shift Responses

In the 1970s, sociologist Charles Derber at Boston College began studying how people compete for attention in social settings. After recording and transcribing more than 100 informal dinner conversations, he identified two types of conversational initiatives: one focused on giving attention and the other on seeking attention. He categorized these as *support* and *shift* responses.[33]

A support response is a question or comment that keeps the focus on the speaker, encouraging them to share more. It helps the speaker feel heard and valued, fostering a deeper connection. Instead of offering advice or turning the focus to your own experiences, a support response invites further exploration via open-ended questions like, "How did that make you feel?" or "What happened next?"

A shift response, however, occurs when the listener redirects the conversation back to themselves, often by sharing something personal or related to the topic. One caveat: while shift responses can strengthen connections and build mutual understanding, they do risk overshadowing the speaker's moment if overused and should be employed thoughtfully and in moderation. Examples include phrases like "That reminds me of when I . . . " or "I've been through something similar." While these contributions can enrich the conversation, it's important to ensure the speaker still feels heard. Therefore, after sharing your insight, be sure to circle back to the other person, giving them space to elaborate or feel validated. This keeps the dialogue balanced and ensures both parties are genuinely listened to.

When two or more people in a conversation have space to share and be heard, the interaction feels comfortable and enriching. However, if one person dominates with too many shift responses, the others may feel overlooked. Similarly, if the listener only uses support responses without contributing their own thoughts, the conversation can become one-sided—more like a talk show interview or even an interrogation. As Derber explained, "The quality of any interaction depends on the tendencies of those involved to seek and share attention," adding, "Competition develops when people seek to focus attention mainly on themselves; cooperation occurs when the participants are willing and able to give and take."[34]

Mirroring and Labeling

Additional techniques for enhancing a leader's active listening come from an unexpected source: hostage negotiators. Chris Voss, a former FBI negotiator, offers simple yet powerful strategies he developed through years of high-stakes negotiations. Two of the most impactful techniques—*mirroring* and *labeling*—can help leaders foster deeper understanding, influence others, and strengthen relationships.[35]

Mirroring

Let's start with mirroring. In a conversation or negotiation, mirroring involves subtly repeating a few key words or phrases the other person has just said. This technique helps build rapport, shows that you're fully engaged, and encourages the other party to elaborate further. For example, if a colleague says, "I've been under a lot of pressure lately with this project," you might respond with, "A lot of pressure?

Tell me what's going on." This not only signals that you're actively listening but also invites them to dive deeper into their experience.

Mirroring can also extend to body language. For instance, if someone leans forward during a discussion, gently mirroring their posture can create a sense of alignment and mutual understanding. Similarly, matching the tone, volume, and pace of their speech can subtly reinforce a connection. The key is to reflect the other person's cues without overdoing it—this fosters trust and encourages open, more meaningful communication.

Labeling

Labeling, as we've discussed previously, is a simple yet powerful tool for building connection. Here, it involves recognizing and acknowledging the other person's emotions or perspective, helping to either ease negative feelings or reinforce positive ones. Using phrases like "It seems like . . ." or "It sounds like . . ." helps validate the other person's experience and show empathy. For example, if a team member says, "This new hybrid work model has been a real challenge for me," a leader might respond, "It sounds like you're struggling with the transition and could use some support." This shows attentiveness, builds trust, and invites further conversation.

Research shows that managers who listen effectively help employees feel more relaxed, self-aware of their strengths and weaknesses, and open to reflecting without defensiveness. These leaders also build trust, enhance job satisfaction, and boost team productivity.[36] Techniques like mirroring and labeling can help leaders establish rapport, ease tension, and create more productive dialogue.

Reviving the Lost Art of the Conversation

One of the fundamental principles of networking and building relationships is to give more than you take. Many people see conversations only as opportunities to get something for themselves. This is a mistake. As Adam Grant has written, "Success depends heavily on how we approach our interactions with other people. Every time we interact with another person at work, we have a choice to make: do we try to claim as much value as we can, or contribute value without worrying about what we receive in return?"[37]

Networking should be a chance for mutual benefit, where everyone involved gains value. It's an opportunity to show what you can offer—whether it's support, expertise, or connections—rather than focusing solely on what others can do for you. Approaching networking with a mindset of contribution fosters stronger, more meaningful relationships. "Whereas takers tend to be self-focused, evaluating what other people can offer them, givers are other-focused," explains Grant. "If you're a giver at work, you simply strive to be generous in sharing your time, energy, knowledge, skills, ideas, and connections with other people who can benefit from them."[38] Demonstrating how you can add value begins with asking questions like "How can I help?" or "How do you see me adding value?" When spoken sincerely, these simple yet impactful phrases not only demonstrate your willingness to contribute but also help build trust and rapport swiftly. By putting the focus on the other person's needs, you create a memorable impression and position yourself as someone generous and ready to offer support.

In today's hybrid work landscape—where face-to-face interactions compete with screens and shifting schedules—the way we connect has fundamentally changed. The traditional rhythms of office life have given way to a more fluid, often unpredictable dynamic. And while this evolution brings flexibility and autonomy, it also risks eroding the everyday social interactions that build trust, belonging, and community.

But there's good news: even in a hybrid world, meaningful connection is still within reach. In fact, it's more important than ever.

Cultivating Authentic Dialogue

Simple, authentic moments—whether they're coffee chats, spontaneous video calls, or quick Slack messages—can help rebuild the social capital that keeps teams resilient and people engaged.

So don't wait for the perfect moment or the ideal setup. Start small. Reach out. Talk to a colleague you don't usually interact with. Share a bit more than just project updates. It might feel awkward at first, but research shows that people consistently underestimate how positive and rewarding these interactions can be.[39]

In an ever-changing work environment, connection isn't just a nice-to-have—it's a foundation for thriving teams. One conversation at a time, you can help shape a more human, collaborative, and connected workplace.

In Chapter 18, we'll explore how to transform these relationships into a powerful engine for collaboration—united by a shared vision. When a team is grounded in trust and mutual understanding, it becomes truly unbreakable.

Chapter 18

Building Unbreakable Teams

It takes two flints to make a fire.

—Louisa May Alcott

Sweet Serendipity: The Origin of Nerds Candy

In the early 1980s, Bob Lambert, a seasoned marketing executive with a wealth of experience at industry giants like Nestlé and Quaker Oats, made a daring leap into entrepreneurship. He cofounded Marketing Edge, a boutique marketing firm that promised to fuse creativity with strategic insight to transform how brands connected with consumers. The risk was immense, but Lambert's knack for relationship building quickly paid off. Through his expansive network, Marketing Edge secured a game-changing client in 1984: Willy Wonka Candy, a playful and beloved brand inspired by Roald Dahl's whimsical tale *Charlie and the Chocolate Factory.*

At the time, Willy Wonka Candy, owned by Sunmark, was already known for its imaginative, movie-inspired creations such as Everlasting Gobstoppers. Yet the brand was looking to capture the attention of an increasingly competitive market and needed fresh ideas. Lambert and his team were tasked with creating something that would resonate with kids and stand out in the crowded candy aisle.

But despite countless brainstorming sessions, nothing seemed to click. Lambert knew they needed something extraordinary—something that embodied the same sense of magic and wonder as the Wonka

259

name itself. Little did he know, the breakthrough would come when he least expected it.

The moment of inspiration came during a visit to the Willy Wonka factory just outside of Chicago. While touring the busy production line with the Wonka brand manager, Lambert noticed something unusual: buckets filled with tiny, irregular white candy pebbles scattered beneath the machines. These weren't part of the finished products, but rather waste materials—discarded fragments from the candy-making process, known in the industry as "renderings."

Curious, Lambert asked, "What happens to these?"

"Nothing," the brand manager replied. "They're swept up and thrown away."

In that moment, Lambert had an epiphany. The discarded candy pebbles, once considered waste, had untapped potential. What if these tiny fragments could be repurposed into something entirely new? Something fun, colorful, and irresistible to kids?

The wheels of innovation started turning quickly. Lambert and the Willy Wonka team wasted no time, diving straight into experimentation with *enrobing*—the process of coating small pebbles with a vibrant candy shell to enhance both their visual appeal and taste. Once they perfected the production process, the team shifted their focus to branding.

After several rounds of brainstorming, they struck gold. The name "Nerds" was chosen—a cheeky, playful term that perfectly captured the quirky, mischievous spirit of the Wonka brand. But they didn't stop there. To make the product even more unique, they designed a signature box with two separate compartments—each filled with a different flavor of Nerds. This dual-flavor packaging gave kids the excitement of variety and a sense of control over their candy experience, further setting it apart from other candy products on the market.

The launch of Nerds in 1985 was nothing short of a phenomenon. Kids were drawn to the vibrant colors, the crunchy texture, and the endless flavor combinations. In an era dominated by traditional candies, Nerds offered something entirely new. The marketing campaign, which included a sweepstakes and collectible prizes (a nostalgic nod to Cracker Jack), only fueled the excitement.

The result? Nerds quickly became a cultural sensation. It was named Candy of the Year by the National Candy Wholesalers Association in 1985, a prestigious accolade that cemented its status as a household name. The success of Nerds didn't stop there. Over the years, the brand expanded into a wide range of products, from Nerds Ropes and Nerds Clusters to collectible Nerds Dolls—there was even a lucrative licensing deal for a Nerds cereal. Lambert's vision had come to life—what started as a waste product had transformed into a billion-dollar brand.[1]

Lambert's ingenuity, combined with his seamless collaboration with the team at Willy Wonka, demonstrates the incredible value of working together to unlock creativity and innovation. Their partnership reveals how sparks of brilliance can fly when diverse minds come together, each contributing their unique perspective to solve challenges. The story behind Nerds isn't just about a candy; it's a powerful reminder that the most revolutionary ideas often emerge when people unite with a shared vision. It all starts with one simple question: *what if?* It's in these moments of collective curiosity that truly groundbreaking concepts are born.

Building Alignment Through Clarity and Purpose

To effectively manage a team, a leader must establish a clear vision and ensure it is communicated consistently to all stakeholders involved. Transparency is key—leaders should articulate both specific goals and expectations, as employees cannot read their mind. This involves not only outlining the vision but also specifying the approach they expect the team to follow, along with a realistic timeline for achieving the objectives.

A leader who hoards information or lacks transparency can hinder a team's success by creating an environment of distrust, confusion, and disengagement. When team members are kept in the dark or feel excluded from critical knowledge, they struggle to make informed decisions, collaborate effectively, or align their efforts with broader goals. This lack of transparency can lead to misunderstandings, inefficiencies, and missed opportunities, as team members may duplicate efforts or work at cross-purposes. Additionally, withholding information undermines morale, as it signals a lack of trust and openness, which in turn diminishes motivation, creativity, and commitment. For a team to succeed, leaders must foster an open flow of communication, empowering members with the knowledge they need to contribute fully and collaborate effectively.

A famous example of a leader intentionally withholding crucial information occurred during the reign of the Roman emperor Caligula. Serving from CE 37 until his assassination in CE 41, Caligula famously posted newly created Roman laws on high columns throughout the empire, with the text written in such small letters that ordinary citizens could not read them. This deliberate obfuscation was not a mere oversight—it was a calculated tactic to maintain control.

By ensuring that the laws were inaccessible to the average person, Caligula left the Roman populace in a constant state of fear and uncertainty, unsure whether they were unknowingly breaking the law or committing a crime. This created an atmosphere of paranoia, where citizens lived in constant dread of unknowingly offending the emperor's unpredictable legal changes. The tactic was effective in keeping the people powerless and submissive, as they could never be certain if they were in compliance. By creating a climate of confusion and distrust, Caligula reinforced his grip on power, manipulating the populace through their fear of the unknown.[2]

This approach mirrors the effects of poor communication in modern organizations. When leadership fails to clearly communicate the company's goals and objectives, employees are left confused and unsure of what's expected of them. Without clarity, they may struggle to align their efforts with the company's mission, leading to inefficiencies and missed opportunities.

Much like Roman citizens who lived in fear of unknowingly breaking the law due to unclear or constantly changing rules, employees may feel uncertain about their priorities. For example, if a marketing team isn't sure whether to focus on social media or content marketing, some may waste time on outdated tasks, while others move in a different direction.

This lack of communication breeds resentment, anxiety, and disengagement. Employees may feel like they're doing their best, but without a clear understanding of success, they're left questioning whether their efforts matter. Over time, this uncertainty leads to frustration and stifles innovation, as employees hesitate to take initiative for fear of missing the mark.

Gallup research shows that 84 percent of US employees now work in "matrixed" environments—collaborating across multiple departments or reporting to several managers, a dynamic often referred to as *multiteaming*. In such work environments, effective collaboration and teamwork become not only more challenging but also, arguably, far more critical to success. The rise of distributed work—where employees operate from diverse locations like home, coworking spaces, or while traveling—only adds to the difficulty, making effective communication and coordination even more critical.[3] Sadly, while 97 percent of employees and executives believe a lack of alignment affects their work,[4] only 62 percent of workers feel well-informed about how their company is doing against its goals, strategies, and tactics.[5]

A study published in the *Harvard Business Review* revealed that since the early 2000s, the time that managers and employees spend on collaborative activities has increased by more than 50 percent. In some companies, employees can now spend up to 80 percent of their time communicating with colleagues.[6] For this reason, achieving *organizational clarity*—ensuring a clear and shared understanding of the company's goals, roles, priorities, and processes—is essential at every level of the organization. This alignment helps foster cohesion, streamlines decision-making, and drives collective success. As Amy Edmondson aptly puts it, "Distributed work is making us realize we have to be more deliberately—more proactively—open. We have to be explicit in sharing our ideas, questions, and concerns, because we can't just overhear what's happening in the next cubicle."[7]

Understanding the dynamics of a team, as well as the individual personalities that comprise it, is also essential for a leader. I spoke with Dr. Marcus Robinson, a leading expert on team dynamics in the corporate world with nearly three decades of experience, and asked him why diversity in the workforce is crucial for effective leadership. "There's a paradox to diversity," Robinson explained, "because on one level we are like no one else, and then at another level, we are just like everybody else. Diversity is about race, ethnicity, and gender. It's also about age and differing abilities. It's about sexual orientation and gender identity. But it doesn't stop there, because it's also about a person's education and background, their geographic location, their role, function and status within an organization. These are all different dimensions of diversity, as well as someone's personality, their communication style, their management style, as well as the culture—the mythos and ethos—of an organization. These are all components of diversity in the human ecology of work now."[8]

The realization that most people share more common ground than differences can empower a leader to manage their team with greater empathy and effectiveness. Robinson explains, "Diversity is like the circles in a Venn diagram. And to the extent that there's no overlap in our circles, then there can be difficulty in communicating across differences. But as we find spaces of overlap, where we can stand on common ground together, this is where we can build and continue to grow the overlap until there's sufficient space for us to belong to each other and include one another in an equitable way."[9]

Indra Nooyi takes the idea even further, pointing out how diversity not only benefits a team but also the entire organization. In a speech to the Economic Club of Washington, DC, the former PepsiCo CEO put it like this: "The world we do business in is changing ever so fast. The social environment we operate in is changing, too. We need to make sure that as good companies, we reflect the society we live in. Diversity and inclusion has to be taken to a new level. It needs to become multitalented, multicultural, multiregional, multiethnic, but most importantly, multigenerational. No group in society can or should be excluded."[10] To foster effective collaboration and manage team dynamics, leaders must understand two key dimensions of human motivation: *agency* and *communion*.

Agency refers to the drive to define one's identity, achieve personal goals, and exert control over one's life. It's characterized by traits like competence, assertiveness, and independence, which empower individuals to take initiative and influence their environment. For example, a team member motivated by agency might seek career advancement, master new skills, or aspire to take on a leadership role. These actions reflect a desire for recognition, autonomy, and achievement.

In psychological terms, agency emphasizes self-confidence, decision-making, and the ability to act proactively—qualities often seen in leaders, entrepreneurs, and high-achieving professionals. For individuals motivated by agency, leaders can foster autonomy by assigning challenging projects that allow personal decision-making and goal setting. Additionally, regular feedback and recognition of accomplishments help reinforce their sense of competence.

By contrast, communion centers on the desire to connect with others, belong to a group, and contribute to its well-being. It is driven by qualities like empathy, cooperativeness, and benevolence, which foster social harmony and mutual support. Team members driven by communion are motivated by connection, empathy, and a strong sense of belonging. They prioritize building meaningful relationships, supporting others, and contributing to the team's overall well-being and success. For instance, a communion-oriented individual might volunteer to help without being asked, offer assistance to a colleague in need, or put the team's goals ahead of their own personal interests. This dimension reflects the deep human need for belonging, social connection, and emotional reciprocity. For team members driven by communion, leaders should promote collaboration and empathy by encouraging teamwork, open communication, and mutual support.

Research has consistently shown that, in general, boys and men tend to focus more on agency strivings, while girls and women are more oriented toward communion strivings.[11] Effective leadership requires understanding the balance of these two key dimensions and adjusting one's approach accordingly. Kevin Kruse, the best-selling author of *Great Leaders Have No Rules*, puts it like this: "Good leaders know each person. They know their strengths, their limitations, their styles. And so you start there. The classic saying goes something like this: the average manager plays checkers, treating team members as mere pieces on the board, while great leaders are playing chess. Different pieces have different names and they move in different ways. Great leaders take a strengths-based approach to their leadership and try to match people to things that they're going to be great at and that give them energy."[12]

Leaders must be adaptable, understanding that individual motivations can shift over time, requiring an evolving approach. This is why building trust and maintaining strong connections with your team members is essential. By recognizing and balancing both agency and communion, leaders can foster a dynamic, engaged team where individual success aligns with collective synergy to drive performance.

Take a moment to assess your team's motivations. Some may value autonomy and challenge, seeking independence, while others may prioritize connection and collaboration. By recognizing these differences, you can adjust your leadership style: offering autonomy to those driven by independence and fostering teamwork for those motivated by connection. What small changes can you make to support both individual growth and team unity? By aligning your approach on these motivations, you can boost personal engagement and enhance overall collaboration.

Scaling the Heights: How Patagonia Built a Purposeful Workforce

Yvon Chouinard, the founder of Patagonia, offers a compelling example of how steadfast values and a strong sense of purpose can shape a successful, values-driven organization. What began as a supplier of rock-climbing gear has evolved into a global leader in sustainable outdoor apparel, thanks to Chouinard's unwavering commitment to his principles. From the outset, Chouinard built Patagonia on a foundation of quality, sustainability, integrity, and social responsibility—principles he refused to compromise, even in the face of pressure to prioritize short-term profits.

At the core of Patagonia's success is its unwavering focus on people. Chouinard recognized that an organization's true strength is rooted in its people. In his book *Let My People Go Surfing*, he emphasized the importance of employees becoming part of a team committed to making a meaningful impact. "We're not in isolation," Chouinard wrote. "The problems we're facing now . . . can only be solved by people working together and staying tough together."[13]

This philosophy has shaped Patagonia's distinctive culture, one built on autonomy, respect, and trust. For instance, employees are encouraged to make decisions that align with the company's core values—such as environmental sustainability and ethical sourcing—without needing constant approval from higher-ups. This autonomy fosters a deep sense of ownership and commitment to the company's broader mission.

One notable example is Patagonia's "Let My People Go Surfing" policy, which allows employees to take time off to surf, hike, or engage in outdoor activities that reflect the company's values.[14] This freedom encourages a work-life balance while reinforcing the company's commitment to outdoor activism. Additionally, the company's decision to donate 1 percent of sales to environmental causes is a clear reflection of the trust and respect they place in their team to uphold these values in every aspect of their work.[15]

Patagonia's success is not just reflected in its financial growth—the company is currently valued at more than $3 billion—but in its ability to remain steadfast in its mission to creating lasting change. In 2023, a poll by Axios Harris ranked Patagonia as the most reputable brand in the United States, a recognition that highlights Chouinard's steady leadership over five decades.[16] By connecting his workforce to the brand's core values and empowering them to act on those values, Chouinard has cultivated a highly engaged organization that continues to thrive, driven by a shared purpose.

Applying the Six-of-One Rule in Leadership

Ron Howard is widely regarded as one of the most accomplished and successful figures in Hollywood. Howard began his career as a child actor in 1959, portraying Opie on the iconic television series *The Andy Griffith Show*. Years later, he found continued success as an adult, playing Richie Cunningham on the beloved sitcom *Happy Days*. Howard transitioned to directing in 1978 and went on to helm such classic films as *Splash*, *Apollo 13*, and *A Beautiful Mind*, for which he won an Academy Award for best director.

When asked who taught him the most valuable lessons about acting, Howard pointed to his father, explaining how he "taught me the simplest version of the Method—Stanislavski's technique. It was all about putting yourself into the character and the situation and understanding it on a personal, emotional level as much as you could and then executing on the written material through that lens and filter."[17] Years later when he transitioned to the director's chair, Howard realized it would require him to employ a different, more advanced set of leadership skills. "I learned a lot more about filmmaking and taking responsibility for an entire production," he said, adding, "I've always had an ability to create an environment where people could flourish."[18]

As Howard developed his leadership approach over the years, he came up with a principle that he used when overseeing various multimillion-dollar movie projects—something he called the *six-of-one rule*. Howard's theory suggested that, in many cases, different approaches can achieve similar results, and it's the experience and growth along the way that truly matter.

Howard explained how he employs the six-of-one rule in his work:

> If I'm working with somebody—whether it's an actor, writer, cinematographer, editor, composer, key production person—who wants to approach a scene in a certain way, not the way I visualized it, I hear that person out on why. Then I ask myself, "What do I need for the scene? Does this conflict with that? Support that?" If it does achieve everything that my idea would have or more, I say, "Yes, great idea." If it's gray—six of one, half a dozen of another—I always try to go that artist's way, because you get an organic X factor in the execution. They're not responding to the director; they're expressing themselves.[19]

269

Building Unbreakable Teams

Another reason Howard embraces the six-of-one rule with his team is that by saying yes often, he establishes a culture of trust and openness. This makes it easier to say no when necessary, ensuring that he can overrule a collaborator's suggestion without damaging the relationship.

Corporate leaders can apply the six-of-one rule by recognizing that, in many decision-making situations, there is rarely a single "right" choice; multiple approaches can lead to similar outcomes. Embracing this mindset enables leaders to foster flexibility and innovation within their teams, shifting the focus from a rigid "the boss is always right" mentality to one centered on receptivity, experimentation, and learning. Rather than fixating on minor differences in strategy or process, leaders can empower team members to explore diverse ideas, trusting that the collective effort will drive meaningful results. This approach not only boosts creativity and morale but also helps teams avoid decision paralysis, promoting quicker action and a focus on progress over perfection.

Disagree and Commit: A Tool for Stronger Decision-Making

Great leaders recognize the importance of fostering an environment where every team member's ideas are heard and valued. However, they also understand that in fast-paced environments, decisions must ultimately be made to maintain momentum. Whether driven by timelines, budget constraints, or other practical limitations, leaders must know when to move from discussion to action. Striking the right balance between inclusivity and decisiveness is key to keeping projects on track and ensuring the team remains focused on achieving the organization's goals.

One effective way to strike this balance is by embracing the *disagree-and-commit rule*, pioneered by Jeff Bezos for his teams at Amazon. At Amazon, Bezos encourages his team members to voice their differing opinions openly during decision-making processes. "Most decisions should probably be made with somewhere around 70 percent of the information you wish you had," notes Bezos. "If you wait for 90 percent, in most cases, you're probably being slow."[20] When it's time to make a decision, even if the group hasn't reached full consensus, Bezos applies the disagree-and-commit rule. "This phrase will save a lot of time," says Bezos. "If you have conviction about a particular direction, even when there's no agreement, it's helpful to say, 'Look, I know we disagree on this, but will you gamble with me on it? Disagree and commit?'"[21]

By asking this question and gaining commitment to move forward from those who disagree, Bezos helps prevent the all-too-common "meeting after the meeting" scenario, where unresolved issues linger and slow down progress. His approach ensures that once a decision is made, everyone—regardless of their initial feelings—fully commits to executing the plan. This not only fosters a sense of unity and focus but also eliminates the potential for any "I told you so" finger-pointing if things don't unfold as expected; the team collectively owns the outcome. "I 'disagree and commit' all the time," says Bezos.[22]

As a leader, you can embrace the disagree-and-commit strategy by ensuring that the voices of every team member are heard during discussions. This approach encourages the sharing of diverse viewpoints, enabling your team to voice concerns, ideas, and alternative solutions. Once the discussion is concluded and a decision is made, the team is then primed to fully commit and align behind it.

By balancing constructive disagreement with decisive action, leaders foster an environment where team members feel safe to voice their opinions, yet understand the need to move forward together once a decision is made. This balance not only ensures efficient and effective implementation of decisions but also drives organizational success. Through the disagree-and-commit principle, teams

Building Unbreakable Teams

are encouraged to innovate and solve problems while maintaining cohesion and a unified sense of purpose and direction.

For a leader, achieving team alignment is crucial to an organization's success. When alignment is strong, it prevents chaos and dysfunction, paving the way for progress. An aligned team shares a common purpose, grounded in shared values, a unified mission, and a strategic road map that everyone understands and supports. While alignment can be challenging, it starts with a leader who defines a clear and compelling strategy that resonates with the company's culture and vision.

However, alignment alone isn't enough to unlock your team's full potential. To drive meaningful progress, you must also cultivate a culture of open communication where every voice is heard and valued. This openness creates synergy, enabling individual strengths to merge into something greater than the sum of its parts. In such an environment, creativity thrives, fueling innovation and growth.

But these sparks of innovation can only take hold if you, as a leader, build trust and empower your team to push beyond their comfort zones and solve problems collaboratively. When you believe in your team's potential and foster this dynamic, the results can be extraordinary: transforming open dialogue and collaboration into powerful, impactful outcomes.

Afterword

One year before his death at the age of 40, as the story goes, Franz Kafka—the introspective, unmarried, and childless German-speaking Jewish writer from Prague—was walking through a park in Berlin when he encountered a young girl in tears. Turns out, she had lost her favorite doll. Seeing her distress, Kafka offered his help, and together they searched for the doll. But despite their efforts, they had no luck. Needless to say, the girl was devastated.

That's when Kafka made a promise. He told the girl to meet him in the park the next day, and they would continue looking. When they met again and the doll was still missing, Kafka gave the girl something unexpected: a letter "written" by the doll. In the letter, the doll explained that she had gone on an adventure, encouraging the girl not to cry because she would send letters to tell her all about her travels. And this wasn't a one-time gesture. Kafka continued to meet with the girl, reading her beautifully crafted letters from the doll, each one describing whimsical adventures from far-off lands. The girl, completely captivated, felt connected to her doll through Kafka's words, even though the doll was gone.

Finally, after many months, Kafka returned with a doll. But it was not the same one the girl had lost. At first, the girl hesitated and was resistant, noting that this new doll looked different. In response, Kafka handed the girl another letter from the doll. In it, the doll explained, "My travels have changed me." Gradually, over time, the girl accepted the new doll, realizing that while it wasn't exactly the same, it still carried the essence of what she had once loved. This new version of the doll eventually became part of the girl's life, and she found happiness once again.

Years later, after Kafka had passed away, the girl, now an adult, found a tiny note inside the doll, written by Kafka. It read: "Everything you love will probably be lost, but in the end, love will return in another way."[1]

Kafka's story is one of profound change. It teaches us that nothing in life remains as it is. Change—whether in the form of loss, transformation, or growth—is an inevitable force we must all encounter and experience. Yet, as Kafka subtly revealed through his letters, it's not the change itself that defines us but how we respond to it. The lesson here is clear: Change and growth aren't to be feared; they are opportunities to be embraced.

The journey to becoming a more effective leader and communicator unfolds daily, over months and years, shaped by each conversation, presentation, and meeting. Just as the doll returned transformed, so too are we continually evolving—our relationships, experiences, abilities, and even our sense of self. The challenge is to meet these moments of change fearlessly, with resilience and grace, allowing them to shape us into a fuller version of who we are ultimately meant to be.

In your life and career, you will undoubtedly face moments of uncertainty, loss, and reinvention. But just as Kafka's doll adapted to its changing circumstances, so too can you. As a leader, you must rise to meet each moment in order to shape it. Let the insights and lessons in this book serve as a personal guide, offering you both clarity and direction. And remember, *Synergy and Sparks* is more than a one-time read—it's a resource you can return to again and again, providing ongoing support as you continue to evolve and refine your communication and leadership skills. Remind yourself of the mantra highlighted in this book: *focus on progress, not perfection.* Give yourself the grace and space to make mistakes and occasionally fall short of your hopes and expectations, despite your best efforts. Be kind to yourself, and when possible, offer that same grace to those around you.

Use the tools and insights in this book to chart your course and navigate the challenges ahead, to not only help you thrive during times of change but also actively shape your future with passion and purpose. As every great leader knows, the first step to getting somewhere is deciding you're not going to stay where you are. The journey begins now, and the path you take is yours to define.

Get out there and be amazing. Let your spark light up the world.

Notes

Introduction

1. Katherine A. Karl, Joy V. Peluchette, and Navid Aghakhani, "Virtual Work Meetings During the COVID-19 Pandemic: The Good, Bad, and Ugly," *National Library of Medicine*, June 2022.
2. Jim Harter and Ryan Pendell, "Global Engagement Falls for the Second Time Since 2009," gallup.com, April 23, 2025.
3. Kritika Langhauser, "HubSpot's 2023 Hybrid Work Report Uncovers Connection as Key Theme Driving the Future of Work," hubspot.com, January 30, 2023.
4. National Alliance on Mental Illness, "The 2024 NAMI Workplace Mental Health Poll," January 9, 2024.
5. Ben Wigert, Jim Harter, and Sangeeta Agrawal, "The Future of the Office Has Arrived: It's Hybrid," Gallup, October 9, 2023.
6. Russ Fradin, "The Surprising Reason Why the Majority of Employees Are Ready to Quit Their Jobs," hrdailyadvisor.blr.com, April 15, 2019.
7. Harter and Pendell, "Global Engagement Falls for the Second Time Since 2009."
8. Jim Harter, "U.S. Employee Engagement Inches Up Slightly After 11-Year Low," gallup.com, July 26, 2024.
9. Harter and Pendell, "Global Engagement Falls for the Second Time Since 2009."
10. Liz Elting, "Managers Don't Want to Hire Gen-Z Workers, Citing a Lack of Soft Skills—Survey Says," forbes.com, December 23, 2024.
11. Ibid.
12. Ana Djurovic, "22 Inspiring Leadership Statistics for a Successful 2023," goremotely.net/blog, March 7, 2023.

277

13. Declan Donnellan, *The Actor and the Target* (Theatre Communications Group, 2006), 2.
14. Nicolo Bicego, "Are We All Actors? Erving Goffman's Analysis of Social Interactions," thecollector.com, July 3, 2024.
15. William Egginton, *How the World Became a Stage: Presence, Theatricality, and the Question of Modernity* (SUNY Press, 2002), 21.
16. Nicolo Bicego, "Are We All Actors?"
17. Cofer Black, "American Manhunt: Osama bin Laden," episode 1, netflix .com, May 16, 2025.
18. Keld Jensen, "Intelligence Is Overrated: What You Really Need to Succeed," *Forbes*, April 12, 2012.
19. Marcel Schwantes, "Warren Buffett Said What Separates Successful People from Everyone Else Comes Down to Three Words," *Inc. Magazine*, October 31, 2024.

Chapter 1: The Stagecraft of Leadership

1. Constantin Stanislavski, *An Actor's Handbook* (Theatre Arts, 1963), 137.
2. Ken Howard, *Act Natural: How to Speak to Any Audience* (Random House, 2003), 189.
3. James J. Murphy, "Demosthenes: Greek Statesman and Orator," *Encyclopedia Britannica*, www.britannica.com, July 20, 1998.
4. Jesse Walker, "Arthur Penn, RIP," *Reason Magazine*, September 9, 2010.
5. Polly Dunbar, "How Laurence Olivier Gave Margaret Thatcher the Voice That Went Down in History," *Daily Mail*, October 29, 2011.
6. Constantin Stanislavski, *An Actor Prepares*, 334.
7. Steve Bartlett, LinkedIn, September 2024.
8. Arnaud Chevallier, Frédéric Dalsace, and Jean Louis Barsoux, "The Art of Asking Smarter Questions," *Harvard Business Review*, May–June 2024.
9. Bill Wilder, "Don't Build a Ship; Create a Yearning for the Seas," industryweek.com, November 7, 2013.
10. John Pitonyak and Rob DeSimone, "How to Engage Frontline Managers," gallup.com, August 9, 2022.

11. Robin Roberts, "Robin Roberts Teaches Effective and Authentic Communication" Master Class, March 31, 2020.

12. Tasha Eurich, "Working with People Who Aren't Self-Aware," *Harvard Business Review*, October 19, 2018.

13. Heather V. MacArthur, "Harnessing Our Brainpower to Navigate Uncertainty," forbes.com, May 28, 2020.

14. David Dunning, "The Dunning-Kruger Effect: On Being Ignorant of One's Own Ignorance," *Advances in Experimental Social Psychology* 44 (2011): 247–96.

15. Steven Bartlett, "Gymshark CEO: How I Built a $1.5 Billion Business at 19!" *The Diary of a CEO* podcast, December 27, 2021.

16. Ben Francis, "Why I Stepped Down as Gymshark CEO," gymshark.com, 2020.

17. Jon Robinson, "Gymshark Founder Reveals Reasons Behind Stepping Down as CEO," *Insider Media*, May 14, 2020.

18. Elizabeth Chuck, "Black Men Arrested at Philadelphia Starbucks Say They Feared for Their Lives," *NBC News*, April 19, 2018.

19. Kevin Johnson, "Starbucks CEO: Reprehensible Outcome in Philadelphia Incident," Starbucks.com, April 14.

Chapter 2: Solving the Attention Dilemma

1. Lindsey Leake, "17 Years of Your Adult Life May Be Spent Online. These Expert Tips May Help Curb Your Screen Time," fortune.com, March 6, 2024.

2. Nir Eyal, *Indistractable: How to Control Your Attention and Choose Your Life* (BenBella Books, 2019), 13.

3. Jonathan Haidt, *The Anxious Generation* (Penguin Press, 2024), 54.

4. Ibid., 227.

5. Kate Murphy, *You're Not Listening* (Celadon Books, 2021), 174.

6. Haidt, *The Anxious Generation*, 34.

7. Michelle Delgado, "From 'the Brick' to the iPhone, the Cellphone Celebrates 50 Years," *Smithsonian Magazine*, April 23, 2023.

8. Felix Richter, "Charted: There Are More Mobile Phones Than People in the World," World Economic Forum, April 11, 2023.

9. Haidt, *The Anxious Generation*, 34.
10. Gloria Mark, *Attention Span: A Groundbreaking Way to Restore Balance, Happiness and Productivity* (Hanover Press, 2023), 143.
11. Johann Hari, *Stolen Focus: Why You Can't Pay Attention and How to Think Deeply Again* (Crown, 2022), 37.
12. Adrian Ward, "The Mere Presence of Your Smartphone Reduces Brain Power, Study Shows," *UT News*, June 26, 2017.
13. Catherine Price, "Putting Down Your Phone May Help You Live Longer," *New York Times*, April 24, 2019.
14. Madeline Holcombe, "Your phone may not be the problem when it comes to distraction, study says," cnn.com, March 28, 2025.
15. Haidt, *The Anxious Generation*, 56.
16. Ibid., 122.
17. Ibid., 135.
18. Mark, *Attention Span*, 36.
19. Hari, *Stolen Focus*.
20. Gloria Mark, gloriamark.com, November 4, 2024.
21. L. P. McAvinue, F. M. O'Keeffe, D. McMackin, and I. H. Robertson, "Sustaining Attention to Simple Tasks: A Meta-Analytic Review of the Effects of Age and Task Demand," *Psychological Bulletin*, 141, no. 4 (2015): 946–68.
22. Mark, *Attention Span*, 46.
23. Hari, *Stolen Focus*, 41.
24. Chryssa Themelis, "Digital Well-Being: Are Devices Overwhelming or Extending Our Minds?" *AACE Review*, December 10, 2018.
25. Florida State University, "Cell Phone Notifications May Be Driving You to Distraction," *Science Daily*, July 9, 2015.
26. Lisa Quast, "Want to Be More Productive? Stop Multi-Tasking," *Forbes*, February 10, 2017.
27. Mark, *Attention Span*, 42.
28. Ibid., 112.
29. Ashley Lee, "Broadway Star Patti LuPone Seizes Phone from Texting Audience Member, Threatens to Quit Theater," *The Hollywood Reporter*, July 9, 2015.
30. Hari, *Stolen Focus*, 41.

31. Mark, *Attention Span*, 100.

32. Shani Murray, "Regaining Focus in a World of Digital Distractions," UCI Department of Informatics, January 26, 2023.

33. Bailey Johnson, "Study: 3-Second Distractions Double Workplace Errors," cbsnew.com, January 15, 2013.

34. Mark, *Attention Span*, 111.

35. Bill Gates, "Mosquitos, Malaria and Education," ted.com, 2008.

36. Todd B. Kashdan, David J. Disabato, Fallon R. Goodman, and Carl Naughton, "The Five Dimensions of Curiosity," *Harvard Business Review*, September/October 2018.

37. Karen Wilson and James H. Korn, "Attention During Lectures: Beyond Ten Minutes," Saint Louis University, May 1, 2008.

38. N. Nurmi and S. Pakarinen, "Virtual Meeting Fatigue: Exploring the Impact of Virtual Meetings on Cognitive Performance and Active Versus Passive Fatigue," *Journal of Occupational Health Psychology* 28, no. 6 (2023): 343–62.

39. Carmine Gallo, "Scientists Pinpoint Exact-Moment People Lose Interest in a Presentation," *Inc. Magazine*, February 27, 2024.

40. Barbara Field, "The Health Benefits of Humor and Laughter," verywellmind .com, January 30, 2024.

41. Constantin Stanislavski, *An Actor's Handbook* (Theatre Arts, 1963), 182.

42. Kay Vandette, "Surprise Can Be an Effective Tool in Impacting Change," earth.com, April 5, 2018.

43. Pierre Baldi, "Bayesian Surprise Attracts Human Attention," *National Library of Medicine*, May 1, 2010.

44. Taryn Hillin, "Science Explains Why Surprise Brings Us Pleasure," splinter.com, April 1, 2015.

45. Interview over Zoom with David Goldrake and the author, January 7, 2025.

Chapter 3: Thriving During Uncertainty

1. Email correspondence with Frank Evers, 2019.

2. Interview with Frank Evers, February 2019.

3. Nacho De Marco, "Soft Skills Are Dead—Long Live 'Skills,'" fastcompany.com, September 13, 2024.

4. Jonathan Haidt, *The Anxious Generation* (Penguin Press, 2024), 177.

5. Michael Weiss, "Where Change Management Fails," Robert Half Management Resources, February 3, 2016.

6. Jim Harter, "U.S. Employee Engagement Inches Up Slightly After 11-Year Low," gallup.com, July 26, 2024.

7. From a conversation with Michael Clayton McCarthy, 2015.

8. Cyril Delarama, "Digital Transformation Is Racing Ahead and No Industry Is Immune," *Harvard Business Review*, June 19, 2017.

9. Shobhit Seth, "BlackBerry: A Story of Constant Success and Failure," www.investopedia.com, April 14, 2024.

10. Stuart Heritage, "The Rise and Fall of the BlackBerry," *Paris Tech Review*, October 15, 2023.

11. Amit Varma, "How Nokia, Blackberry, and Kodak Fell Behind: Timeless Lessons on Adaptation, Bold Decisions, and Innovation," LinkedIn, September 9, 2024.

12. Jacquie McNish, "The Rise and Fall of BlackBerry," *Intelligencer*, January 5, 2016.

13. Raoul Davis, "How Ego Tanks Branding and Marketing Professionals' Progress and Jeopardizes Companies," forbes.com, October 23, 2017.

14. Arnaud Chevallier, Frédéric Dalsace and Jean Louis Barsoux, "The Art of Asking Smarter Questions," *Harvard Business Review*, May-June, 2024.

15. Mark Murphy, "Leadership Styles Are Often Why CEOs Get Fired," forbes.com, July 15, 2016.

16. Elizabeth Kübler-Ross, ekrfoundation.org, December 15, 2024.

17. Gu Zhenjing and Supat Chupradit, "Impact of Employees' Workplace Environment on Employees' Performance: A Multi-Mediation Model," National Library of Medicine, *PubMed Central*, May 13, 2022.

18. Daisy Auger-Dominguez, "Finding Joy as a Manager—Even on Bad Days," *Harvard Business Review*, August 22, 2024.

19. Klaus Schwab, "Future of Jobs Report," World Economic Forum, 2020.

20. Jessica Stillman, "Einstein and Adam Grant Agree: The Puzzle Principle Will Make You Instantly Smarter," *Inc. Magazine*, January 6, 2025.

21. Neil Mulac, "Del Close's Improv Philosophy: A Relevance Beyond Improvisers," Everything Cinema Productions, May 22, 2023.

22. Naina Dhingra and Bill Schaninger, *The Search for Purpose at Work* podcast, June 3, 2021.

23. Thomas Frank, "Three Cheers for George Scialabba," *The Baffler*, October 2015.

24. Walter Isaacson, "How Steve Jobs' Love of Simplicity Fueled a Design Revolution," *Smithsonian Magazine*, September 2012.

25. Sergey Brin and Larry Page, "Founders' IPO Letter," August 18, 2004.

26. Ibid.

27. Ibid.

28. Jennie Weber, "Retail Media at the Center of CES," *The CMO* podcast, Episode 327, January 29, 2025.

29. Constantin Stanislavski, *An Actor Prepares* (Theatre Arts, 1936), 43.

Chapter 4: Boosting Confidence and Maintaining Credibility

1. Arwa Mahdawi, "What the Chaotic Launch of Tesla's Cybertruck Tells Us About Elon Musk," *The Guardian*, November 26, 2019.

2. Mark Sweney, "Cybertruck: Tesla Unveils New Pickup Truck but Windows Break During Demo," *The Guardian*, November 22, 2019.

3. Mahdawi, "What the Chaotic Launch of Tesla's Cybertruck Tells Us About Elon Musk." *The Guardian*, November 26, 2019.

4. *Joe Rogan Experience*, episode 1470, May 7, 2020.

5. Patrick Carroll, Pablos Brinol, Richard E. Petty, and Jed Ketcham, "Feeling Prepared Increases Confidence in Any Accessible Thoughts Affecting Evaluation Unrelated to the Original Domain of Preparation," *Journal of Experimental Social Psychology* 89 (July 10, 2020).

6. Kate Murphy, *You're Not Listening* (Celadon Books, 2021), 121.

7. Ibid., 56.

8. John Koetsier, "Why Every Amazon Meeting Has At Least 1 Empty Chair," *Inc. Magazine*, April 5, 2018.

9. New York Film Academy, "Stanislavski In 7 Steps: Better Understanding Stanislavski's 7 Questions," December 2, 2105.

10. Elaine Bernalyn S. Cercado, "The Formula to Radiate Confidence," LinkedIn.com, November 22, 2014.

11. Alexandre Heeren, "Assessing Public Speaking Fear with the Short Form of the Personal Report of Confidence as a Speaker Scale: Confirmatory Factor Analyses Among a French-Speaking Community Sample," National Library of Medicine, May 3, 2013.

12. Taylor Nicioli, "Rejection Therapy Is Trending on TikTok. Here's What Experts Have To Say About It," cnn.com, October 17, 2024.

13. Minda Zetlin, "A World-Famous Neuroscientist Says This 1 Mindset Is the Key to Happiness and Wealth," *Inc. Magazine*, October 31, 2024.

14. Marney A. White, "What the Yerkes-Dodson Law Says About Stress and Performance," healthline.com, October 20, 2020.

15. Kevin Cokley, "It's Time to Reconceptualize What 'Imposter Syndrome' Means for People of Color," *Harvard Business Review*, March 14, 2024.

16. D. M. Bravata et al., "Prevalence, Predictors, and Treatment of Impostor Syndrome: Systematic Review," *Journal of General Internal Medicine* 35, no. 4 (2020): 1252–1275.

17. Matt Hussey, "A Brief History of Imposter Syndrome," Medium, February 13, 2024.

18. Emily Moskal, "Physicians Experience Imposter Syndrome More Often Than Other U.S. Workers," med.standford.edu, September 15, 2022.

19. Alvin Powell, "Study: Doctor Burnout Costs Health Care System $4.6 Billion a Year," *The Harvard Gazette*, July 12, 2019.

20. Brené Brown, "10 Life-Changing Quotes from Brené Brown," Medium, March 11, 2022.

21. Lee Strasberg, *Old Friends, New Friends*, episode 201; interview with Fred Rogers, August 1, 1980.

22. Julia Cameron, *The Artist's Way: A Spiritual Path to Higher Creativity* (Tarcher, 1992).

23. Carmine Gallo, "A Long-Time Apple Designer Reveals Steve Jobs's 6-Step Rehearsal Process He Used For Every Presentation," *Inc. Magazine*, October 8, 2018.

24. Mel Robbins, *The Let Them Theory* (Hay House, 2024), 63.

25. Cindy Mason, "The Science of Physiological Sigh: Insights from Huberman Lab," *Psych Solutions*, October 2, 2023.

Chapter 5: Elevating Your Leadership Impact

1. "Michael Bay Movie Box Office Results," boxofficemojo.com, November 18, 2024.

2. Nick Morgan, "Michael Bay Melts Down—And Everyone's Worst Speaking Fear Is Realized," Forbes.com, January 7, 2014.

3. Konstantin O. Tskhay, Rebecca Zhu, and Nicholas O. Rule, "Perceptions of Charisma from Thin Slices of Behavior Predict Leadership Prototypicality Judgments," *The Leadership Quarterly* 26, no. 4 (August 2017): 555–562.

4. Ibid.

5. Nicholas Rule, Anne Krendl, Zorana Ivcevic, and Nalini Ambady, "Accuracy and Consensus in Judgments of Trustworthiness from Faces: Behavioral And Neural Correlates," *National Library of Medicine*, March 2013.

6. Rob Capps, "First Impressions: The Science of Meeting People," Wired, November 20, 2012.

7. Lee Strasberg, *Old Friends, New Friends*, episode 201; interview with Fred Rogers, August 1, 1980.

8. Quintilian, "Institutio Oratoria," *The Orator's Education*, vol. IV, book, VI, chapter 3 (Loeb Classical Library Edition, 1920).

9. Neil deGrasse Tyson, "Neil deGrasse Tyson Teaches Scientific Thinking and Communication," Master Class, 2020.

10. Susan Goldin-Meadow, "Expert Tips on Using Gestures to Think and Talk More Effectively," psych.co, September 25, 2024.

11. Tim David, *Magic Words: The Science and Secrets Behind Seven Words That Motivate, Engage, and Influence* (Prentice Hall, 2014).

12. Sam Westerich, PhD, "How Trying to Sound Smart Can (And Will) Backfire," The Startup, January 25, 2021.

13. Stephanie Vozza, "20 'Big' Words That Can Make You Sound Smarter," *Fast Company*, October 19, 2024.

14. Richard Maxwell and Robert Dickman, *The Elements of Persuasion: Use Storytelling to Pitch Better, Sell Faster & Win More Business* (Harper Collins, 2009), 134.

15. Barry Demp, "Language Exerts Hidden Power, Like the Moon on the Tides," LinkedIn.com, September 9, 2020.

16. Art Markman, "What Do (Linguistic) Hedges Do?" *Psychology Today*, October 30, 2012.

17. Jonah Berger, "Finding Your Voice: Why Confidence Is Key to Persuasion," *Knowledge at Wharton* podcast, October 15, 2019.

18. Kit Pang, "15 Poignant Public Speaking Quotes," medium.com, July 7, 2017.

19. Noah Zandan, "How to Stop Saying 'Um,' 'Ah,' and 'You Know,'" *Harvard Business Review*, August 1, 2018.

20. Kate Murphy, *You're Not Listening* (Celadon Books, 2021), 189.

21. Zandan, "How to Stop Saying 'Um,' 'Ah,' and 'You Know.'"

22. Husson University, "Convey Confidence as a Leader by Perfecting Your Body Language," husson.edu, October 8, 2022.

23. Ronald E. Riggio, "There's Magic in Your Smile," *Psychology Today*, June 25, 2012.

24. Ibid.

25. Tim Sanders, *The Likeability Factor* (Three Rivers Press, 2005), 175.

26. Paul Ekman, *Emotions Revealed: Recognizing Faces and Feelings to Improve Communication and Emotional Life* (Times Books, 2003).

27. Kate Murphy, *You're Not Listening* (Celadon Books, 2021), 166.

28. David Robson, "Your Hand Gestures Can Help Make You More Charismatic," bbc.com, August 27, 2018.

29. Ruth Umoh, "These 5 Simple Body Language Tricks Can Help You Build Trust with Anyone," cnbc.com, August 8, 2018.

30. Bill McGowan and Juliana Silva, "Biden's Secret Body Language Weapon," cnn.com, September 30, 2020.

31. Ibid.

Chapter 6: Why Authenticity Matters

1. In-person interview with Christopher Gerber and author on January 5, 2025.
2. Roger J. Kreuz, "Merriam-Webster's Word of the Year—Authentic—Reflects Growing Concerns over AI's Ability to Deceive and Dehumanize," theconversation.com, November 28, 2023.
3. Kate Wild, "Rizz Crowned Oxford Word of the Year 2023," Oxford University Press, December 4, 2023.
4. *Merriam-Webster Dictionary*, November 20, 2024.
5. Interview with author and Bob Lambert over Zoom, November 18, 2024.
6. Galen Stocking and Luxuan Wang, "America's News Influencers," Pew Research Center, November 18, 2024.
7. Gili Malinsky, "57% of Gen Zers Want to Be Influencers—but 'It's Constant Monday Through Sunday,' Says Creator," cnbc.com, September 14, 2024.
8. Mauricio Viladegutt, "What Is Jake Paul's Net Worth After Mike Tyson Fight?" newsweek.com, November 18, 2024.
9. John Antonakis, Marika Fenley, and Sue Liechti, "Learning Charisma," *Harvard Business Review*, June 2012.
10. John Antonakis, Marika Fenley, and Sue Liechti, "Can Charisma Be Taught? Tests of Two Interventions," *Academy of Management Learning and Education* 10, no. 3 (February 10, 2012).
11. Sophia Kunthara, "A Closer Look at Theranos' Big-Name Investors, Partners and Board as Elizabeth Holmes' Criminal Trial Begins," news.crunchbase.com, September 14, 2021.
12. Bobby Allyn, "Elizabeth Holmes Has Started Her 11-Year Prison Sentence. Here's What to Know," npr.org, May 30, 2023.
13. Catherine Thorbecke and Jennifer Corn, "Former Theranos COO Ramesh 'Sunny' Balwani Reports to Prison, Attorney Says," cnn.com, April 20, 2023.
14. Psychologist Robert Greene, robertgreeneofficial Instagram post, July 23, 2024.

15. Tom Peters, "The Brand Called You," *Fast Company*, August 31, 1997.
16. Today Show, "Watch Hoda's Full Interview with Rosalind Brewer, The Newest CEO Of Walgreens," youtube.com, May 5, 2021.
17. Kelsey McKeon, "5 Personal Branding Tips for Your Job Search," themanifest.com, April 28, 2020.
18. Matthew Thomas, "The World Will Ask Us Who We Are," medium.com, January 31, 2024.
19. Gabe Cohn, "Artists We Lost in 2024: In Their Words," *New York Times*, December 20, 2024.

Chapter 7: Unlocking the Science of Engagement

1. Waquar Haider, "Apple Earned $1.65 Trillion from iPhone Sales in last Ten Years; Report," me.mashable.com, February 20, 2024.
2. Sydney Boyo, "How the Apple iPhone Became One of the Best-Selling Products of All Time," cnbc.com, January 27, 2024.
3. Don Reisinger, "Remembering the iPhone Launch 10 Years Later," fortune.com, January 9, 2017.
4. Zameena Mejia, "Steve Jobs Almost Prevented the Apple iPhone from Being Invented," cnbc.com, September 12, 2017.
5. Adam Grant, "Persuading the Unpersuadable," *Harvard Business Review*, March–April 2021.
6. Gerald Zaltman, "The Subconscious Mind of the Consumer (and How to Reach It)," *Working Knowledge*, Harvard Business School, January 3, 2003.
7. Carmine Gallo, "The Art of Persuasion Hasn't Changed in 2,000 Years," *Harvard Business Review*, July 15, 2019.
8. "Buy Now: The Shopping Conspiracy," Netflix.com, November 18, 2024.
9. Cole Helbling, "Why You Should Arouse in Others an Eager Want," medium.com, September 26, 2020.
10. NeuroLeadership Institute Staff, "The Neuroscience of Storytelling," neuroleadership.com, September 30, 2021.

11. Jonah Berger, "Finding Your Voice: Why Confidence Is Key to Persuasion," *Knowledge at Wharton* podcast, October 15, 2019.

12. Christina Steindl, "Understanding Psychological Reactance," *National Library of Medicine*, December 8, 2015.

13. Lisa Barrett, *Seven and a Half Lessons About the Brain* (Mariner Books, 2021), 89.

14. C. H. Miller, L. T. Lane, L. M. Deatrick, A. M. Young, and K. A. Potts, "Psychological Reactance and Promotional Health Messages: The Effects of Controlling Language, Lexical Concreteness, and the Restoration of Freedom," *Human Communication Research* 33 (2007): 219–240.

15. B. L. Quick and J. R. Considine, "Examining the Use of Forceful Language When Designing Exercise Persuasive Messages for Adults: A Test of Conceptualizing Reactance Arousal as a Two-Step Process," *Health Communication* 23 (2008): 483–491.

16. Barrett, *Seven and a Half Lessons About the Brain*, 89.

17. Johann Hari, *Stolen Focus: Why You Can't Pay Attention—and How to Think Deeply Again* (Crown, 2023), 131.

18. Ibid.

19. David Axelrod, "David Axelrod & Karl Rove Teach Campaign Strategy and Messaging," masterclass, October 23, 2018.

20. Meridith McGraw, "It's Been Exactly One Year Since Trump Suggested Injecting Bleach. We've Never Been the Same," Politico, April 23, 2021.

21. Carmine Gallo, "A Brain Scientist's 8-Word Secret for Better Public Speaking and Presentation Skills," inc.com, January 14, 2025.

22. "Helen Fisher Tells Us Why We Love + Cheat," TED: Ideas Worth Spreading, February 2006, www.ted.com/talks/helen_fisher_tells_us_why_we_love_cheat.html.

23. Constantin Stanislavski, *An Actor's Handbook* (Theatre Arts, 1963), 39.

24. Chai M. Tyng and Hafeez U Amin, "The Influences of Emotion on Learning and Memory," *National Library of Medicine*, August 24, 2017.

25. Matt Johnson, "How Two Brains Synchronize in Conversation," psychologytoday.com, December 8, 2024.

Chapter 8: Creating Outcomes by Design

1. Lean Enterprise Institute, "Clarifying the '5 Whys' Problem-Solving Method," lean.org, July 19, 2018.
2. David E. Sprott, "The Question–Behavior Effect: What We Know and Where We Go from Here," *Social Influence*, Vol. 1, Issue 2, February 3, 2006.
3. Maggie Jackson, "How to Live in Uncertain Times," *The Gray Area* podcast, March 17, 2025.
4. Arnaud Chevallier, Frédéric Dalsace, and Jean Louis Barsoux, "The Art of Asking Smarter Questions," *Harvard Business Review*, May–June 2024.
5. The American Presidency Project, UC Santa Barbara, June 27, 2024.
6. Ibid.
7. Richard Nisbett, Henry Zukier, and Ronald Lemley, "The Dilution Effect: Nondiagnostic Information Weakens the Implications of Diagnostic Information," *Cognitive Psychology* 13, no. 2 (1981): 248–277.
8. Brian Stelter, "This Infamous Steve Bannon Quote Is Key to Understanding America's Crazy Politics," cnn.com, November 16, 2021.
9. Frankie Taggart, "Trump Floods the Zone, Leaving Opposition Drowning," barrons.com, January 29, 2025.
10. Jonathan Rauch, *Don't Give Up on Truth* podcast, June 19, 2021.
11. Kathryn Hew, "The Murder Board: Getting Comfortable with Discomfort," audaciastrategies.com, October 30, 2023.

Chapter 9: How Leaders Drive Passion and Purpose

1. Matty Bates, "How Sara Blakely Went from Disney Goofy to Spanx Billionaire," startupgeek.com, November 7, 2013.
2. Sara Blakely, "How to Find Your Higher Purpose," LinkedIn post, March 8, 2019.
3. Sara Blakely, Facebook post, May 30, 2019.
4. Sydney Lake, "Spanx Founder Sara Blakely's $1 billion Idea Started with just $5,000 in Savings and Wanting to Solve Her Own Problem," fortune.com, February 27, 2024.

5. Blakely, Facebook post.

6. Jim Harter, "U.S. Employee Engagement Sinks to 10-Year Low," gallup .com, January 14, 2025.

7. Jim Harter and Amy Adkins, "Employees Want a Lot More From Their Managers," gallup.com, April 8, 2015.

8. Mel Robbins, *The Let Them Theory* (Hay House, 2024), 67.

9. Nona Momeni, "The Relation Between Managers' Emotional Intelligence and the Organizational Climate They Create," *Public Personnel Management* 38, no. 2 (June 1, 2009).

10. Andrew Hearle, "50 Great Acting Quotes," stagemilk.com, October 3, 2019.

11. Jim Harter, "Engage Your Workforce By Empowering Your Managers First," gallup.com, June 12, 2024.

12. Laurel S. Morris and Mora M. Grehl, "On What Motivates Us: A Detailed Review of Intrinsic *v.* Extrinsic Motivation," *National Library of Medicine*, July 7, 2022.

13. Muhammad Ali, Instagram video post, mybestlifeonline, November 20, 2024.

14. Chris Sheridan, "Great Motives Elevate Champs," espn.com, August 11, 2006.

15. Marcel Schwantes, "3 Sure Ways Leaders Can Unleash Their People's Success," *Inc. Magazine*, August 5, 2020.

16. Jingjing Li, Jian Zhang, and Zhiguo Yang, "Associations Between a Leader's Work Passion and an Employee's Work Passion: A Moderated Mediation Model," *National Library of Medicine*, August 28, 2017.

17. Jon M. Jachimowicz, "When Your Passion Works Against You," Harvard Business School, November 25, 2019.

18. Paul J. Zak, "The Neuroscience of Trust," *Harvard Business Review*, January–February 2017.

19. Ibid.

20. Jawad Khan, Qingyu Zhang, "Gamification in hospitality: Enhancing workplace thriving and employee well-being," sciencedirect.com, June 2024.

21. William Arruda, "The Most Important Ingredient For Employee Engagement—And It's Not What You Think," *forbes.com*, September 10, 2024.

22. Marina Astakhova and Violet Ho, "Passionate Leaders Behaving Badly: Why Do Leaders Become Obsessively Passionate and Engage In Abusive Supervision?" *Journal of Occupational Health Psychology* 28, no. 1 (November 3, 2022): 40–51.

23. Jachimowicz, "When Your Passion Works Against You."

24. Astakhova and Ho, "Passionate leaders Behaving Badly."

25. Ibid.

26. Jacqueline Mayfield and Milton Mayfield, *Motivating Language Theory: Effective Leader Talk in the Workplace* (Palgrave Macmillan, 2017).

27. Jacqueline Mayfield and Milton Mayfield, "Embracing Agility with Hands, Heart, and Spirit with Jacqueline & Milton Mayfield," *YouTube*, August 30, 2021.

28. Ibid.

29. Ibid.

30. Zoom interview on February 20, 2025, with the author and Jacqueline and Milton Mayfield.

31. Jacqueline Mayfield and Milton Mayfield, "Embracing Agility with Hands, Heart, and Spirit with Jacqueline & Milton Mayfield."

32. Guoxia Wang, Yi Wang, and Xiaosong Gai, "A Meta-Analysis of the Effects of Mental Contrasting with Implementation Intentions on Goal Attainment," *National Library of Medicine*, May 11, 2012.

33. Ryan Holiday, "What Everyone Gets Wrong About Stoicism Is Exactly Why You Need It," observer.com, November 3, 2015.

34. Andreas Kappes, "Mental Contrasting Changes the Meaning of Reality," *Journal of Experimental Psychology* 49, no. 5 (September 2013): 797–810.

Chapter 10: The Undeniable Power of Narrative

1. Nancy Duarte, *DataStory: Explain Data and Inspire Action Through Story* (Ideapress Publishing, 2019), 5.

2. Professor Scott Galloway, Instagram post, December 1, 2024.

3. Pallab Ghosh, "World's Oldest Cave Art Found Showing Humans and Pig," bbc.com, July 3, 2024.
4. Carmine Gallo, "The Neuroscience of Storytelling," *Inc. Magazine*, October 27, 2023.
5. Grace Eliza Goodwin, "Reddit Cofounder Alexis Ohanian Predicts Live Theater and Sports Will Become More Popular Than Ever as AI Grows," businessinsider.com, December 20, 2024.
6. Jim Stratton, "How Can We Elevate Uniquely Human Skills in the Age of AI," weforum.org, January 20, 2025.
7. Ananya Mandal, "Researchers Find Talking About Ourselves Triggers Sensation of Pleasure," *News Medical*, May 8, 2012.
8. Robin Dunbar, "Gossip in Evolutionary Perspective," *Review of General Psychology* 8, no. 2 (June 2004).
9. David Ludden "Why You Were Born to Gossip," *Psychology Today*, February 27, 2015.
10. Backlinko Team, "Podcast Statistics You Need To Know," backlinko.com, September 16, 2024.
11. "TED (Conference) Facts," kickassfacts.com, November 1, 2023.
12. Carmine Gallo, "I've Analyzed 500 TED Talks, and This Is the One Rule You Should Follow When You Give a Presentation," carminegallo.com, May 31, 2016.
13. Carmine Gallo, "The Science of Storytelling," *Inc. Magazine*, October 27, 2023.
14. Uri Hasson, "Speaker–Listener Neural Coupling Underlies Successful Communication," *Inc. Magazine*, July 26, 2010.
15. Jonathan H. Westover, "The Power of Storytelling: How Our Brains Are Wired for Narratives," January 11, 2024.
16. Paul J. Zak, "Why Your Brain Loves Good Storytelling," *Harvard Business Review*, October 28, 2014.
17. Andrew Stanton, Biography from imdb.com.
18. Andrew Stanton, "The Clues to a Great Story," ted.com, February 2012.
19. Michele Delattre, "Monomyth: Hero's Journey Project," Hero's Journey Project, UC Berkeley, December 2024.

20. Robert McKee, "Q&A: Nothing Moves Forward Except Through Conflict," Robert McKee's *YouTube* channel, September 2, 2010.
21. John August, "Structure, and How to Enjoy a Movie," *ScriptNotes* podcast, episode 673, January 28, 2025.
22. Kyle Deguzman, "What Is Aristotle's Poetics—Six Elements of Great Storytelling," studiobinder.com, November 26, 2023.
23. MasterClass, "Freytag's Pyramid: Definition, Elements and Example," masterclass.com, February 15, 2023.
24. MasterClass, "Tips and Examples of *In Medias Res* in Writing," September 3, 2021.

Chapter 11: Managing Change Through Storytelling

1. Ben Wigert and Corey Tatel, "The Great Detachment: Why Employees Feel Stuck," gallup.com, December 3, 2024.
2. Garth Japhet and Warren Feek, "Storytelling Can Be a Force for Social Change. Here's How," World Economic Forum, June 27, 2018.
3. Melissa Burke, "88% of Business Transformations Fail to Achieve Their Original Ambitions; Those That Succeed Avoid Overloading Top Talent," Bain & Company, April 15, 2024.
4. Tahir Abbas, "8 Leadership Skills for Organisational Change," Change Management Insight, March 30, 2022.
5. Marie-Lou Almeida and Camilla Frumar, "Help Your Employees Cope with Stress," gallup.com, August 23, 2023.
6. Jon Kabat-Zinn, Instagram post, May 3, 2024.
7. Jacqueline Novogratz, "Learn the Art of Storytelling to Tell Stories That Matter," blog.acumenacademy.org, December 10, 2024.
8. Annie Fields, *Atlantic Monthly: A Magazine of Literature, Science, Art, and Politics*, vol. 78, August 1896 (Forgotten Books, 2018), 148.
9. Caleb Naysmith, "Blockbuster Had The Opportunity to Buy Netflix for $50 million but 'Laughed Them Out of the Room,'" finance.yahoo.com, May 25, 2023.

10. Victoria Craig, "Deep Dish: Domino's CEO Talks Turnaround Success," foxbusiness.com, April 9, 2014.

11. Bill Taylor, "How Domino's Pizza Reinvented Itself, *Harvard Business Review*, November 28, 2016.

12. Jeff Haden, "10 Years Ago, 'Cardboard' Pizza Almost Killed Domino's/ Then Domino's Did Something Brilliant," *Inc. Magazine*, January 14, 2023.

13. Craig, "Deep Dish."

14. Aaron Allen, "How Domino's Turnaround Gained Nearly $12b in Enterprise Value," aaronallen.com, December 12, 2024.

15. Tim Creasey, "Organizational Agility as a Strategic Imperative," prosci .com/blog, January 9, 2024.

16. Madhurima Bhatia, "PM Modi's Approval Rating (AR) Remains Steady at 70% in November, 2024," ipsos.com, December 1, 2024.

17. Narendra Modi, x.com, April 20, 2025.

18. Mujib Mashal, "What Makes PM Modi's Narratives Reach Out to the Heart and Catapult His Popularity?" *Economic Times*, June 22, 2023.

19. John Blake, "'Civil War' Sends a Message That's More Dangerous Than the Violence It Depicts Onscreen," cnn.com, May 12, 2024.

20. Mashal, "What Makes PM Modi's Narratives Reach Out to the Heart and Catapult His Popularity?"

21. John Blake, "'Civil War' Sends a Message That's More Dangerous Than the Violence It Depicts Onscreen."

22. Ibid.

23. Ibid.

24. Stephen Collinson, "America Has Never Had a Presumptive Nominee Like Donald Trump," cnn.com, March 6, 2024.

25. Donald Trump, "Full Text: 2017 Donald Trump Inauguration Speech Transcript," politico.com, January 20, 2017.

26. Frances X. Frei and Anne Morriss, "Storytelling That Drives Bold Change," *Harvard Business Review*, November–December 2023.

27. Carmine Gallo, "The Art of Persuasion Hasn't Changed in 2,000 Years," *Harvard Business Review*, July 15, 2019.

28. Jonathan Berliner, "Barack Obama's Landscapes: The Unfolding Road as Metaphor of American Unity," *American Studies* 59, no. 1 (2014).

29. Carmine Gallo, "The Metaphors That Played A Role in Trump's Victory," forbes.com, January 9, 2017.

30. Jason Hellerman, "What Is a Thematic Echo in Screenwriting?" nofilmschool.com, April 23, 2024.

31. Ronald Reagan, "Farewell Address to the Nation," Ronald Reagan Presidential Foundation & Institute, January 11, 1989.

32. Priyanka Aribindi, "Barack Obama's 11 Most Inspirational Quotes," time .com, August 4, 2016.

33. Sam Dangremond, "Who Was the First Politician to Use 'Make America Great Again' Anyway?" *Town & Country*, November 14, 2008.

34. Carmine Gallo, "The Art of the Elevator Pitch," *Harvard Business Review*, October 3, 2018.

35. Hellerman, "What Is a Thematic Echo in Screenwriting?"

Chapter 12: Choosing a Business Story to Tell

1. Kyle Pearce, "10 Brand Storytelling Tips from Innovative Business Leaders," socialcreators.com, October 2, 2024.

2. Ibid.

3. Douglas A. Ready, "How Storytelling Builds Next-Generation Leaders," *MIT Sloan Management Review*, July 15, 2002.

4. Joshua Foer, *Moonwalking with Einstein: The Art and Science of Remembering Everything* (Penguin Press, 2011), 23.

5. Alan Weiss, "Logic and Emotion," alanweiss.com, April 2, 2019.

6. Scott Van Voorhis, "Looking to Leave a Mark? Memorable Leaders Don't Just Spout Statistics, They Tell Stories," *Harvard Business Review*, June 20, 2023.

7. Ibid.

8. Eddie Merla, "Storytelling Is for Kids—and Project Managers," Project Management Institute, February 11, 2009.

9. Email received on April 23, 2025.

10. Tommy Vietor, "Kamala Crushed It," *Pod Save America*, August 22, 2024.

11. "Why Is It Called Airbnb? The Origin Story and Its Impact Today," airdna .co/blog, June 18, 2024.

12. Airbnb, "Celebrating Our Community Milestone of 5 Million Hosts," news.airbnb.com, February 15, 2024.
13. Hayley Peterson, "The Bizarre Inspiration Behind Nike's First Pair of Running Shoes," *Business Insider*, July 6, 2015.
14. Amir Vera, "Colin Kaepernick's Nike Ad Wins Emmy for Outstanding Commercial," cnn.com, September 19, 2019.
15. Anupriya Dhonchak, "Nike's 'Dream Crazier'—A New Brand of Self Objectification," *Engenderings*, blogs.lse.ac.uk, May 28, 2019.
16. Charlotte Alter, "How Whitney Wolfe Herd Turned a Vision of a Better Internet Into a Billion Dollar Industry," time.com, March 19, 2021.
17. Ibid.
18. Ibid.
19. Ibid.
20. Joanne Chen, "American Dreamers: Zoom Founder Eric Yuan on Making His Mark in Silicon Valley," forbes.com, July 11, 2022.
21. Dominic Kent, "The History of Eric Yuan's Zoom," *Mio* blog, August 12, 2020.
22. Emily Ayshford, "Why Your Next Brainstorm Should Begin with an Embarrassing Story," insight.kellogg.northwestern.edu, December 2, 2019.
23. David Vallance, *How to Overcome Negativity Bias*, blog.dropbox.com, January 27, 2020.
24. Ibid.
25. James Estrin, "Kodak's First Digital Moment," *New York Times*, August 12, 2015.
26. Vallance, *How to Overcome Negativity Bias*.

Chapter 13: Establishing Trust and Mutual Respect

1. Ira Glass, "403: NUMMI," *This American Life*, March 26, 2010.
2. John Shook, "How NUMMI Changed Culture," lean.org, September 30, 2009.
3. Glass, "403: NUMMI."

4. Gloria Mark, *Attention Span: A Groundbreaking Way to Restore Balance, Happiness and Productivity* (Hanover Press, 2023), 177.

5. Keith Ferrazzi, *Leading Without Authority* (Crown Currency, May 26, 2020), 167.

6. Tom Nolan, "The No. 1 Employee Benefit That No One Is Talking About," gallup.com, October 12, 2017.

7. Pumble Team, "Communication in the Workplace Statistics 2024," pumble.com, December 1, 2024.

8. Interview with Frank Evers and the author, February 2019.

9. Ferrazzi, *Leading Without Authority*, 167.

10. Debra Mashek, "College Graduates Lack Preparation in the Skill Most Valued by employers—Collaboration," hechingerreport.org, June 23, 2021.

11. Vania Martinez, Alvaro Jimenez-Molina, and Monica M. Gerber, "Social Contagion, Violence, and Suicide Among Adolescents," *National Library of Medicine*, February 15, 2023.

12. Elsie Boskamp, "35+ Compelling Workplace Collaboration Statistics [2023]: The Importance of Teamwork," zippia.com, July 6, 2023.

13. Matt Given, "Mark Zuckerberg's JFK Quote is a Master Class on the Role of a Unified Purpose," *Inc. Magazine*, July 10, 2017.

14. Scott Jaschik, "Well-Prepared in Their Own Eyes," insidehighered.com, January 19, 2015.

15. Boskamp, "35+ Compelling Workplace Collaboration Statistics [2023]."

16. Alain Hunkins, "The #1 Obstacle to Effective Communication," forbes.com, September 15, 2022.

17. Meredith Wholley, "*7 Workplace Collaboration Statistics and Advice*," blog.clearcompany.com, September 3, 2017.

18. Michael Chui and James Manyika, "The Social Economy: Unlocking Value and Productivity Through Social Technologies," mckinsey.com, July 1, 2012.

19. Seth Godin, Facebook post, August 16, 2019.

20. Sarah Pollock, "*The Importance of Employee Feedback*," blog.clearcompany.com, June 22, 2021.

21. Patricia Satterstrom, Michaela Kerrissey, and Julia DiBenigno, "The Voice Cultivation Process: How Team Members Can Help Upward Voice Live on to Implementation," *Administrative Science Quarterly* 66, no. 2 (October 5, 2020).

22. Kristin Bain, Tamar A. Kreps, Nathan L. Meikle, and Elizabeth R. Tenney, "Research: Amplifying Your Colleagues' Voices Benefits Everyone," *Harvard Business Review*, June 17, 2021.

23. Ibid.

24. Morgan Smith, "Try This Simple, Research-Backed Trick if You Want to Get Ahead at Work," cnbc.com, October 25, 2021.

25. Melissa Summer, "Introverts and Leadership—World Introverts Day," themeyersbriggs.com, January 2, 2020.

26. Adam Grant, Francesca Gino, and David A. Hofmann, "The Hidden Advantages of Quiet Bosses," *Harvard Business Review*, December 2012.

27. Rachel Cohn and Sara Silverstein, "Adam Grant Explains Why Introverts Make Better Leaders," businessinsider.com, March 4, 2019.

28. Jeff Haden, "Why Introverts Make Great Leaders," *Inc. Magazine*, March 3, 2023.

29. Jessica Andrews-Todd and Carol M. Forsyth "Collaborative Problem Solving," sciencedirect.com, 2023.

30. Cherry Collier, "How to Adopt a Collaborative Problem-Solving Approach Through 'Yes, and' Thinking," forbes.com, November 21, 2016.

Chapter 14: Enhancing Performance Through Feedback

1. Sukanya Sharma, "Under Indra Nooyi's Tenure, PepsiCo's Revenue Grown by More Than 80 Percent," financialexpress.com, August 6, 2018.

2. Arbora Johnson, "Indra Nooyi," National Women's History Museum, December 1, 2024.

3. Brian Kropp, "Be a Leader at All Levels: A Conversation with Indra Nooyi," betterworks.com, December 20, 2021.

4. Indra Nooyi, Twitter post from Association for Talent Development (ATD), May 21, 2020.

5. Vijay Govindarajan and Indra K. Nooyi, "Becoming a Better Corporate Citizen," *Harvard Business Review*, March–April 2020.

6. Ben Wigert and Corey Tatel, "The Great Detachment: Why Employees Feel Stuck," gallup.com, December 3, 2024.

7. Caitlin Jones, "2023 Engagement and Retention Report," achievers.com, February 7, 2023.

8. Mark Murphy, "Fewer Than Half of Employees Know if They're Doing a Good Job," forbes.com, September 4, 2016.

9. Josh Horvath, "32+ Employee Feedback Statistics 2024," explodingtopics .com, January 31, 2024.

10. Cate Tarr, "Gen Z and Millennial Workers Are Bringing Their Need for 'Likes' into the Office," cnbc.com, July 23, 2024.

11. Ibid.

12. Elina Landman, "Four Strategies for Building Trust in the Workplace," forbes.com, July 30, 2024.

13. John Eades, "The Role of Humility at Work (And Why the Best Leaders Embrace It)," *Inc. Magazine*, August 23, 2019.

14. Andrea Christensen, "Delivering Bad News? Don't Beat around the Bush," *Science Daily*, October 5, 2017.

15. Erick Mott, "New Study Uncovers Major Gap in Employee and Employer Expectations for Performance Management and Growth," reflective .com, April 4, 2018.

16. Marco Margaritoff, "Sarah Paulson Trounces Actor for 'Outrageous' 6-Page Email of Notes on Her Performance," huffingtonpost.com, May 14, 2024.

17. Christine Porath, "Nine Tips for Giving Better Feedback at Work," *Greater Good*, March 9, 2022.

18. Bettye Miller, "Good News First, or Bad News?," universityofcalifornia .edu, November 4, 2013.

19. Amy Kan, "The Art of Giving Effective Feedback: Best Practices for Leaders," wpinitiative.com, July 17, 2024.

20. Denise Mclain and Bailey Nelson, "How Effective Feedback Fuels Performance," gallup.com, January 1, 2022.

21. Erick Mott, "New Study Uncovers Major Gap in Employee and Employer Expectations for Performance Management and Growth," reflective .com, April 4, 2018.
22. Todd Thornock, "How the Timing of Performance Feedback Impacts Individual Performance," researchgate.net, November, 2016.
23. Goldie Chan, "Why Asking Questions Is Good for Your Brand and Your Career," forbes.com, February 1, 2021.

Chapter 15: Mastering Challenging Conversations

1. Jack Kelly, "The Rise and Fall of Better.com's Controversial CEO," *Forbes YouTube* channel, January 13, 2022.
2. Ibid.
3. Ibid.
4. Jack Kelly, "Better.com's CEO Called Workers 'Dumb Dolphins'—Three Executives Quit," forbes.com, December 8, 2021.
5. Mary Ann Azevedo, "Better.com CEO Vishal Garg Steps Back as Employees Detail How He 'Led by Fear,'" techcrunch.com, December 10, 2021.
6. Kelly, "The Rise and Fall of Better.com's Controversial CEO."
7. Kelly, "Better.com's CEO Called Workers 'Dumb Dolphins.'"
8. Ibid.
9. Ibid.
10. Anna Brown, "What Is Psychological Safety at Work?" futureforum.com, September 16, 2022.
11. Amy Edmonson, "Psychological Safety and Learning Behavior in Work Teams," *Administrative Science Quarterly* 44, no. 2, (June 1999): 350–383.
12. Charles Duhigg, "What Google Learned From Its Quest to Build the Perfect Team," *New York Times Magazine*, February 25, 2016.
13. Jared Lindzon, "Why Psychological Safety at Work Is Key to Preventing Employee Burnout," fastcompany.com, February 19, 2021.
14. Ibid.

15. Beth M. Schwartz, "What Is Psychological Safety at Work? Here's How to Start Creating It," American Psychological Association, December 4, 2023.

16. Amy C. Edmondson, "What People Get Wrong About Psychological Safety," *Harvard Business Review,* May–June 2025.

17. Amanda Cross, *26 Employee Recognitions Statistics You Need to Know in 2024,* nectarhr.com/blog, October 30, 2024.

18. Jeff Haden, "Steve Jobs Wanted What Every Remarkably Successful Person Wants," *Inc. Magazine,* August 11, 2020.

19. Gary Klein, "Performing a Project Premortem," *Harvard Business Review,* September 2007.

20. Redbooth Team, "Pre-mortems and Post-mortems: The 2 Most Important Parts of Any Project," redbooth.com, March 28, 2018.

21. Howard Schultz, "Howard Schultz on Business Leadership," masterclass .com, September 17, 2019.

22. Rita Hudgens, "Having Difficult Conversations," transformuniversity.net, January 25, 2023.

23. Schultz, "Howard Schultz on Business Leadership."

24. Thomas Oppong, "The Ability to Regulate Your Emotions Is Quickly Becoming the Premier Skill of the 21st Century," thriveglobal.com, November 14, 2019.

25. Susan David, "3 Ways to Better Understand Your Emotions," *Harvard Business Review,* November 10, 2016.

26. Groucho Marx, "Speak When You're Angry and You'll Make the Best Speech You'll Ever Regret," quoteinvestigator.com, May 17, 2014.

27. Amy Gallo, "How to Control Your Emotions During a Difficult Conversation," *Harvard Business Review,* December 1, 2017.

28. Ibid.

29. David, "3 Ways To Better Understand Your Emotions."

30. Heather V. MacArthur, "Harnessing Our Brain Power to Navigate Uncertainty," forbes.com, May 28, 2020.

31. Adam Grant, LinkedIn post, April 8, 2025.

32. Oppong, "The Ability to Regulate Your Emotions Is Quickly Becoming the Premier Skill of the 21st Century."

33. Rachel Wells, "To Email or Not? 90% of Workplace Misunderstandings Start via Email," forbes.com, January 1, 2024.

34. Maggie Mulqueen, "Texting Really Is Ruining Personal Relationships," nbcnews.com, December 7, 2019.

35. Ibid.

36. Ibid.

37. Ibid.

38. Robyn Short, "The Cost of Workplace Conflict," workplacepeaceinstitute .com, August 6, 2024.

39. Robyn Short, "State of Workplace Conflict in 2024: Insights and Solutions," workplacepeaceinstitute.com, September 16, 2024.

40. Travis Bradberry, "6 Ways Nice People Can Master Conflict," *Huffington Post*, May 14, 2016.

41. Todd Bishop, "Full text: Microsoft CEO Satya Nadella Explains Big Job Cuts," geekwire.com, July 17, 2014.

Chapter 16: The Case for Empathy in Leadership

1. Alex Nichols, "Businessolver Study Reveals Decline in Workplace Empathy," businessolver.com, June 21, 2022.

2. Ilitch Holdings, Inc., "Mike Ilitch (1929–2017)," ilithcholdings.com, December 30, 2024.

3. Ibid.

4. Eric Levenson, "Little Caesar's Founder Quietly Paid Rosa Parks' Rent for Years," cnn.com, February 15, 2017.

5. Christopher Botta, "Ilitch Aids Civil Rights Pioneer Rosa Parks, Others," sportsbusinessjounral.com, February 24, 2014.

6. Jennifer Rubin, "We Are Suffering from an Empathy Gap, but We Can Fix It," washingtonpost.com, February 15, 2023.

7. United Way NCA, "Surveying Americans on Empathy Burnout," unitedwaynca.org, April 7, 2022.

8. Na'amah Razon and Jason Marsh, "Empathy on the Decline," *Greater Good Magazine*, January 28, 2011.

9. Vivek H. Murthy, "Surgeon General Urges Americans to 'Rethink How We're Living Our Lives' in Closing Letter to the Country (Exclusive)," people.com, January 7, 2025.

10. Ronni Abergel, "The Origin of the Human Library," humanlibrary.org, January 7, 2025.

11. Lauren Gunderson, "How Theater for Young People Could Save the World," *Huffington Post*, March 19, 2012.

12. Kate Murphy, *You're Not Listening* (Celadon Books, 2021), 79.

13. Lynn Vavreck, "How Kamala Beat Trump," *The Wilderness* podcast, August 18, 2024.

14. James Liddell, "Allstate CEO Tom Wilson Faces MAGA Backlash Following Bizarre Sugar Bowl Ad in the Wake of New Orleans Attack," yahoo.com, January 3, 2025.

15. Christine Porath, "The Hidden Toll of Workplace Incivility," mckinsey.com, December 14, 2016.

16. Mahita Gajanan, "Read Meryl Streep's Powerful Golden Globes Speech," time.com, January 9, 2017.

17. Travis Bradberry and Jean Greaves, *Emotional Intelligence 2.0* (Talent Smart, 2009), 169.

18. Ernest J. Wilson III, "Empathy Is Still Lacking in the Leaders Who Need It Most," *Harvard Business Review*, September 21, 2015.

19. Kirk Dando, Lessons from Colin Powell," medium.com, May 16, 2017.

20. Alan Henry, "New Study Shows Audience's Hearts Synchronize at the Theatre," broadwayworld.com, November 27, 2017.

21. Brand Genetics, "Empathy Stats and Facts for Business," brandgenetics.com, October 10, 2019.

22. Gajanan, "Read Meryl Streep's Powerful Golden Globes Speech."

23. Patrick Healy, "The Fundamental Attribution Error: What It Is & How to Avoid It," online.hbs.edu, June 8, 2017.

24. Linda Tucci, "Servant Leadership," techtarget.com, September 2023.

25. Amanda Cross, "26 Employee Recognition Statistics You Need to Know in 2024," nectarhr.com, October 30, 2024.

26. Katelyn Hedrick, "Despite Employer Prioritization, Employee Well-Being Falters," gallup.com, November 4, 2024.

27. David Mattson, "Unlock Leadership Success: Why Gratitude Is Your Best-Kept Strategy," go.sandler.com, November 25, 2024.
28. Arthur C. Brooks, "Build the Life You Want: Arthur Brooks and Oprah Winfrey Share Happiness Tips," Harvard Business School, October 3, 2023.
29. Samuel Patrick Smith, "The Deepest Principle in Human Nature," LinkedIn.com, July 13, 2016.
30. Reuters Fact Check, "Fact Check: Photo Shows Runners Farah and Rupp, not Mutai and Fernández," reuters.com, August 16, 2021.
31. Ibid.

Chapter 17: Cultivating Authentic Dialogue

1. SK Weekly Staff, "No Way Out," sfweekly.com, January 27, 2010.
2. Ibid.
3. Lonnie Morris and Donald Frazier, "BOSS Talks," *YouTube*, April 17, 2024.
4. Ibid.
5. Ibid.
6. No More Tears, nomoretearssq.com, January 1, 2025.
7. Zoom interview by author with Lonnie Morris on January 13, 2025.
8. Bobby Powers, "The Complete Guide on How to Receive Feedback," medium.com, October 16, 2019.
9. WCNC Staff, "More Than Half of People Wear Headphones Just to Avoid Talking to Other People, Researchers Say," wcnc.com, July 8, 2019.
10. Kate Murphy, *You're Not Listening* (Celadon Books, 2021), 9.
11. Ibid., 11.
12. Ibid.
13. Youri Benadjaoud, "US Surgeon General Warns About the Dangers of Loneliness," abcnew.com, June 12, 2024.
14. The HR Observer, "Gallup Study Finds Loneliness on the Rise in Workplaces," thehrobserver.com, June 13, 2024.
15. Pete Buttigieg on Rolling Stone Instagram page, December 2024.
16. Ryan Pendell, "1 in 5 Employees Worldwide Feel Lonely," gallup.com, June 12, 2024.

17. David Sturt and Todd Nordstrom, "10 Shocking Workplace Stats You Need to Know," forbes.com, December 10, 2021.

18. Ryan Pendell, "1 in 5 Employees Worldwide Feel Lonely," gallup.com, June 12, 2024.

19. Gian Casimir, Karen Lee, and Mark Loon, "Knowledge Sharing: Influences of Trust, Commitment and Cost," *Journal of Knowledge Management*, September 7, 2012.

20. Annamarie Mann, "Why We Need a Best Friend at Work," gallup.com, January 15, 2018.

21. Paul J. Zak, "The Neuroscience of Trust," *Harvard Business Review*, January–February 2017.

22. Adrian Ward, "The Neuroscience of Everybody's Favorite Topic," scientificamerican.com, July 16, 2013.

23. Jacqueline Mayfield, "Embracing Agility with Hands, Heart, and Spirit with Jacqueline & Milton Mayfield," *YouTube*, August 30, 2021.

24. Philip Burnard and Paul Morrison, "Self-Disclosure and Nursing Students: The Replication of a Jourard Study," *International Journal of Nursing Studies* 21, no. 2 (April 1995).

25. Karen Huang, Michael Yeomans, Alison Wood Brooks, Julia Minson, and Francesca Gino, "It Doesn't Hurt to Ask: Question-Asking Increases Liking," *Journal of Personality and Social Psychology* 113, no. 3 (2017), 430–452.

26. Murphy, *You're Not Listening*, 63.

27. Ibid.

28. Ibid., 115.

29. Marvin R. Shanken, "One-on-One with Michael Jordan," *Cigar Aficionado*, July/August 2005.

30. Murphy, *You're Not Listening*, 22.

31. Joy Victory, "Hearing Loss Is Common in the U.S. The Good News? Hearing Aid Satisfaction Is High, Surveys Show," healthyhearing.com, February 26, 2024.

32. Bassey BY, "Bill Nye Says, 'Everyone You Will Ever Meet Knows Something You Don't,'" medium.com, September 29, 2021.

33. Murphy, *You're Not Listening*, 136.

34. Brett McKay and Kate McKay, "How to Avoid Conversational Narcissism," artofmanliness.com, January 20, 2020.

35. Carmine Gallo, "Win People Over with 2 Simple, Powerful FBI Tactics," *Inc. Magazine*, February 6, 2020.

36. Guy Itzchakov and Avraham N. (Avi) Kluger, "The Power of Listening in Helping People Change," *Harvard Business Review*, May 17, 2018.

37. Maria Popova, "Givers, Takers, and Matchers: The Surprising Psychology of Success," themarginalian.org, April 10, 2013.

38. Ibid.

39. David Sax, "Why Strangers Are Good for Us," nytimes.com, June 12, 2022.

Chapter 18: Building Unbreakable Teams

1. Interview over Zoom with Bob Lambert on November 17, 2024.

2. Neil Gorsuch and Jane Nitze, *Over Ruled: The Human Toll of Too Much Law* (Harper, 2024).

3. Jake Herway, "The Hidden Earnings Potential in Matrixed Organizations," gallup.com, March 8, 2019.

4. David Hassell, "Four Steps for Building a Culture of Open Communication," forbes.com, October 3, 2014.

5. People Insight, "50 Employee Engagement Statistics for 2025," peopleinsight.co.uk, January 23, 2025.

6. Kate Murphy, *You're Not Listening* (Celadon Books, 2021), 105.

7. Anthony Wing Kosner, *Amy Edmondson on the Power of Psychological Safety in Distributed Work*, blog.dropbox.com, March 27, 2020.

8. Dr. Marcus Robinson interviewed by the author on the *Pinnacle Presents* podcast, November 2020.

9. Ibid.

10. Indra Nooyi, Economic Club speech, March 12, 2009.

11. Jonathan Haidt, *The Anxious Generation* (Penguin Press, 2024), 150.

12. Kevin Kruse interviewed by the author on the *Pinnacle Presents* podcast, September 2021.

13. Yvon Chouinard, "A Letter from Our Founder Yvon Chouinard," onepercentfortheplanet.org, April 22, 2020.

14. Rebecca M. Brossoit, "Engaging with Nature and Work: Associations Among the Built and Natural Environment, Experience Outside, and Job Engagement and Creativity," *National Library of Medicine*, January 11, 2024.

15. Yvon Chouinard, "Our Story: Business as Usual Is Failing People and the Planet," onepercentfortheplanet.org, September 14, 2022.

16. Axios, "The 2023 Axios Harris Poll of Reputation Rankings," axios.com, March 23, 2023.

17. Alison Beard, "Life's Work: An Interview with Ron Howard," *Harvard Business Review*, January/February 2023.

18. Ibid.

19. Ibid.

20. Don Reisinger, "All Companies Should Live by the Jeff Bezos 70 Percent Rule," *Inc. Magazine*, June 27, 2020.

21. Justin Bariso, "In Just 3 Words, Amazon's Jeff Bezos Taught a Brilliant Lesson in Leadership," *Inc. Magazine*, April 13, 2017.

22. Jeff Bezos, "2016 Letter to Shareholders," aboutamazon.com, April 11, 2016.

Afterword

1. Mary Benatar, "Kafka and the Doll: The Pervasiveness of Loss," *Huffington Post*, December 3, 2011.

Acknowledgments

The research and writing that went into *Synergy and Sparks* would not have been possible without the contributions, knowledge, and generosity of every member of the Pinnacle team—starting with my Pinnacle cofounder and collaborator for the past 20 years, David Lewis. Many of the topics or ideas discussed in these pages were developed and refined over time in various Pinnacle trainings and workshops across the globe.

I would like to gratefully acknowledge the contributions of our core group of Pinnacle team members, some of whom have been with us from the beginning: Vicky Albertelli, Sally Al Shafey, Cheryl Avery, Yvonne Blackwell, Betty Blok, Alice Bussey, Lucas Calhoun, Chanel Carmichael, Jay Collins, Charlotte Cornwall, Jason Denuszek, Darci Elam, Brandon Garcia, Kate Garassino, Lubet Garrido, Gabriel Garzón, Chris Gemerchak, Sarah Gitenstein, Aarti Gupta, Radhika Gupta, Matt Harrison, Sara Holser, Jessica Kadish-Hernandez, Tim Kasper, Hayley Koch, Jim Krag, Brad Lawrence, Gerri Leon, Han Ee Lim, Scott Lowell, James Mackey, Marquese Martin-Hayes, Connor McNamara, Brian McNeany, Claudio Medeiros, Corin Mellinger, Jo Mills, Sadie Mills, Christian Mortensen, Naomi Ouellette, Olivia Porter, Ben Schlotfelt, John Schuler, Jay Schwartz, Craig Tafel, Petra Tramp, Krysta Van Ranst, Andrew Weir, Jay Wong, and Lizzie Yirrell-Smith. I'd also like to acknowledge the great Phil Davison, who has been so generous with his time, talent, and passion over the years.

To everyone mentioned, your commitment, dedication, and input have been invaluable in the process of developing and writing this book. I'd also like to extend my thanks to *Forbes*, where I'm a member of their Coaches Council and where some of the content in *Synergy and Sparks* first appeared.

To my family—especially my wife Jo, my daughters Sadie and Sawyer, my parents Gary and Marlys Mills, my brothers Mark Mills and Paul Besso, as well as my in-laws Beth Love, Dionicio and Jona Borja, Simon Borja, and Celestina Borja—thank you for the support and understanding you have provided me as I disappeared for weeks on end to work on this book, often spending extended periods of time working out of town or overseas.

To my network of friends and supporters—specifically Rami Abushhab, Ryan Adkins, Jacob Alexander, Hassan Al Juaidi, Scott Becker, Emily Bennett, Desmon Berry, Daniel Bird, Brandan Burgess, Tyler Burke, Joe Borja, Juliet Borja, Darren Callahan, Benson Chang, Max Chang, Ralph Covert, Pancho Demmings, Tramel Dodd, Kevin Douglas, John Dugenske, Alicia Flores, David Flores, Linda Habjan, Rick Hamilton, Bill Hoversten, Patti Hoversten, Chuck Huber, Nicholas Jeffries, Zubin Kammula, Guy Kawasaki, Lee Kirk, Ryan Lance, Charles Loggins, Butch Mills, Anthony Moseley, David Murray, Harish Naidu, Jeanene O'Brien, Shanna Olness, Treshan Weerasooriya Pereira, Lataryion Perry, Greg Porcaro, Jackie Price, Mark Reisetter, Cameron Raasdal-Munro, Kurt Rolle, Willie Round, Marquis Simmons, Johnathan Simmons, Cameron Smith, Matt Sullivan, Joe Urbinato, Scott Vehill, Kristen Vehill, DawnMarie Vestevich, Betsy Williams, Anthony Wolf, and Roy Youman—thank you for being a part of this adventure.

I'd also like to thank my agent Eric Lupfer at United Talent Agency for seeing the potential of this project from the start, as well as the team at John Wiley & Sons—especially Zachary Schisgal, Susan Geraghty, Michelle Hacker, Amanda Pyne, Rachel Rozar, and Kim Wimpsett. I am humbled by the invaluable guidance you have provided in shaping this project throughout the entire process. I'm grateful to call Wiley my home for the third time with this book.

I'd also like to thank those who provided me interviews and stories for the book: Christopher Gerber, David Goldrake, Kevin Kruse, Bob Lambert, Jacqueline Mayfield, Milton Mayfield, Lonnie Morris, and Dr. Marcus Robinson. Thank you for your time and generosity.

Finally, I want to thank our various Pinnacle clients and partners across the globe, specifically Philip Altschuler, Sherri Beck, Kianna Boatswain, Dr. Ray Bowmen, Alex Boykin, Owen Clanton, Alistair Cumming, Jenn Devenyns, Therese Dickerson, Erin Doyle, Bridget Dunn, Richard Fletcher, Lauren Fregonese, Rolando Garcia, Andrea Gillman, Christine Gilmore, Mark Gitenstein, Mahipal Goud, Sarah Greeley, Pankaj Gupta, Arti Gusain, Rohullah Hassani, Wanda Hayes, Scott Hamilton, Jason Hess, Bill Joiner, Ramesh Kaushik, Butch Kinsey, Laleh Malek, Cynthia Marsh, Clemente McWilliams, Paula Miller, Sergio Obregon, General Manoj Pande, Githesh Ramamurthy, Diane Reeves, Mario Rizzo, Mark Salisbury, Prathyusha Sebastian, Michael Sheehan, Heidi Smith, Luke Sokolowski, Kelly Spring, David Walsh, Sarah Wang, Melanie Waters, Jennie Weber, and Monique Williamson. I am truly grateful for the opportunity you've given both myself and Pinnacle to collaborate with you.

About the Author

G. Riley Mills is an Emmy Award–winning producer, writer, and the cofounder of Pinnacle Performance Company, a globally recognized communication skills training firm. As the coauthor of *The Bullseye Principle* and *The Pin Drop Principle* (both published by Wiley), Mills has influenced communication practices worldwide. Named among *Inc. Magazine*'s "Top Leadership Speakers," he has provided communication training to executives and CEOs across six continents. His TEDx Talk, "Are We Killing Communication?," was presented at the Shanghai American School in China. Mills won a 2024 Emmy Award, his third, for Outstanding Regional Documentary for his work on NBC's *The Lost Story of Emmett Till: Then & Now*.

Mills has delivered guest lectures and keynotes at prestigious institutions and events worldwide, including Columbia University, London Business School, the ATD International Conference, the London Chamber of Commerce, the SHRM International Conference, New York University, Utrecht University of Applied Sciences

(Netherlands), Singapore Management University, and the MENA Conference in Saudi Arabia. He has also consulted on communication for high-profile clients, including the Ministry of Defence in the United Kingdom, Manchester United, and The Royal Household at Buckingham Palace.

As a writer, Mills has contributed to *Forbes*, *Fast Company*, and *Inc. Magazine*. His accomplishments in theater include winning two Joseph Jefferson Awards for Best New Work and receiving the 2022 Distinguished Play Award from the American Alliance for Theatre and Education for his play *Lift Every Voice* (cowritten with hip-hop artist Willie Round). In film, Mills wrote and produced *Broke Down Drone* (also with Round), which won "Best of the Fest" at the 2022 Chain Theatre Film Festival in New York City and was showcased at the iconic TCL Chinese Theatre in Los Angeles. Mills recently served as executive producer of the feature film *Blood Shine*, which is set to premiere at the FrightFest film festival in London in fall 2025.

For bonus content, including exercises based on the material presented in *Synergy and Sparks*, scan the QR code provided here.

For author appearances or speaking inquiries, please visit grileymills.com. To learn more about Pinnacle Performance Company, go to pinper.com.

Index

Page numbers followed by *f* refer to figures.

Achatz, Grant, 81
Achievement, 62, 126–132, 134, 170, 193, 200, 265
Active listening, xx, 23, 45, 250–255. *See also* Effective listening
Adaptability, xix–xx, 34–38, 43, 90–91, 102, 205, 266
Agency, 265–266
Agility, xvii, 34, 38, 46, 90–91, 115, 223
Airbnb, 174–176
Alcott, Louisa May, 159
Ali, Muhammad, 84–85, 129–130
Alighieri, Dante, xv
Alignment:
  through clarity, 261–267
  importance of, 272
  mirroring for, 256
  neural entrainment for, 110

questioning for, 115
storytelling for, 158, 170, 173, 180
Amazon, 54, 100, 271
Amplification, 195–197
Anecdotes, 30, 86, 158, 161–164, 172, 182
Antioco, John, 160
Apple, 46, 63, 88, 97–98, 102, 108
Archer, William, 149
Aristotle, 152, 167, 201
Assumptions, 53, 89, 93, 109, 124, 211, 238
Attention, capturing of, 24–28
Atwood, Margaret, 143
Auerbach, Red, 215
Aurelius, Marcus, 137
Authentic dialogue, 245–258

315

Authenticity, xxii
  and charisma, 83–87, 89
  eye contact for, 79
  importance of, 81–94
  and perfectionism, 61
  and self-awareness, 12–15
  smiling for, 75
  in storytelling, 143, 174, 182
Axelrod, David, 107

Bain, Kristin, 196–197
Balsillie, Jim, 38
Balwani, Ramesh "Sunny,"
    87–89
Bannon, Steve, 119
Bartlett, Steven, 10
Bateson, Mary Catherine, 167
Bay, Michael, 67–68
Beecher Stowe, Harriet, 159
Before/event/result formula,
    163–164
Berger, Jonah, 73, 103
Berkman, Lisa, 249
Best Buy, 46–47
Better.com, 215–217, 226
Bezos, Jeff, 54, 270–271
Biden, Joe, 116–118, 166
Bill Nye the Science Guy, 254
BlackBerry, 38–41
Blake, John, 165
Blakely, Sara, 125–126
Blecharczyk, Nathan, 175

Blockbuster, 160
Body language:
  and charisma, 86
  as conveyance, 106
  eye contact in, 80
  hand usage in, 78
  as influence, 56
  in mirroring, 256
  modification of, 91
  as nonverbal cue, 70
  and self-awareness, 12
  texting vs., 225
  in visual channel,
    74–75
Bowerman, Bill, 177
Box breathing, 65, 65*f*
Bradberry, Travis, 236
Branson, Richard, 131, 171
Breathwork, 6, 28, 64–66
Brehm, Jack, 103
Brett, Jeanne, 223
Brewer, Rosalind, 92–93
Bridging, 121–122
Brin, Sergey, 46
Brooks, Arthur C., 241
Brown, Brené, 61, 231
Brown, Rita Mae, 72
Buffett, Warren, xxi
Bumble, 178–180
Burnout, xvii–xviii, 25–26,
    40, 59, 61, 87, 133
Bush, George H. W., 169

316

Index

Caligula, 252
Cameron, Julia, 62
Campbell, Joseph, 149
Carnegie, Dale, 7, 101
Carnegie Institute of
    Technology, xxi
Cause/effect/remedy formula,
    163
Charisma, 7, 68, 84–87, 89–90,
    125, 171
Checkbacks, 120–121
Chesky, Brian, 175
Chouinard, Yvon, 267–268
Clance, Pauline, 60
Climax (of a story), 148, 154
Clinton, Bill, 7, 169
Close, Del, 45
Collaboration:
    adaptability for, 35–36
    amplification in, 195–196
    in communication, 190–195
    creative, 37
    cross-cultural, 187–190
    cross-generational, 16
    in performances, 44–47
    questioning for, 111–115
    and self-awareness, 13
    teamwork as, 197–200
    technology's effect on, 22–23
Collaborative communication,
    190–195
Communication:

collaborative, 190–195
and culture, 135
hit-and-run, 225
and intention, 9–11
intentional, 10
as leadership strategy,
    238–240
nonverbal, 11, 20, 69–71, 76,
    78, 80, 121, 235
objectives for, 8–9
Pinnacle Method of, 11–12
self-awareness for, 12–15
social awareness for, 15–17
spontaneous, 120–123
Communion, 265–266
Confirmation bias, 234, 238. *See
    also* Negativity bias
Conflict, 9, 13, 104, 134,
    148–150, 153–154, 221–225
Conflict resolution, 223, 224,
    227, 228
Congruence, 11, 12, 68–70, 72,
    76
Connection:
    and authenticity, 81–83
    and body language, 75,
        79–80
    and charisma, 84
    and compassion, 231–232
    and competition, 242–244
    emotional, 81–83, 85,
        102, 109–110

Connection: *(continued)*
  and empathy, 105, 238–240
  humor for, 31
  intentional communication
    for, 10
  need for, 233–237
  and servant leadership,
    240–242
  spatial, 77
  through storytelling, 143,
    164, 174, 182
  technology's effect on, 20–21,
    23, 27, 225
Connector statements, 120–121
Consistency, 93, 168, 221
Constructive disagreement, 271
Continuous improvement, 62,
    111, 188–189, 207. *See also*
    Kaizen
Controlling language, 104
Conversational narcissists, 254
Conversational sensitivity,
    252–253
Conveyance, 106
Costa, Marena, 100
COVID-19 pandemic, xvi–xviii,
    34, 36, 46, 107, 165,
    180–181, 233
Creative conflict, 191, 194, 222.
    See also Conflict
Crucible stories, 178–180

Cuddy, Amy, 69
Customer-centric
    decision-making, 54
Cybertrucks, 51–52

David, Susan, 223
Davis, Daryl, 146
Decisive action, 150, 271
Demosthenes, 6
Derber, Charles, 254–255
Desired outcomes, 8, 12, 31, 137
Dilution effect, 118–120
Directive feedback, 207. *See
    also* Evaluative feedback;
    Exploratory feedback
Disagree-and-commit rule,
    20–271
Disclosure, 252
Disengagement, 31, 36, 40, 191,
    263. *See also* Engagement
Distress, 40–41
Dodson, John Dillingham, 58
Domino's Pizza, 160–161
Donnellan, Declan, xx
Dostoevsky, Fyodor, 171
Doyle, Patrick, 160–161
Dramatic structure, 152–154,
    153*f*
Dunbar, Robin, 146
Dunning-Kruger effect, 13
Dweck, Carol, 204

Eames, Charles, 245
Edmondson, Amy, 218–219, 264
Effective listening, 252–253. *See also* Active listening
Einstein, Albert, 33, 44
Ek, Daniel, 112
Ekman, Paul, 76–77
Elizabeth, Queen, 3–5
Emotional agility, 223–224
Emotional contagion, 127
Emotional intelligence, 14, 17, 79, 82, 90, 102
Empathy:
  body language for, 80
  and collaboration, 192–193
  and connection, 105, 238–240
  during COVID, 233
  expressions of, 135
  feedback for, 203
  importance of, 235–237
  as influence, 101
  in leadership, 231–244
  in motivational speeches, 135
  questioning for, 54, 113
  social awareness for, 15
  in storytelling, 173
  strategies for boosting, 238–240
  technology's effect on, 21, 145
Empty chair concept, 54

Engagement. *See also* Disengagement; Reengagement
  active listening for, 250–254
  and adaptability, 37
  with audiences, 29, 86
  through consistency, 242
  decline in, 157
  emotional, 128, 144
  employee, 208, 231, 236, 241
  humor for, 30
  in hybrid work, 35
  importance of, 189
  incentives for, 129, 131
  of introverts, 198
  language's influence on, 134
  morale for, 43
  nonverbal cues for, 78, 80, 128
  and passion, 134, 151
  and pattern interrupt, 31–32
  personal, 267
  questioning for, 112
  science of, 97–110
  and self-awareness, 13
  through storytelling, 155, 165
  studies on, xvii–xviii, 36, 126, 214
  with technology, 21–22, 26, 39, 85
  "Yes, and" model for, 45

English, Bill, 234

Enrobing, 260

Eustress, 40–41

Evaluative feedback, 206. *See also* Directive feedback; Exploratory feedback

Evers, Frank, 33–34

Executive presence, 69

Experience blockers, 20–21

Exploratory feedback, 206–207. *See also* Directive feedback; Evaluative feedback

Exposition, 152–153, 155

Extrinsic motivation, 129

Facebook, 21, 26, 105

Falk, David, 253

Falling action, 154

Farson, Richard, 252

Feedback, 201–214
  and amplification, 197
  as collaborative communication, 193
  constructive, 37
  directive, 207
  for Dominos, 160–161
  embracing, 14–15, 213–214
  and empathy, 203
  evaluative, 206
  exploratory, 206–207
  eye contact as, 80
  from groups, 124

for growth, 203–204

for improved performance, 207–212

during integration phase, 43

and intention, 209

mindset for, 204–206

rehearsal for, 63

resistance to, 90

soliciting, 31

timing of, 211

types of, 206–207

Fernández Anaya, Iván, 243

Finding Nemo, 149

Fisher, Helen, 109

Fixed mindsets, 204

Flooding (of information), 119

Forman, Miloš, 132

Francis, Ben, 14–15

Freud, Sigmund, 77

Freytag, Gustav, 152

Freytag's pyramid, 152, 155, 161

Fundamental attribution error, 238

Futuring, 33–34

Galloway, Scott, 144

Garg, Vishal, 215–217, 224, 226

Gates, Bill, 28–30

Gebbia, Joe, 175

Gen Z, xix, 21, 85

General Motors (GM), 187–190

George VI, King, 6
Gerber, Christopher, 81–83
Ghoshal, Sumantra, 10
Gilligan, Vince, 155
Glossophobia, 57
Godin, Seth, 195
Goffman, Erving, xxi, 190
Goldrake, David, 32
Gore, Al, 146
Gossip, 146
Gottman, John, 71
Graeber, Thomas, 172
Grant, Adam, 209, 224, 257
Grazer, Brian, 111
Great Detachment, 157
Great Resignation, xviii
Greaves, Jean, 236
Greenfield, David, 22
Greenleaf, Robert K., 240
Growth mindset, 204–205
Gymshark, 14

Harris, Kamala, 8, 118
Hasson, Uri, 147
Hastings, Reed, 160
Hawkins, Trish, 209
Hedging language, 72
Hero's journey, 148–151
Hit-and-run communication, 225
Hoke, Dirk, 40
Holmes, Elizabeth, 87–89

Home base position, 77
Homer, 155
Hooks, 29–30
Howard, Ken, 5
Howard, Ron, 268–270
Huberman, Andrew, 66
Humor, 30–31, 86, 162, 182
Hybrid work, xvii, 35, 126, 157, 181, 250, 256–257

Ilitch, Michael, 231–232
Imagination, 39, 44, 47, 88, 132
Imes, Suzanne, 60
Imposter syndrome, 60–62.
    See also Speech anxiety
In Medias Res, 155–156, 161
Inciting incidents, 153
Influence:
    emotional, 5
    and intrigue, 108–110
    language for, 104–108,
        134–137
    of leaders, 106, 174, 212, 236
    motivations for, 129
    neuroscience of, 98–102,
        109–110
    and persuasion, 97–98
    resistance to, 103–104
    social, 32
    and storytelling, 148
    vocalization for, 73

321

Index

Influencers, 85–86
Insight questions, 113
Instagram, 26, 85, 108
Intention. *See also* Objectives
and charisma, 87, 89
communicating, 120
and effective listening, 253
(*See also* Objectives)
explanation of, 9–11
and feedback, 209
and gratitude, 242
and insight, 181
mindset for, 205
and objectives, 5, 12, 56, 63
questioning for, 115
and reengagement, 250
in style flexing, 90
and teamwork, 200
technology's effect on, 23–24,
28, 225
and visual cues, 76–78
and vocalization, 73–74
Intention cues, 8, 70
Intentional breathing, 64–65
Intentional communication, 10
Intentional connections, 82–83
Intentional interruptions, 28
Intentional listening, 197
Intrigue, 108–110
Intrinsic motivation, 129
Introversion, 197–199
iPhones, 21, 38–39, 46, 97–98

Jachimowicz, Jon M., 133
Jackson, Ketanji Brown, 7
Jackson, Maggie, 112
James, William, 24, 242
Jobs, Steve, 21, 46, 63, 88, 97–98,
102, 108, 219
Johnson, Kevin, 16
Jordan, Michael, 85, 253
Jung, Carl, 93

Kabat-Zinn, Jon, 158
Kaepernick, Colin, 177–178
Kafka, Franz, 273–274
Kaizen, 188. *See also* Continuous
improvement
Kappes, Andreas, 137
Keith, Damon, 232
Kennedy, John F., 6–7, 192
Kim, Chloe, 178
Kinetic attention, 26
The King's Speech, 6
Knight, Phil, 177
Kodak, 181–184
Kruse, Kevin, 266
Kübler-Ross, Elisabeth, 41–42
Kübler-Ross Change Curve,
41–43, 42*f*

Labeling, 223, 255–256. *See also*
Mirroring
Lambert, Bob, 84, 259–261
Lazaridis, Mike, 38

Le, Tan, 147

Lee, Kris, 224

Lembke, Anna, 23

Lemley, Ronald, 119

Lewis, David, xxii

Lincoln, Abraham, 159

Loewenstein, Jeffrey, 31–32

Logue, Lionel, 6

Loneliness, 247–250

LuPone, Patti, 27–28

McCarthy, Michael Clayton, 37

McKee, Robert, 150

Magnetism, 84–90

Main character energy, 83

Manipulative leaders, 89–90

Mark, Gloria, 24–26

Marx, Groucho, 223

Matrixed environments, 263

Mayfield, Jacqueline, 134–137, 251

Mayfield, Milton, 134–137

Meaning making, 135, 136

Medina, John, 30, 169

Meisner, Sanford, 127

Mental contrasting, 134, 137–139

Metaphors, 24, 86, 167–170

Miller, Earl, 22

Mindfulness, 24, 64, 76, 79, 106, 163, 254

Mirroring, 20, 27, 76, 255–256. *See also* Labeling

Mitchell, David, 187

Modi, Narendra, 164–165

Monomyths, 149

Morgan, Lewis, 14

Morris, Lonnie, 247

Motivating Language Theory, 134–137

Muhammad, Ibtihaj, 178

Mulqueen, Maggie, 225

Multiteaming, 263

Murder boards, 123–124

Murthy, Vivek, 233, 248

Musk, Elon, 51–52

Mutai, Abel Kiprop, 243

Mutuality, 212, 218

Myers-Briggs, 197, 226

MySpace, 37

Nadella, Satya, 226–227

Negativity bias, 105, 241. *See also* Confirmation bias

Nerds, 259–261

Nerurkar, Aditi, 64

Netflix, 144, 160

Networking, 156–157

Neural entrainment, 110, 147

Neuroscience, xx, 8, 98–102, 109

Nike, 92, 176–178

Nisbett, Richard, 119

Nixon, Richard, 6

No More Tears program, 245–247

Nolan, Christopher, 155

Nonverbal communication, 11, 20, 69–71, 76, 78, 80, 121, 235

Nooyi, Indra, 201–203, 208, 265

Novogratz, Jacqueline, 158

NUMMI (New United Motor Manufacturing, Inc.), 187–190

Obama, Barack, 38, 86, 116, 166–168

Objectives:
communicating, 263
defined, 8–10
and goal-setting, 55–56
importance of, 5
and influence, 101
instructions for, 199
and intentions, 12
and intrigue, 109
in meetings, 63
in pre-mortems, 220
strategies for using, 121
timelines for, 262 (*See also* Intention)

Oettingen, Gabriele, 137–138

Ohanian, Alexis, 145

Ohno, Taiichi, 111

Organizational clarity, 264

Origin stories, 174–176

Pacifiers, 77

Page, Larry, 46

Parker, Sean, 21

Parks, Rosa, 232

Passionate leaders, 128, 132–134

Passive-aggressive behavior, 225

Past/present/future formula, 163

Patagonia, 267–268

Pattern interrupts, 31

Paul, Jake, 85–86

Pausch, Randy, 157

Pavlou, Paul, 22

Penn, Arthur, 6

PepsiCo, 201–203, 208, 265

Perfection paradox, 61–62

Personal branding, 91–94

Personas, xxi, 7, 87–88, 107

Persuasion, 97–101, 103–104, 120. *See also* Resistance

Peters, Tom, 92

Physiological sighs, 66

Pie-in-the-face stories, 181–184

Pinnacle Method, xxi, 8, 11–12, 53, 90

Pinnacle Performance Company, xv–xvi, xix, xxii, 3

Pitch Fest, 46

Poetics (Aristotle), 152

Post-mortems, 220–221

Powell, Colin, 237

Pre-mortems, 220–221

Presence:

324

Index

and anxiety, 57–58
breathwork for, 64–66
charisma as, 7, 84–87
executive, 69
eye contact for, 80
and imposter syndrome, 60–61
and perfection, 61–62
questioning for, 54–57
spatiality for, 77
and stress, 58–59
and success, 53–54
The Presentation of Self in Everyday Life (Goffman), xxi
Prism of priority, 53
Project Purple, 97
Psychological safety, 217–219
Push/pull approaches, 143, 153

Question design, 112
Quintilian, 70

Rapport-building questions, 113, 115
Reactance, 103–104. *See also* Resistance
Reagan, Ronald, 7, 166–169
Reengagement, 31, 250. *See also* Engagement
Reframing, 62, 122–123

Rehearsing, 35, 63–64, 66, 115, 124, 132
Repetition, 122, 168–170
Resistance, 13, 39–40, 103–104, 158, 160, 173. *See also* Persuasion
Resolution (of a story), 154
Retention, 31–32, 171–173, 213, 242
Richardson, Ralph, 73
Riley, Pat, 130
Rising action, 153–154
Rizz, 83. *See also* Charisma
Roberts, Robin, 11
Robinson, Marcus, 264
Rock, David, 13, 223
Rogers, Carl, 252
Rosen, Hannah, 35

Saint-Exupéry, Antoine de, 10
Samsung, 67–68
Sandberg, Sheryl, 60, 146
Sartre, Jean-Paul, 19
Sasson, Steven, 182–183
Satyrus, 6
Schmiedl, KeyAnna, 204
Schultz, Howard, 221–222
Scialabba, George, 45
Scott, Sophie, 72
Scrub-downs, 123
Self-awareness, 12–15, 55, 74, 182, 206–207, 224

Self-doubt, 4, 57, 126

Senju, Atsushi, 79

Servant leadership, 240–242

Shakespeare, William, 78

Shields, John and Karen Urie, 82

Shift responses, 254–255

Signaling theory, 68–70

Sills, Paul, 45

Simon, Herbert A., 20

Sincero, Jen, 97

Six-of-one rule, 268–270

Smartphones, 21–24, 26–27, 38–39, 97, 163

Smith, Kevin, 3

Smith, Maggie, 94

Social actors, xxi

Social awareness, 15–17, 236

Social contagion, 192

Social influence, 32, 103

Soft skills, xix

Solution stories, 180–181

Spanx, 125–126

Spatiality, 77

Speech anxiety, 57–58, 60, 62, 65, 74. *See also* Imposter syndrome

Spolin, Viola, 45

Spontaneous communication, 120–123

Spotlighting, 121, 122, 163

Spotlights, 24, 64, 100, 116, 209, 252, 253

Stanislavski, Constantin, 5, 9, 31, 47, 54–57, 75, 109, 269

Stanislavski's Seven Questions, 54–57

Stanley, Andy, 248

Stanton, Andrew, 148–149

Starbucks, 16–17, 221

Stated needs, 113–114

Stinziano, Joe, 67–68

Stone-face syndrome, 77

Stopping power, 84

Storytelling:

anecdotes vs., 161–162

appeal of, 143–148

brains' response to, 102, 147

facial, 76

of hero's journey, 149–151

influencing through, 148

metaphors in, 167

origins of, 144–145

as retention booster, 171–173

structure of, 151–154

thematic echoes in, 169

types of, 173–184

Strasberg, Lee, 61, 69

Streep, Meryl, 236–237

Style-flexing, 90–91

Sullivan, Jeremiah, 134

Support responses, 254–255

Surprise, 28–32, 41
Sustained attention, 25
Suzuki, Wendy, 58
Switch cost effect, 28

Teasers, 108
TED Talks, 29, 146–147
Thatcher, Margaret, 7
Thematic echoes,
    167–169
Theranos, 87–88
Thomas, Eric, 125
Thornock, Todd, 211
TikTok, 85, 108
Toyota, 111, 187–190
Toyota Production System (TPS),
    111, 187–188
Transient attention, 25
Transitions, 63–64, 78,
    157, 170, 256
Transparency:
    and alignment, 261–262
    during conflicts, 221–222
    fostering, 165
    improvisation vs., 108
    lack of, 39
    during layoffs, 215–216,
        226–227
    radical, 161
    trust-building through, 194
    through value stories, 176

Transportation, 147
Trump, Donald, 8, 84, 86, 107,
    116–119, 166–169, 234–235
Turkle, Sherry, 22
20 Percent Time initiative, 46

Unjudging, 233
Unstated needs, 113–114

Value stories, 176–178
Vavreck, Lynn, 235
Verbal channel, 71–72
Verbal viruses, 74
Vietor, Tommy, 175
Visual channel, 74–80
Visualization, 61, 137, 169, 223
Vocal channel, 73–74
Von Holzhausen, Franz,
    51–52

Weber, Jennie, 47
Wezowski, Kasia and Patryk,
    78–79
Wilde, Oscar, 81
Wilmer, Taylor, 58
Wilson, Tom, 235
Winfrey, Oprah, 7, 171
The Wizard of Oz, 9, 152–154
Wolfe Herd, Whitney,
    179–180
Woolf, Virginia, 53

Yerkes, Robert, 58
Yerkes-Dodson law, 58–59, 59*f*
"Yes, and" technique, 44–47
YouTube, 85–86
Yuan, Eric, 181

Zak, Paul J., 148
Zaltman, Gerald, 99
Zelenskyy, Volodymyr, 7
Zoom, xvii, 180–181
Zukier, Henry, 119